BIGGER FASTER STRONGER.

The Total Program

By

Dr. Greg Shepard

Dedication

To my lovely and patient wife, Diana
To my children — Andrea, Matthew,
    Shauna Sue, and Mark
To my wonderful mother, Carolyn Shepard
To my dad, Maurice Shepard

Acknowledgements

The author would like to acknowledge the men who have helped him throughout the years in developing his knowledge in strength and conditioning with athletes. These men are Dr. Phil Allsen, Dr. Lavon Johnson, Dr. L. Jay Silvester, Dr. Ed Reuter, Don Tollefson, George Frenn, Coach Al Decoria, Coach Herb Langeman, Coach Verl Shell, and Coach Gerald Crittenden. Thanks to Stefan Fernholm who has added a great dimension to Bigger Faster Stronger. Thanks to Coach Jim Brown, Jeff Scurran, Len Walencikowski, Rick Bojak, Bob Doyle, Doug Ekmark, Dennis Dunn and Bob Bozied who are BFS Clinicians. Special thanks to my Bigger Faster Stronger partners Rick Anderson and Bob Rowbotham and the thousands of coaches and athletes who have participated in the Bigger Faster Stronger program and clinics.

Preface

Bigger Faster Stronger is not so much just a weight program but an attitude. An attitude which can propel both coach and athlete to their upper limit. It's called achievement of potential. The fulfillment of one's potential is a coach's greatest challenge. It is the athlete's most challenging goal. It is a noble cause.

This book is not a bodybuilding or competitive lifting book, for that is a completely different aspect of training. The reader will become an expert in the field of strength and conditioning for those involved in mainstream high school and collegiate sports. State–of–the–art concepts will be presented and put together into one complete total package.

Literally thousands of hours and decades of experience have gone into the BFS program. Bigger Faster Stronger has access to perhaps the largest amount of written material from the Russian and East European countries of any entity in the United States. Coach Shepard has been a true pioneer in the strength and conditioning field. All the way from being a major college football strength coach at three universities in the mid-sixties and early seventies, to being the first strength coach in the NBA to have a continuous program.

Included in this book is a complete speed, plyometric, agility, flexibility and, of course, weight training program. All these programs are integrated into the total BFS program.

Great care has been taken to present what has worked over and over again. It is what world class, self–made athletes have been doing for years. This total program has been perfected and continuously improved upon every year to give the coach and athlete a true, concise picture of what has to be done. This book is purposely designed to give any athlete and coach the ABSOLUTE WINNERS EDGE.

About the Author

Greg Shepard trained his first group of athletes in 1964 after graduating from Oberlin College. During the next thirty some years he has been a strength coach at three major universities (Oregon State University: 1965, University of Oregon: 1967 and Brigham Young University: 1971-73) and the strength coach for the Utah Jazz from 1982 to 1997. Every situation has been a pioneering effort.

Coach Shepard received a Masters degree from the University of Oregon with an emphasis in physiology, and Doctorate in Physical Education from Brigham Young University. His first love is football, both as a player and especially as a coach.

Coach Shepard has coached football in five different states and turned two different high schools with previous winless records into immediate winners. He was the Football Coach of the Year in Utah in 1975. Coach Shepard also guided Brigham Young University's Power Lifting team to a national championship in 1973.

**Greg Shepard in 1966 in the 198 lb. class
working on the Olympic lifts**

In 1962, Greg spent a year in Salzburg, Austria and was introduced to Olympic lifting. While there, he became a member of the local team. Greg received medals from the Austrian government for his competitive efforts. He has also won many power lifting trophies in the 198–, 220– and 242–pound weight classes. Greg has even run in some marathons. He still competes several times a year in Olympic lifting and has three state Master's records.

Greg Shepard has been president of Bigger Faster Stronger since 1977. Through BFS, Greg has written four books and produced twenty-three videos. In addition, he has published the BFS Journal four times yearly. As a result, he has written volumes - making him, most likely, the most prolific writer in strength and conditioning history.

Through Bigger Faster Stronger, over 100 BFS clinics are held nationwide each year. As illustrated in the photo below, it is here the special BFS attitude and spirit are passed on to thousands of athletes. Nearly 200 high schools have gone on to win their football state championships after their clinics. Clinics also produce 20% more victories in all boys and girls sports while cutting injuries in half.

Greg Shepard gets his greatest pleasure and emotional feeling when he sees young athletes set high goals and then totally commit themselves to make it happen. The crowning fulfillment is when the individual through this commitment learns a better way of life and becomes an "Upper Limit" person: A leader, an example, and a person being the best they can, be it athletically, academically, socially or spiritually.

500,000 athletes do all or part of the BFS program. Bigger Faster Stronger: The Nation's Leader in Athletic Fitness.

**Greg Shepard Dead Lifting 685
in the 242 lb. class in 1973**

Table of Contents

I. Introduction

Today the Upper Limit coach who desires a state-of-the-art program must be acutely aware of the importance of a total program concept for his athletes. You can no longer just emphasize lifting a few weights and workout a few months in the off-season. It is much more complicated than that. A state-of-the-art program must include not only a lifting program but also just the right balance of flexibility, speed, plyometric, agility and technique of sport(s) training.

The origin of athletic training programs began in the late 1950's with track athletes, specifically with the throwers. Shot put, discus, hammer and javelin throwers discovered that by lifting heavy weights their performance would improve. This improvement did not come by little bits, but came in huge chunks once the athlete caught on and had access to "the secret". By the late 1960's, many throwers weighed 265-plus pounds while running a 4.6 forty. In contrast, pro football linemen were much smaller, weaker and slower at this time. Shot put distances for the top twenty throwers increased by about ten feet and nearly twenty-five feet in the discus. To put it simply, if you didn't know "the secret" you couldn't compete.

As a football coach, I was fascinated by these huge, fast throwers. Since I had some friends who were world class throwers, I made it my business to learn "the secret". I'd spend my summers in the late 1960's in Los Angeles where the great throwers assembled. It was great fun to train on this program but even greater fun to bring it back to Sehome High School in Bellingham, Washington where I coached football and track.

We were the only ones in the state, high school or college, who had access to "the secret". Wow, what an advantage! We had fifty football players running between 4.5-5.0 in the forty. Many players weighed over 200 pounds while benching 300–plus, squatting 400–plus and dead-lifting 500–plus. Naturally, we wiped up in football. Sehome High School had an enrollment of 1400 in the top four grades and we played a number of schools with significantly greater enrollment. In a kind of mythical state championship post-season game, we clobbered Snohomish 27-7 and held them to minus yards rushing. In track, I had eleven discus throwers between 140 and 180 feet. That's better than some entire states even today.

During this time of the 1960's and early 1970's, athletes and coaches from other sports dabbled in strength training. Basketball and baseball shunned weights like the plague, while football coaches flitted about from one thing to another. It wasn't so much of trying to keep "the secret" a secret but more of just not broadcasting your advantage to the world. Also, it seemed that football coaches were looking for three things: something quick, something easy to administer and something safe. Since less than one percent of football coaches at that time had any self experience in weight training, they were, of course, terribly naïve and gullible.

ISOMETRICS

Hettinger and Müller, two German "scientists," came out with astounding statistics with isometrics. They claimed that strength gains of 3% a week could be made by pushing or pulling against an immovable object. All you had to do was go hard for six seconds, repeated three times. It certainly was appealing: Quick, easy and no coaching experience needed or necessary.

What a joke! It took football coaches about a year during this mid-sixties fiasco to figure out that isometrics were a real waste of time. During this isometric episode, the throwers remained with their free weight, heavy core lift approach while shaking their heads in disbelief that football coaches could do something that crazy. It was found years later that Hettinger and Miller had their subjects on steroids.

EXER–GENIE

At about the same time, the Exer–Genie came upon the scene. Thousands of coaches purchased these gadgets. Again, a short amount of time was required for a workout, it was safe and any coach by reading one page of instruction could administer the program. Perfect? Well, yes, except for one thing. It didn't work very well at all. The throwers kept shaking their heads.

UNIVERSAL GYM

Later in the 60's decade, the Universal Gym exploded upon the athletic world. The sales pitch went like this: It's safe, your loose weights won't get stolen, your kids just go around the circuit and it's easy. Administrators really liked the sales part. I was praying that every school I coached against would buy a Universal Gym for the tremendous advantage my kids would have. My prayers were profoundly answered. Every high school in America, including mine, bought one. My administrator thought it would be a good idea. We used it for some auxiliary work. I thought, "Pretty expensive auxiliaries. The stupid thing cost more than all my free weight equipment."

Probably the majority of high school athletes until the mid-seventies used a Universal Gym or a similar machine like a Marci for their primary training mode. As more and more high schools were becoming aware of "the secret", they began to turn away from their machines. To appease the women coaches, many football coaches would say, "OK, how about if we give you our Universal Gym." It may have seemed like a good idea at the time but it was a great disservice to women's sports because they can't reach their potential without also training with "the secret".

Shot Put World Record Holder (71–5 1/2) Randy Matson knew "the Secret" in the 1960's

**Randy Matson Squatting in the 1960's.
While at Texas A&M, he threw
the shot over 70 feet!**

Many football coaches then decided to give their
Universal Gym to the junior high schools. This too seemed
like a good idea, but now we find that "the secret" should be
started at the seventh grade level. The Universal Gym
people were smart. They recognized their machine was
shifting to an antique status and they began building free
weight equipment towards the end of the 1970's.

NAUTILUS

Football coaches were not prepared to deal with Arthur Jones and his Nautilus machines. We have never seen such . advertising before or since the Nautilus machines arrived in the early 1970's. Thirty-six and forty-eight pages of advertising were put into journals like Scholastic Coach. Arthur Jones paid for it, so under our American capitalistic rules, he was able to say anything to promote his machines. Since the vast majority of coaches had little or no experience in weight training, the advertising claims were taken in as the gospel. It took about ten years for the majority of coaches to figure out that these elaborate, expensive Nautilus machines were no way for an athlete to reach his potential.

The throwers just laughed and again shook their heads. Their secret seemed safe. However, for four reasons machines began to dwindle in popularity, until today machines are almost entirely used for auxiliary exercises.

First, high schools couldn't afford $5,000 per machine so they used free weights. At first, these coaches wished they could have a shiny blue machine, but then their kids began having some great results. If the difference between machines and free weights were not so dynamically obvious, machines would have snuffed out free weights entirely.

Second, the advent of the strength coach played a significant role in doing things right. Before the strength coach, it was usually administrators or the football coach who made strength training decisions. By the early 1980's, nearly all major colleges had a strength and conditioning coach. Boyd Epley of Nebraska, an ex-track athlete, started the National Strength and Conditioning Association (NSCA) in the late 1970's. Books and publications like the NSCA and BFS journal were being published. As a result, a much more knowledgeable strength and football coach emerged. No longer were vast majorities of coaches gullible.

Machine people still get asked to speak at clinics because they pay for booth space, but recently it has become embarrassing. Football coaches will make jokes and speak out during a machine presentation. To stay in business, the machine people have softened their claims considerably. Some have also started producing a free weight line or taken a stand that you need both.

Third, we began learning about Russian and Eastern European training techniques which were almost identical with the throwers but now coaches were listening because of some marvelous results with athletes from a variety of sports.

Fourth, the giants in powerlifting and Olympic lifting scorned machines. Even bodybuilders preferred free weights. Simply put, the machine people could never get the best athletes in any phase of the strength game to go with their program.

BFS Consultant and Clinician Stefan Fernholm. NCAA Discus Record Holder and also had World's farthest throw for most of 1987.

Stefan Fernholm took "the secret" to another level

HT.: 6–1 1/2   WT.: 270   40: 4.3

SQUAT: 820   POWER CLEAN: 475

POWER SNATCH: 350   VJ: 40 INCHES

SLJ: 11–3   BOX JUMP: 58 1/2 INCHES

ISOKINETICS — MINI-GYM — LEAPER

To differentiate between isometrics and regular free weight training in the late 1960's, several terms became popular. Isotonics was used to describe normal free weight movements. Isokinetics described equal resistance provided by a machine throughout a full range of motion. On paper and in theory, it looked good but in reality it just didn't help an athlete reach his full athletic potential. Terms like Isonetic and Variable Resistance were also used in describing isokinetic principles. Nautilus, Mini-Gym and the Leaper used the isokinetic principle. They claimed each other was different but it was basically the same.

THE DREAM! THE GOAL! THE GLORY!

To become an "Upper Limit" athlete and to reach one's fullest potential, an athlete must squat, bench, clean, stretch, sprint, vary his sets and reps, do agilities and plyometrics. Attention must be given to a great diet, proper rest and keeping exact records of progress. Workouts must be attacked with a war-like intensity and a game day attitude. Coaches should supervise their athletes' workouts like they would a football practice.

Athletes in mainstream high school or collegiate sports should never train exactly like a bodybuilder or a competitive lifter. The total BFS program for mainstream athletes is complex, with each phase interrelated in perfect harmony.

Most strength coaches and athletic programs now do all or a major part of what we do with the BFS program. It's no longer a secret. So you're either already on our BFS program or we're on yours.

It isn't so much of *what* to do anymore but *how* to do each intricate phase correctly and then weave those phases into an exciting, workable, state-of-the-art TOTAL TRAINING PROGRAM.

I promise to those who follow the exact BFS program an athletic career that will propel you to your fullest potential. It is fun and rewarding. Every athlete and coach will make so much day-to-day progress that emotional highs and great bonds of friendship will be commonplace.

Athletes, teams and coaches. . .work together—dream together. Totally commit yourselves to a common goal. As you progress upward, you will see that all the sweat, the work and the pain was worth every second.

Brian Blutreich 6–5 1/2, 250, used "the secret" to produce the best double in High School history in 1986. Shot: 69–6 1/2. Discus: 210–8. Bench: 405, Squat: 515, Clean: 320, Snatch 200. 40: 4.8. VJ: 33. SLJ: 10–0. GPA 3.1.

John Godina: (6–4, 247) Followed the BFS Program exactly, and as a 16-year-old junior threw 194-8 in the discus in 1989. He was also a Wyoming All-State Football player. GPA 4.0. At U.C.L.A. John won the World Championship in 1995.

Christy Ward: (5–6, 164) Best Shot Put in the nation in 1988 at 49 plus. From North Valley High School in Oregon, Christy also followed the BFS Program exactly. She benched 210, Squatted 355, Power Cleaned 180. VJ: 30 1/2. 40: 5.13. She received special coaching from Stefan.

Kami Keshmiri, 6–4, 220, used "the secret" for the National High School Record in the Discus in 1987. Kami threw 225–2. Parallel Squat: 530, Bench: 395, Snatch: 225. 40: 4.3, VJ: 36. Shot: 65–9 1/2, GPA: 3.5.

II. The Total Program
An Overview

The weight training part of the Total BFS Program is divided into two basic segments: the Core Lifts and the Auxiliary Lifts. Core Lifts are those exercises which are deemed to be the most important for developing athletic potential. Core Lifts are the big exercises which work more than one muscle group and require a greater emphasis of time and energy. The basic BFS Core Lifts are the Squat, Clean, Bench Press and Dead Lift.

Auxiliary Lifts are also important in the development of athletic potential. However, these exercises usually involve only one muscle group and require less time and energy than core lifts. An example of a football auxiliary would be a neck exercise.

An athlete should do flexibility exercises every day and do them all year long. The BFS 1–2–3–4 Flexibility Program will be presented which emphasizes speed improvement. It is easy to learn and is most effective. The BFS 1–2–3–4 Flexibility Program takes only ten minutes per day.

The BFS Plyometric Program also only takes ten minutes per workout. It is done twice per week with an optional individual workout which can be done on Saturdays. Plyometrics can bridge the gap between strength and power as explosiveness is created. Accurate records on the vertical jump, standing long jump and box jumps should be kept and tested on a regular basis.

Speed and sprint work is done in conjunction with Plyometrics. A complete program will be presented which will include the BFS Sprint Technique System. Sprinting should be done all-year round with either running forty or twenty yard sprints for time. Sprints should be timed twice per month. Accurate records and charts should be kept.

YOUR BFS TOTAL PROGRAM

MONDAY	TUESDAY	WEDNESDAY	THURSDAY	FRIDAY
Squat Variation	Sprint Work	Power Clean	Sprint Work	Parallel Squat
Bench Variation	Plyometrics	Trap Bar	Plyometrics	Bench Press
Auxiliary Lifts	Flexibility	Auxiliary Lifts	Flexibility	Auxiliary Lifts
Flexibility	Agility	Flexibility	Agility	Flexibility
Agility	Technique	Agility	Technique	Agility

* This is the BFS Off-Season Program. During the
In-Season, lifting is done twice per week.

You Must Get Great on the Parallel Squat

The Bench Press: A Big Core Lift

Technique is Critical on the Power Clean

An easy way to get an edge is to use video analysis of speed technique. When an athlete combines the above with Plyometrics, Flexibility Exercises, Parallel Squats and light Straight-Leg Dead Lifts it is easy to improve speed.

The BFS Dot Drill is a fantastic way to develop agility and it only takes one minute a day. Plus, we have national standards, so as the athlete gets timed, he'll have goals and standards. Every athlete needs quick feet and agility.

Technique training is an integral part of the Total BFS Program. A quarterback should not wait until August to throw a football. A basketball player shouldn't take six months off to dribble or shoot. A discus thrower needs to work on his technique more than just in April and May. It doesn't take a lot but it does take consistency.

The Dead Lift with a Spot: An Optional Football Core Lift

Stefan Stretching for Speed

Speed Technique Training   **Plyometric Bounding**

The Total BFS Program involves lifting weights all year round. An athlete either is in an off-season or an in-season program. Most programs try to maintain during the in-season, while the BFS Program allows every athlete to make great gains and break many personal records during each week of the sport season.

The BFS Set–Rep System is a vital key to the overall success of the total program. It is absolutely imperative that sets and reps be varied from workout to workout. The BFS System creates unbelievable intensity and progress in the weight room. In fact, we guarantee that every athlete will break at least eight or more records per week. They will do this week after week, month after month and year after year.

Plyometric Box Jumping: BFS Total Program

**Coach Shepard Teaching the
BFS 1-2-3-4 Flexibility Program**

Vertical Jump
Stefan has 40" VJ

Dan Santhouse:
Widener University
BFS Dot Drill
National Record Holder:
36.6 seconds

Nutrition and rest are also tremendously important in aiding the ultimate progress of each athlete. About 30 percent of all high school athletes will eat nothing or drink a Coke for breakfast. The BFS Nutrition System is an easy, fun way to upgrade every athlete's diet. The BFS 30 point nutrition will be presented along with some additional upper limit nutritional information.

The total BFS Program can work miracles and it can literally change lives, but these great things cannot take place without the final ingredient. Every coach, every team and every individual must have an intense desire to succeed. The best program in the world will fail with an improper attitude.

Top Priority Auxiliary Exercise: The Jerk Press

Everyone involved must be totally committed, dedicated and persistent. The athlete must enter his workouts with a game-day attitude and refuse to fail. The coach must conduct his team's workouts like he would a regular practice. He should be involved, organized and demanding. True success won't happen unless you make it happen. Everyone must take on a leadership role. Every athlete should learn the coaching points of every exercise and then be willing and able to help his teammate get through every phase of the program with great technique. Everyone must follow this great quote: "If it is to be, it is up to me." As this attitude permeates your very being then, and only then, will you become a true Upper-Limit athlete.

Coach Shepard Spotting a High School Athlete on a 500 lb. Dead Lift at a BFS Clinic.

If it is to be — It is up to me!

The Dream! The Goal! The Glory!

III. The Core Lift Concept

I have used a Core Lift concept since 1967 and began calling certain exercises Core Lifts soon thereafter. Part of "the secret" is utilizing this concept.

The Core Lift concept is now universally accepted and many strength coaches use this term. The concept is simply understanding that some exercises are more important than others. Which is more important to success in football, your legs or arms? Obviously, most coaches are going to answer that legs are the most important. If that is so, then which exercise is most important, squats or curls? Should an athlete do two sets of 10 reps on both the Squat and the Bicep Curl exercises or should more emphasis be placed on the Squat?

The answer appears to be quite obvious, yet you can bet that several teams in any high school conference will not use a Core Lift concept. Do you get it! Even though "the secret" is out and has been out for many years, you can still gain an edge at every turn. Why? Well, some coaches and athletes don't want to put forth the effort while some believe something else. Isn't that wonderful? You can gain a big edge on some opponents just by putting the BFS Core Lift Concept into practice!

Some schools or programs are going to do ten or fifteen different exercises and do the same sets and reps with each of those exercises. What we're going to do is select several multi–muscle group exercises and then really get after those exercises. We will emphasize the legs and hips for that is the foundation of strength and power for an athlete. We will call these exercises: <u>The Core Lifts</u>.

The next four chapters will discuss in detail the BFS Core Lifts. First is the Parallel Squat with some excellent variations. Second is the Bench Press with variations. Third is the Power Clean with variations and fourth is the Dead Lift with its variations.

Do the BFS Core Lift concept and you will gain an edge. I call it the "Winner's Edge." There is no other path that will lead you to your "Upper Limit"!

Top photo: **Senior Linebacker, Daniel Cole, squatting 800 pounds.**
Bottom photo: **Daniel as a Freshman, before he learned the Secret of the Eyes.**

Don't Look Up! Look Straight Ahead!

IV. Squats

The parallel squat is the king of all exercises for an athlete. If an athlete were to do nothing but parallel squats, he would have a good program; not great, but good. Leave them out, minimize them or do them incorrectly and it doesn't matter what else is done—what machines are used or what system is used: <u>You simply will not have a good program</u>!

Parallel squats are the basis and foundation of great speed with great size. A 6–4 athlete who weighs 265 and who has good athletic ability can run a 4.6 forty, if an excellent parallel squat program is used. If machines or something else is done, this same athlete would be lucky to run a 5.0 forty. I cannot overemphasize the importance of squatting parallel and performing this exercise correctly. Parallel squats for an athlete are absolutely critical.

Since the majority of high school football programs do squats, you might well ask about the winning edge of "the secret" that was promised. Don't worry! You can make a quantum leap over your opponents by parallel squatting correctly. First of all, many high school programs have their athletes squat high to way high. In an eight team conference, probably four to five schools will squat high. Second, the other two or three schools will have serious technique or spotting problems.

It is absolutely imperative to understand the importance of depth on squats. All known standards are based on a parallel or slightly below parallel depth. The High School All-American Standard is 500 lbs. The All-State Standard is 400 lbs. These standards were designed by BFS to help the athlete and coach understand when something unique has been achieved. It takes a special athlete and a special understanding of how to do squats to reach those levels. If an athlete squats a foot high or three inches high with 500 pounds, it is meaningless. Not a whole lot is really happening and great benefits will be missed.

The Parallel Squat: The King of Exercises

Squatting high will only strengthen the quadriceps, the muscles in the front part of the upper leg. Not until the thighs are parallel or slightly below parallel will the hamstrings be positively affected. As this depth is attained, the hamstrings and the quadriceps will be strengthened in a coordinated manner. It is also critical to understand that running speed improvement of any athlete is directly correlated with hamstring development. To improve speed, the hamstrings have got to be made stronger. Squatting to the proper depth will give you a big edge over many opponents.

TECHNIQUE SECRETS

The best way to get all athletes, beginning and veteran lifters, in a perfect squatting position is to have them sit in an ordinary chair. This is a vital secret because everyone, even the most difficult, can easily experience a perfect rock-solid squatting position. Now, you are going to concentrate on six important technique secrets: Athletic stance, spread the chest, lock-in lower back, toes pointed slightly out, eyes focused straight ahead and sit tall.

A.   Athletic Stance: There are three basic squatting stances: Bodybuilding, Powerlifting and Athletic. Bodybuilders generally use a very narrow stance often with the toes straight ahead and sometimes with a board placed underneath the heels. This method is used to attain certain bodybuilding objectives of thigh development. Many powerlifters will use a very wide stance with the toes flared out. Some powerlifters will use a narrow stance but will point the toes outward quite a lot. Some powerlifters will use an athletic stance. Powerlifters will use whatever stance will allow them to squat the most weight but when I see a very wide stance with the toes pointed out excessively, I refer to that as a powerlifting stance.

A Perfect Parallel Squat

Whenever I read about squatting stances from strength coaches or attend a seminar on the subject, invariably the experts will always say "Assume about a shoulder-width stance." This is meant to be an athletic stance but is there a better way? Yes! This is part of your winning edge. Part of "the secret".

Tell your football players to get in a linebacker stance. Tell basketball players to get in a rebounding stance and baseball players to look like a shortstop. Volleyball and tennis players should be in their ready position. At clinics, we get into a bodybuilder's squatting stance and ask "Does this look like a linebacker?" The kids say, "No. Get your feet wider?" We then get into a wide powerlifting stance with the toes flared way out and ask, "How about this. Does this look like a football, basketball or baseball player?" Everyone always laughs. Then we get into an athletic stance and it's amazing. You can't tell what sport we are in. You see the "ready position" for all mainstream high school sports is essentially the same.

Now, groove and build your power and strength from this athletic stance. As athletes and coaches spot each other they should be making sure lifters look like an athlete at all times with their stance. This is a far superior perspective than saying "about shoulder width." Our way also sends a message that we are athletes and that when the same high school athlete makes a transition from football to basketball to baseball his squatting stance will remain the same.

Now, sit in a chair and place the feet in a perfect athletic stance.

B. Spread the Chest: This is a most fantastic coaching secret which I accidentally discovered while doing a BFS Clinic. I was frustrated because several boys could not lock-in their lower back. I blurted out, "Spread the chest!" To my amazement, the lower back immediately went from poor to great. I now say "spread the chest" to athletes when they dead lift or clean. Once the athlete experiences the lower

Figure 1: Great Squatting Position

    A. Athletic Stance

    B. Spread the Chest

    C. Lock in Lower Back

    D. Toes Pointed Slightly Out

    E. Eyes Focused Straight Ahead

    F. Sit Tall

back locking into place as he spreads his chest while sitting in a chair, he can usually have the same experience without the chair. Sitting in the chair just makes it a whole lot easier.

Several years later, I noticed that some strength coaches were saying "get a big chest." It is the same principle but "spread the chest" seems to be a superior coaching term.

C. Lock-in the Lower Back: Spreading the chest and locking in the lower back go hand-in-hand. However, you must visualize and coach both. The lower back must <u>swoop</u> way in, into a deep concave position. Most coaches have a difficult time seeing the difference between a fair, good and great concave lower back position.

A coach may want to pull back on the lifter's shoulder and push in on the lower back as shown in figure 5. The athlete in that photo has at best only a fair position while in figure 6 he now has a good to great position. There is still room for improvement. So, what do you say? "Spread the chest, lock-in the lower back." I will probably say this 100 times each workout session with groups of athletes. It is a key phrase that spotters should also be using frequently. Athletes need constant reminders. That's a secret unto itself.

D. Toes Pointed Slightly Out: This technique secret is fairly well known but it's still the cause of many mistakes for athletes. Most athletes will point their toes out naturally because it aids in balance. However, many times the athlete will point the toes out too far. No problem. All you do is go back to the athletic stance formula. Ask the question, "Do you look like a linebacker, shortstop or basketball player?" Remember, you must groove your power from an exact athletic stance and this, of course, must include the toes only being pointed <u>slightly</u> out.

E. Eyes Focused Straight Ahead: How many times have you heard, "Look up—look up!" I diplomatically tell athletes and coaches this means to <u>look up straight ahead with eyes focused on a point.</u> Would you sprint looking up

Figure 2: Find Five Major Problems

Figure 3: Find Four Major Problems

Figure 4: Find Three Major Problems

Figure 5: A Coach must be able to recognize problems, then correct them.

at the sky? Would you block or tackle looking up at the sky? Obviously not! You should sprint, block or tackle looking straight ahead. You squat the same way. You also want to focus your eyes on a point. Do not take your eyes off this point which should be straight ahead. If your eyes move, your head moves. If your head moves, your body moves. If your body, head and eyes move, your squat technique will be adversely affected. Not only will you lift less weight, you will do it less safely.

When an athlete looks up at the ceiling while beginning the squatting movement at the top position, everything might seem comfortable and right. However, at the bottom position is when things go bad. It is virtually impossible to look at the same point on the ceiling at the bottom position. Therefore, the eyes move, the head moves and the body moves out of position.

Don't look down at the ground as this can be as dangerous as tackling a ball carrier with your head down. Don't look up and don't look down but stare intensely straight ahead and fix your eyes on a single point completely and totally throughout the entire lift. It is one of the great secrets that will give you a big edge on your opponents.

F. Sit Tall: Every athlete wants to always attempt to squat with the feeling of sitting tall. You do not want to bend over with the head down and hips high. Many athletes will naturally sit tall and keep a beautiful upright position throughout the entire squat. However, many other athletes will have a very difficult time trying to keep upright. This has to do primarily with trunk length versus leg length. Secondarily, the legs could be weak and lower back stronger and the athlete compensates by bending over while squatting.

The solution may never fully be realized but that's perfectly all right. Many great squatters lean over. However, they attempt to sit tall and their eyes fix in on a point with the chest spread and the lower back locked in correctly. Always ATTEMPT TO SIT TALL while squatting. This

Figure 6: Perfect Low Power Position. This athlete will have no problem parallel squatting.

is a key coaching point and you should remind your athletes constantly throughout the squatting movement to sit tall.

Now, sit tall in a chair. Get your feet in an athletic stance with the toes pointed out slightly. Focus your eyes on a point straight ahead and spread the chest and lock-in the lower back. If you can do that, congratulations! You are now ready to experience the low power position.

THE LOW POWER POSITION

Many coaches have remarked after our BFS Clinics that it's amazing how we get young athletes to squat perfectly in just a minute or two even with no previous squatting experience. The trick is to get each athlete into a perfect low power position as illustrated in figure 6. We recommend that even experienced athletes feel this position before each set. I still do even though I've been squatting for over 25 years.

If an athlete cannot assume a perfect low-power position, he is most certainly doomed to failure. A coach must be able to recognize any and all errors. He must also be able to correct these errors before his athlete can be successful. Let's analyze the previous photos and find the major errors.

In figure 2 (pg. 40), there are five major problems. First, the heels are not firmly planted on the floor. Sometimes athletes are told to put a board underneath the heels to help on balance. This is wrong. Get your athletes in a perfect low power position. The second problem is the knees. They are way forward in relation to the toes. Not only is this poor squatting technique, it places unnecessary pressure on the knee joints. To help correct the first two problems, simply have the athlete get his feet closer to the Squatting Stand, which is the third problem in the photo. The next two problems are the lower back not being locked-in tight and the upper body leaning forward. To correct the lower back, tell your athlete to spread his chest. To correct the upper body lean, say "sit tall". The coach may physically push in on the lower back and place the palm of his hand on the athlete's chest and gently pull back. The coach can also physically pull the knees back in helping his athlete get into a perfect low power position.

Figure 3 reveals the same problems except now the athlete's feet are flat and the heels are firmly planted on the floor. The knees are better but this athlete doesn't need to squat quite that low. In figure 4, we find the feet are close to the squatting stand and the knees are back which is good but this athlete has three major problems: First, squatting too low, second the lower back is not locked-in; and third, the upper body has too much forward lean.

Figure 6 shows the perfect low power position. The athlete has his feet close to the Squatting Stand. His feet and heels are firmly planted on the floor. His knees are back and not extended past the toes. The athlete is at a perfect parallel position. His eyes are focused on a point which helps the lower back and upper body position. If you said one of the major problems in figure 2 and 3 was the head position, I wouldn't argue. Notice the difference in the chin position of figure 2 and figure 6. The athlete pictured is my son, Matt, while he was in the 8th grade. At this time, he weighed 125 and Parallel Squatted 225 pounds.

PRE–SQUAT TECHNIQUE

A. Grip: There are two technique guidelines to consider when establishing a proper grip on the squat. First is thumb position. Should you have your thumb around the bar or in back of the bar as illustrated in figure 7? About 60% of powerlifters have the thumb in back while 40% of power-lifters prefer their thumbs around the bar. Obviously both styles are acceptable, but I prefer to coach my athletes with their thumbs in back of the bar. I feel this style is superior as it tends to prevent slippage of the bar. Sometimes athletes will have a problem in keeping the bar on the shoulders.

Figure 7

Figure 8 shows Joe Clifford demonstrating a 726 competition squat. **Notice Joe's wide grip.** Joe was on coach Shepard's powerlifting team.

Sometimes the bar will actually slip off the shoulders and slip down the back. The bar seems to be more secure with the thumbs in back; but if an athlete, after trying both styles, really prefers to have his thumbs around, I don't object.

The second grip guideline to consider is the width of the athlete's grip. This is another one of those secrets which can give you an edge. At clinics, I ask everyone to pretend they have a bar on their shoulders and to get a "very narrow grip." Then, I ask everyone to sit tall, spread their chest and lock-in their lower back. Next, they are asked to take a wide grip and lock-in their lower backs. Now I ask, "Which grip makes it easier to lock-in the lower back?" It's unanimous! It's the wide grip.

Make sure you use the lines which are grooved into most Olympic bars about four inches from the inside collars. Use these lines as reference points. An athlete might put his first finger on each line with his thumb behind the bar. Now, he is properly balanced with a wide grip and has some assurance that the bar will remain secure on his shoulders. He is now ready to place the bar on the shoulders.

B. Bar Position: A very common mistake for athletes who squat is placing the bar too high on the shoulders. In fact, many athletes place the bar right on the neck. This hurts, so they'll use a barbell pad. For most athletes, this also affects proper balance for heavy squatting. The vast majority of athletes will squat more and squat more effectively with more comfort when the bar is placed lower on the shoulders as shown in figure 9. Only a very, very small percentage of athletes will be able to squat more effectively with a high bar placement and this is because of structural differences in bone length and tendon-muscle attachments.

Some powerlifters will place the bar extremely low on the shoulders. Sometimes the bar may be as much as four inches from the top of the shoulders, which is against the rules. For some lifters, this may give a slight anatomical advantage or the advantage may be experienced because of a

Figure 9
Bar Position demonstrated by Eric Leckner
of the Utah Jazz

heavy, tight lifting suit or even lack of flexibility. Whatever the reason, extreme low bar placement squatting will detract from overall leg development which is obviously bad for an athlete.

Most athletes will be able to find a natural groove on the shoulders when they come under the bar in a proper position. "Don't put the bar on your neck; put it on your shoulders. Find a groove." In almost every case, if you say these technique cues, athletes will be able to have excellent bar placement during their squat.

C. Taking the Bar off the Rack: I've seen high school athletes get all psyched to squat and get their shoulders 2–3 inches under the bar. Then, with an explosive movement, jam their shoulders against the bar. Well, jamming your shoulders against a steel bar from this 2–3 inch space will cause the athlete to bruise his neck or shoulders. Besides hurting, it is unlikely the athlete will have the bar placed on his shoulders correctly.

On the other end of the spectrum, I've seen athletes wimp a bar off the rack. Many times this athlete will not be in a good solid squatting position as he backs up to a ready stance.

A far superior way is to come under the bar in a great solid proper power position, making sure everything is correct. Get the bar in the groove on your shoulders. Look straight ahead. Spread the chest. Get in your athletic stance. Now, this next technique point is most critical. Get your athletic stance directly under the bar. Many athletes will stand a foot back and lean forward. This is asking for trouble, especially with heavy weight. Now you're ready. Put some pressure on the bar and make sure everything feels right. If it does, blast off! This explosive movement will not bruise the shoulders because you've already put some pressure on the bar. The advantage you have now is that your position is great and because of the explosive movement, the bar feels light. You are confident.

The bar is now off the rack and the athlete is firmly under the weight. At this point, take a short step back with each foot, and assume an athletic stance. You are ready to squat. In the case of some squat racks, the athlete may have to take several steps backward to clear himself to squat. Some step-squat racks and peg-squat racks may require many long steps for clearance. Some squat racks have a spotting tier which is too high for parallel squats, thus requiring a long walk back for position. Obviously, anything more than a short step back with each foot is a disadvantage.

SQUAT TECHNIQUE

A. The Start: The athlete should be looking straight ahead at a point. His mind should be clear and intense. He should be thinking about technique: chest spread, locking in the lower back and his descent pattern. A huge breath must be taken in just prior to the descent. In the case of a one rep max, I recommend two breaths. First, a huge breath which is held to let the air settle in deep within the rib cavity, and then another quick breath as you begin the descent to expand the chest even further.

B. The Descent: The athlete should descend in an even, controlled pattern. Some athletes will descend inch by inch and take forever, which is a mistake. Some athletes will rapidly crash down out of control, which is dangerous. When the athlete remains in an even and controlled pattern, his technique is more likely to be better.

Throughout the descent, the breath should be held. The athlete, coach and spotters should be mindful of all technique guidelines that have previously been discussed. Always spread the chest, lock-in the lower back, look at your point and sit tall.

C. The Bottom Position: The athlete should squat to the parallel or slightly below parallel position. Keep in

Notice thumb, bar position on shoulders, and wide grip

mind, many athletes will squat high. This is one of your edges. An edge that will give you an advantage over your competition. Therefore, strict adherence to the parallel position must be realized. If you squat high, then no hamstring or glute development takes place. This will greatly hamper your speed and jumping improvement. To hit a correct parallel position is critical for personal and team success. It is one of the greatest secrets in this book.

It is very difficult for most athletes to know when they are parallel. The spotters need to become involved in letting their partner know when he's parallel. This can be done through the marble test. We also have a device called the Safety Squat or Beeper which automatically lets you know when you're parallel.

D. The Marble Test: I use the marble test concept with athletes because they easily visualize a true parallel squat position. I will squat down to a position that is four inches from parallel and ask, "Now pretend that I have a marble on the top of my thigh halfway between my knee and hip. What would it do?" Naturally they say it would roll down towards my knee. This illustrates a squat that is too high. When I squat parallel, the athletes can visualize the marble staying in the middle of my thigh.

Spotters, which are also judges, should position themselves to see their partner's thighs while he's squatting. The spotters should let their partner know exactly how he is doing on every rep as they visualize that marble. Saying things like, "You're one inch too high, perfect depth or you're too low," can be very helpful.

Powerlifters must break parallel. Therefore, the marble would have to roll towards the athlete's hip. Some football and/or strength coaches want their athletes to break parallel. I have no objection to this whatsoever. To get the proper leg development, the athlete must go to at least parallel.

Some coaches don't use the top of the thigh, but use the bottom of the thigh as their parallel squatting reference point.

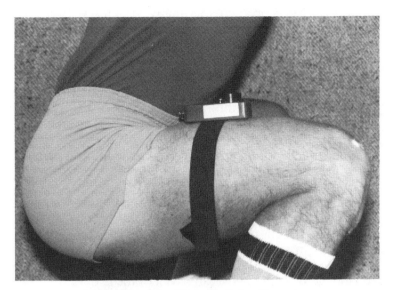

Figure 11: The Safety Squat

The Safety Squat or Beeper can be a useful tool in helping athletes and coaches understand the meaning of parallel. Many times an athlete will argue with a teammate or coach on the question of being parallel. With the Safety Squat, there is no argument.

The Safety Squat works on a mercury switch and when the device is held at a parallel position, it will beep. The athlete simply wraps the velcro straps around his thigh at midpoint making sure the safety squat is placed exactly on top of the thigh.

This creates problems as many athletes will end up squatting 2–3 inches higher than if using the top of the thigh as the parallel point. These athletes would lose hamstring and glute development plus, standards become meaningless.

E. The Upward Drive: You should continue holding your breath when beginning the upward drive from the parallel position. You should picture your hips attached to a giant rubber band. As you go down to parallel, you stretch the rubber band to the limit. The instant the hips hit parallel, you release the rubber band. Your hips pop upward while you maintain perfect technique.

About halfway up, you pass through the "sticking point" which is the point when the squat becomes easier. When you reach this point, you should breathe out. Sometimes, lifters on a heavy squat will let out a yell as they expel the air in their lungs. This is perfectly acceptable and probably helps with the overall psych of the lift.

Sometimes with a heavy lift the hips will come up alright but the athlete will lean over. To correct this position, you may try two techniques. First, scoot the hips forward and try to get the hips underneath the bar. Obviously, you should again reemphasize our previous technique guidelines for the chest and lower back. The second technique guideline which works extremely well with many athletes is to think elbows forward. When lifter presses his elbows forward during a squat, he will tend to have an upright torso with a big chest and a locked-in lower back. The hips will also follow the elbows.

The eyes should remain fixed on the same point throughout the entire upward drive. When the lift and set is completed, take short, controlled steps back to the rack. Always keep in a solid position as you rack the bar.

F. Controlled Psych or Frenzied Psych? I've seen some powerlifters, when attempting an all-time max, work themselves into a screaming psychotic frenzy. They invariably miss and sometimes get hurt. The parallel squat is a tricky lift. Technique and correct position means everything. Every technique guideline must be executed to perfection when attempting a new max. You must be psyched but it must be a controlled psych. Your mind must be clear and mentally preparing and thinking of correct positioning throughout the entire lift.

KNEES AND SQUATS

Are squats bad for the knees? This question is certainly one that has been raised many times. It has appeared to me that many people, not even in the field of athletics or physical education, including women, have heard that squats are "bad for the knees." Many football coaches have in the past taken an extremely firm stand that squats and football do not go together.

On the other extreme, track and field athletes, especially shotputters, hammer, javelin, and discus throwers, have been doing heavy squats for years with no apparent knee damage. The oriental people sit in a deep squat position for hours with no apparent knee problems.

It has always seemed quite a phenomenon that these two extreme views exist. The stand against squats seems to be based generally on hearsay or opinion. The stand for squats seems to be generally based upon personal experience. I have done competition squats for nearly 15 years without knee problems.

Therefore, in the summer of 1971 I conducted a research project to determine, if possible, the facts regarding squats. The following information is selected excerpts from this research project.

Incredibly as it may seem, there has been practically no pertinent scientific research that I was able to locate regarding knees, squats and knees, or exercise and knees. I perused numerous research journals, physical education journals, and medical journals dating back to 1950.

Performing squats going down under complete control to only a parallel position will cause positive changes to take place. First, the leg muscles will become stronger and bigger, especially the quadriceps and hamstrings. Second, the tendons will become thicker and stronger. Third, the knee ligaments will also become thicker and stronger. Fourth, the entire articular capsule of the knee will become thicker. Fifth, the bones of the legs will become stronger and slightly bigger due to increased capilarization. Sixth, the cartilage of the knee will become more resistant to injury (according to Dr. Mel Hayashi). Dr. Hayashi, a sports medicine orthopedic specialist, has been a chief resident at the Mayo Clinic and was the Chief Orthopedic Surgeon in the 1984 Olympic Games. I believe the above positive effects of squats are why athletes who do squats correctly have a far less incidence of knee injuries than those athletes who do not squat at all. This is especially true in football.

I believe there might be some danger to the knee joint in deep squats, especially if the lifter comes down fast, or out of control, or bounces at the bottom position. It seems to me only logical and common sense that if a lifter does deep squats, for example, with 400 pounds, and he comes down hard and bounces at the deep bottom position, he is asking for problems.

However, if the lifter with a heavy weight comes down **under control** to the parallel squat position and then comes up, **there should be no danger to the knee joint whatsoever**. This is a completely natural movement, like sitting in a chair. The bones, ligaments, and muscles were designed and constructed to be able to articulate to a parallel squat position.

Our organization is singularly unique in the fact we are in personal touch with thousands of football coaches. For example, we do over 100 all-day seminars annually throughout the nation, teaching tens of thousands of athletes how to squat correctly. These coaches asked to report positive and negative training effects through our toll-free number. We also publish a journal which goes to every head football coach in America. We are in constant touch with America's football coaches. Our base monthly phone bill is testimony to this fact. The results are overwhelming!

Performing squats correctly seems to greatly reduce the number of knee injuries. Our files are full of coaches who relate their stories of how dramatic the reduction injuries became after including squats in their training program. Believe me, if there were a problem we'd hear about it. We hear about many problems from coaches, but squats adversely affecting the knees is certainly not one of them.

In conclusion, we are firmly and resolutely convinced that performing squats correctly is like taking out an insurance police against injury, especially knee injuries.

SQUATTING ALIGNMENT: I like to sit all my athletes in the bleachers and have them get into an "athletic stance" "sit tall" and "spread their chest". See Figure 12. In this photo, I am checking Luther Elliss' knees for correct alignment.   (Luther is a 6-5 300 pound star Defensive Tackle for Detroit.) My finger is pointing at the middle of his knee. If I were to drop a string straight down, where would it land? In this case, in this photo, the string would land in the middle of his foot which is perfect. If you had 50 athletes in the bleachers, it would take less than two minutes to identify all the athletes who would not fit this perfect alignment format. It would also only take about two minutes to correct any alignment problems. There are three ways to look at knees for correct squatting alignment: Knees out, in or forward.

Knees In: (See Figure 14) This problem is quite common with women athletes and junior high age boys.   When squatting the knees-in problem will surface on the way up. The knees are usually alright on the way down when squatting. The knees-in problem is more difficult to correct and puts unwanted pressure on the medial collateral ligaments.   The first step is to yell "knees" to the athlete

FIGURE #12

FIGURE #13

FIGURE #14

FIGURE #15

FIGURE #16   **FIGURE #17**

while squatting. This is a signal to force the knees out over the toes.

This signal may or may not work the first time. If not, the second correction technique is to lightly slap the inside of the athlete's knee as shown in Figure 15. This gives the athlete a kinesthetic feel of the problem. The cure usually happens after only a few light slaps. If the problem persists, then video taping the athlete squat so he/she can see themselves will almost always do the trick in those few extreme cases.

Knees Forward: (See Figure 16) Many beginning squatters will want to lift their heels off the ground and bring their knees forward as the main part of their descent pattern. This puts too much pressure on the patella area besides being horribly ineffective. You may correct the knee-forward problem by letting the athlete hold on to a partner's hands for balance as in Figure 17. The athlete should "sit tall" and "spread the chest" with the elbows and shoulders back. The athlete will now be able to balance himself with his heels on the ground from a Parallel Squat position. The partner should also let go after a while to let the athlete have a chance to balance himself from that difficult position. It is surprising but most high school athletes can balance themselves after they get the "feel" of the parallel position with the heels on the ground.

Most bodybuilders will squat with the knees forward with the bar position high on the neck. Bodybuilders usually lift with a lighter weight with higher reps and therefore will perhaps never have a problem. However, athletes will usually bring the bar back more on the shoulders and want to lift a lot more weight. If the knees persist on coming forward with heavier and heavier weights, it is my opinion that this is potentially dangerous. It is better to attempt to sit back more on the hips with the lower leg being more vertical as in Figure 17.

SPOTTING TECHNIQUES

Correct spotting techniques are critical to squatting correctly.   A coach has the responsibility of teaching spotting correctly and demanding strict adherence to these spotting techniques. Three spotters should be used to insure success in squatting correctly. A back spotter and two side spotters are used, as in Figure 18. The functions of the three spotters are threefold.   First, the spotters should act as coaches and give correct technique cues.   Second, they should act as judges on proper depth and technique problems. Third, they should be great teammates and offer constant encouragement. Spotters should pull the best from their training partner.

Your competition will not spot this way. This is part of "the secret" that will give you the winner's edge.

The Back Spotter: The back spotter should place his hands firmly on the bar at all times. This includes from the moment the lifter gets under the bar to back out to when he puts the bar back on the rack after squatting. The hands are placed on the bar for two reasons. First, it is very easy to correct technique especially when a lifter leans forward. The back spotter then just pulls back slightly but firmly and that poor position is corrected. Also, the back spotter should be talking and encouraging the lifter through the lift and set. Sometimes powerlifters will spot from behind with their arms going under the lifter's armpits to his chest but this assumes no technique problems.

The Side Spotters: The side spotters should be in a squat position on the sides with their hands underneath the bar. If something happens, it usually happens quick and they need to be ready. You cannot spot on the sides with arms crossed in a standing position. The side spotters also should "yell" something on **each rep** of every heavy set. Here are some suggestions: "One inch high, a little lower, perfect! Looking good, stay tight, eyes, fight it, be fierce, one more rep, too low, spread the chest, etc."   After the set is completed, the side spotter will grasp the bar and assist the lifter back to the rack. I tell the side spotters to put their nose on the rack. This is important because if they remain on the side, they just can't see the rack (see figure 18).

FIGURE #18 Three Spotters Should Always be Used and Side Spotters Should Assist the Lifter in Getting Back to the Rack.

KNEE WRAPS AND BELTS

Knee wraps should be available to all athletes, but should be used sparingly. Some lifters will wrap their knees for every set. This, I believe, is wrong for an athlete. Always squatting with knee wraps hinders the development of the tendons and ligaments of the knee.

However, nearly all powerlifters wear knee wraps in competition. You can squat more with knee wraps. Therefore, when an athlete is going for a heavy set or new one-rep max, knee wraps will give him both physiological and psychological support.

Some athletes will have sore or tender knees. Often knee wraps will make squatting easier and tolerable. Knee wraps will also make and keep the knee joint warm and therefore better lubricated with synovial fluid.

Lifting belts are essential to every weight room. Belts also give physiological and psychological support. There are three kinds of belts: The four-inch tapered Olympic belt, the six-inch belt and the four-inch power belt.

The four-inch or ten centimeter Olympic belt is best for overall lifting. It is the most common belt used and best for power cleans, snatches or Olympic lifting. The six-inch belt cannot be used in competition but some athletes prefer this belt for training because of the greater area of support in the lower back. Some athletes don't like the six-inch belt because it cuts into their sides. The four-inch power belt does not taper in front but is four inches all the way around. Powerlifters used to turn their four-inch tapered belt around so the wide part was in front. This gave them an advantage in the squat. As a result, manufacturers began producing the power belt. All three kinds of belts should be available in any athletic weight training room.

Knee Wrap Guidelines

1. **Wrap tight**

2. **Wrap with a straight leg**

3. **<u>Always</u> wrap from the outside to the inside**

Some situations on some equipment means <u>serious injuries</u> or <u>death</u>!!

I believe 90% of coaches who run weight programs for their athletes have **never** squatted big themselves. The vast majority of people making decisions on purchasing equipment make bad decisions when getting a squat rack. If you haven't had much experience, *please*, please read this carefully and if you have any questions call our Toll Free number or write.

Why? Here's why. I know of two separate serious injury cases where a high school athlete missed a squat while squatting on a rack with a spotting tier. Heavy duty squat racks without a spotting tier are safer if you miss (see page 66). Very few people understood that the pegs on the deluxe rack make it easier for different height athletes to squat but the spotting tier doesn't make it safer.

The two serious injuries happened the same way. The kids couldn't make the lift and they took their hands off the bar and grabbed the spotting tier. The weight rolled forward and over their head landing on their fingers. The fingers were instantly severed and landed on the floor. One kid lost five and the other lost four fingers. Even if you keep your hands on the bar, fingers can be severely pinched. Besides, even if all goes well and the bar hits the spotting tier you'll most likely damage the bar.

If you miss while squatting free, the lifter is much safer. I know it's difficult for a person to understand who hasn't squatted but it's a simple matter to throw the weight forward or back. The bar will also not be damaged. The biggest pain is getting the bar back on the rack. I can live with that. Administrators or purchasing people somehow imagine an athlete sitting in low squat position getting squashed if he can't make his squat. That's absurd.

At a clinic I did, the women's coaches had put a lot of pressure on the high school football coach to buy some squat equipment for the girls. They kept repeating what the salesman had said about his squat machine. "You don't want to squat with free weights," he argued, "Our machine is completely safe. Free weights can be real dangerous." So they paid $400-plus for a squat machine that has a bar moving up and down on a cylinder. A hook attached to the bar on each side is secured on pegs about four inches apart on a vertical shaft. So, when I got ready to do the clinic, here was this squat machine.

To begin with, this school had a sign which said, "When lifting with free weights, you must have a spotter." I asked, "Does this mean when you lift on a machine that it's okay and safe to lift alone?" Boy, were these guys nervous now. I could see their guts twinging. "You see that squat machine—that's a death trap!"

"What do you mean?" came a scared reply.

I got in the apparatus and said, "Picture me squatting alone with 400 pounds. I take the weight on my shoulders by turning the bar and, thus, the two hooks come off the pegs." Then I squatted down to parallel and asked, "What if I get stuck and can't come back up?"

It was plain to see that I was an inch short as I tried to twist the hooks back to the pegs. I was stuck. I couldn't bail out forward or backward. I was a dead man—literally. They gasped and stammered. Their faces were an ashen white, but they were grateful that nothing had happened to a student—yet.

It was also incredibly bad trying to twist the bar to the pegs, even from an upright position. With a heavy weight, a lower-back injury would be very likely. Needless to say, the sign was changed immediately; and during the clinic they paid attention when their athletes were taught how to squat correctly. Manufacturers will always try to build some kind of a leg machine. They're in it to make money. Their sales points will always be safety and simplicity. They will always attempt to make claims about the scientific superiority of their machine. The only thing I can say to you is this. Pray that your competition falls for it. You will always have a decisive edge by doing Parallel Squats with free weights. That's a big part of this whole secret.

IF YOU MISS, WHAT DO YOU DO?

Always use *three spotters* on the squat—but what happens if you're alone or your spotters are lazy and you miss?

OPTION I: The safest situation is NOT to have a spotting tier but being free. Option I is to push the bar forward and over the head.

Option II: is to shove the bar back. It looks scary, but it's quite safe. Both options are instinctual.

BFS Trainer Richard Bates working on Parallel Squats with 7'5" former Utah Jazz Center Mark Eaton without a spotting tier. He made over a million per year. Maybe we were foolish? Maybe we should have had a spotting tier? Maybe we should have had a machine in which the bar goes up and down on a cylinder? After all, can we really afford our stars getting hurt? Sound familiar?

V. Squat Variations

The main reason for including a Squat Variation as a core lift is to help prevent a plateau in strength building from happening. If an athlete were to do parallel squats three times a week for an eight week period, there is no question that a plateau would occur. There are two main ways to prevent plateaus. First, an athlete should cut back. Therefore, only two squat workouts should be done. To parallel squat three times per week is suicide in an over-training sense. The second way to prevent plateaus is to make a change in the method of squatting. You can work just as hard but because you have done the hard work in a different way, you will trick your body. The best solution in preventing plateaus is to squat only twice per week: one parallel squat workout and one squat variation workout.

Many recognize the need for change and decide to have one heavy workout and one light workout. I don't like this philosophy. I don't want my athletes coming in for an "easy" workout. I want to work hard with an all-out intensity every training session. This chapter will discuss acceptable squat variations which would allow an athlete to go all-out and still keep his parallel squat strength progressing month after month at a rapid pace with no plateaus.

THE BOX SQUAT

The Box Squat can be one of the six BFS core lifts. For the development of hip strength, hip explosive power and hip tendon strength, the Box Squat is superior to any other lift or machine. When we get a chance to demonstrate the Box Squat at clinics, we always get the same reaction from coaches. They really like this lift! Why? Because it makes sense, as it duplicates the exact hip movement used in the power sports (football, volleyball, basketball, baseball, etc.). We hear time and time again after our demonstration, Coaches saying, "That's what I want! That's what I want!"

Yet, we find most strength coaches at our colleges and universities do not do the Box Squat. The major reason is simply not knowing about it. We have also heard people say it is dangerous as it will compress or jam the lower vertebrae. We get negative comments on the Box Squat from machine people. One such person voiced his vigorous opposition to other coaches at a recent clinic. He started out ten years ago as a welder of machines and by his own admission has had no lifting or coaching experience. However, since he now sells the machines, he is now an "expert."

I came across the Box Squat twenty years ago while training in Los Angeles with the world's greatest power-lifters and track athletes (shot putters, discus and hammer throwers). Los Angeles at this time was the mecca for amateur power athletes. I'd coach high school track, football and wrestling and then train in L.A. with men like George Frenn and Jon Cole.

George taught me how to Box Squat. For those who don't know about George, he squatted 853 in competition and won the national hammer throw championship three years in a row. That 853 squat was the best of anybody in the world for years even though George only weighed 242 pounds. Frenn would Box Squat once a week and Squat once a week. Doing regular squats twice a week was far too draining on the system and George couldn't throw as well in meets or practice. The Box Squat left him with energy for the next day.

I used this system with great success for not only myself but for my athletes for the next 4-5 years. Then the sport of powerlifting became much more specialized. The national and world champions only powerlifted. As a result, the powerlifters did not Box Squat. They convinced me to do away with the Box Squat and do regular squats twice a week. After all you don't Box Squat in competition. Right?

After squatting the powerlifting way for another 4-5 years, I found out that I'd made a serious mistake. Old George was right! Box Squats once a week were definitely the way to go. You see, powerlifters who squat on Monday don't do anything on Tuesday. However, an athlete needs to do sprints, plyometrics and develop the technique of his sport. This takes a great deal of time and energy. The Box Squat allows an athlete to perform a squatting exercise twice a week while still having the time and energy to develop athletic abilities. I had dinner one summer with Dr. Fred Hatfield, called by many, Dr. Squat. He is super in the sport of powerlifting but this story will amaze coaches. Fred was reluctant to walk three blocks to the restaurant. He had a major competition in two weeks and this would tire him. This obviously is an intolerable situation for an athlete for another sport. However, it does illustrate the big differences which now exist between powerlifting and power weight training for an athlete.

The Box Squat technique is as follows. First assume an athletic stance and squat down carefully under control on a box or a high bench. Take care not to plop down out of control as this could cause injury. Then settle back making sure the lower back remains concave in a "locked-in" position. Your power should then be driven forward and up by using your powerful hip and butt muscles and tendons. If you go down and just touch the box or bench, like most people, then all you develop are the quadriceps. This would be a serious mistake for an athlete. The final coaching point of technique is as the lift is being completed, the athlete should drive up on his toes in an explosive type action. The athlete should have the same feeling of blocking, tackling, rebounding or releasing a track implement at this final stage.

Here are five major reasons we recommend the Box Squat as one of our six BFS possible core lifts.

I. Develop hip and hip tendon strength.

II. The athlete gets used to a heavier weight and this increases confidence on the regular parallel squats.

III. Recuperation is almost immediate and thus allows for 100% energy for practice or games even on the following day!

IV. Alternating regular and Box Squat workouts during the week helps an athlete overcome plateaus more easily. This will in all probability allow the athlete to squat more in the long run anyway than by doing only regular squats all the time.

V. Teaching basic squatting technique is very easy with the Box Squat. The height of a medium Squat Box for athletes 5–8 to 6–1 is 19 1/2 inches. Shorter athletes should use an 18-inch box while taller athletes use a 21–inch box. We therefore recommend very strongly that coaches purchase at least one Box from us before making them on your own.

We have always cautioned that plopping down hard on the box can be potentially dangerous to the lower back. We've always emphasized keeping the lower back in tight and sitting down under control. We must also emphasize that a difference of no more than 100 to 150 pounds should exist between the Box Squat and the Parallel Squat. We have found some athletes using 200 to 300 pounds more on the Box Squat. This is very wrong. If you are using the BFS Set-Rep system, you may want to set a limit of 100 pounds. For example, if your max is 325 pounds on the Parallel Squat, you can't do any more than 425 pounds on the Box Squat on one or more reps. Sometimes it gets a little scary trying to spot a huge Box Squat, if the athlete is shaking and wobbling all over the place.

The 100 pound rule would keep things safer and yet still enable the athlete to keep progressing. Also, there would be greater forced intensity on the Parallel Squat. Box Squat records to be broken would be largely dependent on efforts made on the Parallel Squat. The recovery on Box Squat day would also be more complete and easier.

THE FRONT SQUAT

The Front Squat can be an excellent variation to the Parallel Squat as it can help an athlete stay upright and keep the lower back in a correct position. Front Squats also accentuate development in the lower quadriceps of the thighs and thus are acceptable as one of the six BFS core lifts.

In Box Squats, the athlete will use more weight than the Parallel Squat, while less weight is used on the Front Squat. When an athlete in high school is Box Squatting in the 500 plus range, he may wish to switch to Front Squats. Also, if an athlete has trouble with correct form on the Parallel Squat, he may want to switch from the Box Squat to the Front Squat. Switching because of a big Box Squat, might jolt the athlete to new highs. Switching to Front Squats because of form, might make a huge difference in an athlete reaching his potential.

Front Squats may be done one of three ways. The athlete may hold the bar as in the Power Clean with elbows up and forward and resting the bar on the deltoids. He may also cross his arms and hold the bar again on the deltoids. This method gives additional support by the upper arms. Perhaps the easiest and best way for beginners to do the Front Squat is to use our Sting Ray or EZ Squat device.

OTHER VARIATIONS

Other acceptable Squat variations would be a high-bar bodybuilding or Olympic style squat and the Safe Bar Squat. In the high-bar building squat less weight would be used than on the Parallel Squat. Correct form would have to be stressed. Some athletes who choose this option go several inches below parallel. I personally do not like this variation for the athlete but recognize its acceptability.

The Safe Bar Squat utilizes a uniquely shaped bar. It features padded steel appendages and a padded neck piece.

When the neck is placed between the two appendages, the weight and line of gravity position helps the athlete keep a locked-in lower back and an upright position. You can use more weight because you hold on to the support standards and pull up thus aiding the upward thrust of the legs and hips. Caution should be used in loading big amounts of weight onto the Safe Squat Bar and pulling mostly with the arms. This is wrong and, of course, defeats the purpose of building leg and hip power.

CONCLUSIONS

Do not parallel squat three times per week. You will make more progress and have much less problem with plateaus if you have only two squat workouts per week in-season and during the off-season. You will also further overcome plateaus and make more progress in the long run if you parallel squat on one workout and then use an acceptable squat variation for the other workout. The Box Squat and Front Squat are the two best variations.

ADDITIONAL BOX SQUAT GUIDELINES

To add to the variability of your squat routine and to increase squatting power while controlling the Box Squat poundage systematically, you should use different height boxes.

Obviously, if you use a very high box, you can not only squat more but a beginner can more easily keep his back and body in a better, safer position.

When your Box Squat gets to 100-150 pounds more than your Parallel Squat, lower your box. Call BFS for equipment and/or ideas on how to do this.

The Box Squat with Mark Eaton

BFS Vice-President, Rick Anderson spotting former Utah Jazz Center Mark Eaton early in his career. Eaton got pinned with 145 pounds on the Box Squat in 1981. However, he broke 275 personal weight training records in his first year during the season. Three years later Eaton Box Squatted 500 pounds and became the NBA Defensive Player-of-the-Year.

Sit tall, spread the chest, lock-in the lower back, sit on the box under complete control, settle back slightly and then drive forward and up.

Kent Johnston: Green Bay Packer Strength and Conditioning Coach

"The Box Squat is the best method to train lower body explosion for anybody that is in a power related sport. First, the breakup of the eccentric and concentric movement by coming to a rest and then requiring the explosive hip movement off the box makes this lift superior. Second, I believe it is safer than any other leg-hip exercise. You never have to worry about depth and I've never had an injury doing the Box Squats with our Green Bay team.

Our players are sold on the Box Squat. At this pro level, it's hard to get players to squat but since we incorporated the Box Squat two years ago, they have definitely taken to it. During the season, Box Squats have been especially helpful because our players can do it even if they are sore after a game. I believe it helps on joint stress. You are never in a bad position when you Box Squat."

The Safe Squat demonstrated by Eric Leckner, Utah Jazz Center–Forward.

BFS 5 lb. Training Plates

An absolute must for teaching technique on the power clean or power snatch. Great for readiness athletes, women and even pro athletes.

VI. The Power Clean

Power Cleans or Cleans are of vital importance. An athlete must do some kind of "Quick Lift." Examples of quick lifts are snatches, cleans, and reverse grip cleans. Quick lifts can be done with a squat style or a power style as illustrated in the "Rack" photo. The Power Clean is the most popular quick lift and since our BFS standards are based on this lift, it is the quick lift we recommend.

The Power Clean develops explosiveness and aggressiveness. Every muscle is brought into play and when done correctly every muscle will be fired in proper sequence in executing a maximum summation of force.

Bruno Pauletto, ex-strength coach for the University of Tennessee and past N.S.C.A. Strength Coach-of-the-Year, wrote a series of articles for our BFS journal. In this series, Coach Pauletto wrote the following:

"The Power Clean is an explosive lift in which speed is a very big factor. With speed being so important and heavy weights being moved, the power output is great. The Power Clean just cannot be done slowly. Other lifts like the bench and squat have minimal power out put because speed is not a factor; they basically develop strength. Many coaches still believe that the weight room is the place to develop only strength and the field is the place to develop speed. I believe that some lifting exercises go beyond the strength factor and one of them is the Power Clean.

Similarities between the Power Clean
and Athletic Movements.

Because of the way the Power Clean is executed, it is very similar to many athletic movements.

A) Rotary hip movement: A biomechanical analysis of the Power Clean will show the rotary action of the legs and hips, which is very similar to jumping, running and pulling action common to many sports. All of these movements require the use of a combined leg and hip drive. The big muscles of the legs and hips bring the hips forward and up. Basically the hips and legs have to get underneath the body to push it up and out. It makes no difference whether the action is directly straight up (high jump) or at an angle (tackling). In the Power Clean the legs and hips move under the body by a rotary action to drive the body to a full extension.

B) The pre-stretch: As I just pointed out, in the middle of the pull when the hips are under the bar, the thighs are positioned so that a pre-stretch is placed upon them. Because of this pre-stretch, the muscles of the legs will contract more forcefully. As the athlete perfects this phase his muscles will react more explosively. This pre-stretch is very similar to plyometric jumping.

C) Multi-Joint movement: The Power Clean is a "complete" lift, since all muscle groups work in performing the exercise. It is a multi-joint exercise working the ankles, knees, hips, back, shoulders, elbows and wrists, and most of the muscles associated with these joints. Muscle coordination is improved because the muscles work together in a chain reaction. For a powerful total body movement to occur, each joint and associated muscles must produce proper forces at proper times. When these produced forces are joined the result is a force of great magnitude. The Power Clean is one of a very few resistance exercises that can produce this great force."

I believe in the Clean. I believe the Clean is a great lift for football, basketball, track, baseball and all other sports dealing with explosive power. The Clean is one of the most popular power movement lifts among strength coaches. The Power Clean may also come in the form of Dumbbell Cleans or Hang Cleans. Some feel Dumbbell Cleans simulate football movements better and some feel that Hang Cleans are easier on the lower back. It is my estimate, that about ninety percent of all strength coaches use the clean movement for a basic power building exercise.

I believe the Clean to be a safe lift. There are, for example, many more injuries on the Bench Press than the Clean. Also, weight training in general has proven to be about the safest of all activities. I feel at BFS that we are in touch with what is happening around the country better than anyone. We are doing clinics nearly every week of the year outside of our home base in Utah. Sometimes we do five or more clinics in one day between our staff at BFS. We also have a toll-free number which is constantly used by high school coaches. We are literally in personal touch with tens of thousands of athletes and coaches in every corner of the United States. At this point, *we just do not have anybody complaining about the Clean.* I do not want to recommend something dangerous. It is my conclusion that Cleans are safe!

Now I will address the question of the Clean not developing explosive power. I believe it does! Especially in the marginal athlete. Coaches, how many times have you seen one of your players with a big upper body but he just can't hit? And, conversely, the player who weighs 155 pounds who will just knock your socks off. What the Clean can do, is help the athlete who does not have that natural hitting ability. We also have standards. The varsity high school standard is 175, All-State 235 and All-American is 300. Things do not really start to happen until the 200 pound level is reached. Then, the athlete is forced to execute the lift with correct technique and quickness. He is forced to create a maximum summation of force with his entire body. I really saw this happen when working with Mark Eaton of the Utah Jazz. When he was doing 125, he would wimp it up and that's how he looked rebounding and blocking shots. I thought seriously about getting him a ballerina outfit. But then his technique improved, with a much more aggressive attitude towards the Clean. Later, he Cleaned 250 and would let out a roar and explode through the lift. Mark has led the NBA in blocked shots and was an NBA All-Star in 1989. I wanted to put a football helmet on him.

One strength coach at a powerful football university does not recommend the Clean. The head coach's son was seriously hurt during the Clean and so Cleans are now forbidden. Was it the Clean which was responsible or poor technique or perhaps an already present problem? I would like to present our BFS technique guidelines which will greatly reduce the possibility of injury and increase your chances of success.

TECHNIQUE GUIDELINES

1. Never do more than 5 reps during a set.
2. Only Power Clean heavy once a week.
3. Do not bounce the bar on the floor while doing reps, but pause and make sure of a proper starting position.
4. Maintain a proper position at the start.
   A. Back in concave position: spread the chest.
   B. Feet should be flat on floor especially the heels with the shins placed on the line on the bar where the knurling begins. Get into a *JUMP STANCE!*
   C. Arms straight.
   D. Bar should be touching the shins.
   E. Hands should be placed on the bar very close to the lifter's legs.
5. Maintain a proper position during the lift.
   A. Chin up and shoulders back.
   B. Elbows high.
   C. Bar should be as close to chest as possible.
   D. Start the upward movement in a slow controlled pull. Do not ever jerk the bar from the floor.
   E. As the bar passes the knees, then **jump**.
   F. Pull the bar high and snap explosively under the bar with elbows snapping forward under the bar. The feet should pop out to an Athletic Stance.
   G. As the body surges under the bar, the lower back should be in a concave position.

The most result-producing coaching point that I've found while doing clinics is to yell "Jump" when the bar is brought just past the knees. I can talk about double dipping or using the thighs or ramming the hips forward, but nothing works like yelling "Jump". When an athlete jumps at the right time, the net effect is good technique at a crucial part of this most important lift.

WRIST WRAPS

Many athletes will get sore wrists from doing Power Cleans or even Bench Presses. Oftentimes this soreness is caused by incorrect technique and/or poor flexibility. The Power Clean when done correctly will rest on the deltoids as the athlete racks the bar. The bar should never be fully or primarily supported by the wrists.

I recommend doing a simple wrist flexibility exercise before doing a Power Clean. This exercise takes only 15 seconds with each wrist. This exercise is illustrated on page 88. Pull back on the fingers as shown until the back of the fingers touch the top of the deltoids. Bring the elbow straight out in front as in the finished rack position of the Clean.

In addition, I recommend our *BFS* Wrist Wraps as a helpful training aid to the Clean. They give great support to the wrist and might possibly prevent a wrist injury if an athlete has incorrect technique. I always wear them while doing Cleans. They feel good and also probably give some psychological support. Once you try them you won't want to lift without them.

WRIST STRAPS

Wrist straps could also be used in the Power Clean and Dead Lift or any heavy type pulling exercises. These exercises are not designed to develop wrist and hand strength. Therefore, it would be a big mistake to allow weaknesses in the hand and wrist to deter or hamper total body development in these power exercises. The wrist straps help an athlete to totally focus on the acceleration of the bar and prevents slippage and skin abrasions to the palm area. However, to develop grabbing power, some positions in football might not want to use straps.

Wrist straps should be 1 1/2 inches in width and long enough to wrap around the bar one complete revolution. Straps made from slick materials are not recommended materials. Good straps are made from canvas or leather. All straps will eventually wear out. It is, therefore, very important to check for tears frequently to prevent accidental breakage. Do not lift with worn straps.

The use of Wrist Straps is relatively easy, but an athlete must develop some finger dexterity and coordination to quickly use them efficiently. At first, it may seem a little awkward, but with practice an athlete will soon get the hang of it.

To begin, simply put your hand through the loop. The end of the strap should be on the same side of the bar **as the thumb**. Then, you are ready to wrap the strap around the bar as tight as possible. Now grip the rolled up strap with your fingers and thumb locking the strap into place. Follow the same procedure with the other hand.

SPOTTING

Most strength coaches and lifters prefer not to have spotters. However, you may want to have a spotter in back of the lifter. If he falls backward, the spotter can then push the lifter forward so the weight does not fall on the lifter. Two spotters may be used with one spotter on each side of the bar. However, their principal job would be to assist the lifter in getting the bar down from the finish position. Strict teamwork is a must with this style. High school athletes seem to like this method when done correctly.

The Power Clean

6. The Rack by Stefan Fernholm

1. **The Start:** Head level, eyes straight, hips down, arms locked, spread chest, lower back locked-in, jump stance.
2. **The Beginning Pull:** Head, eyes, and arms the same. Begin lift with legs only. Maintain same back angle. Do not jerk weight off the platform.
3. **The Middle Pull:** Move hips explosively under shoulders. Do not jerk shoulders and head back. Head, eyes, and arms keep the same position.
4. **The Erect Position:** Head straight, eyes level, arms locked, shoulders over hips, bar moves in a straight line. Do not jerk shoulders and head back.

1. The Start

2. The Beginning Pull

3. The Middle Pull

4. The Erect Position

5. The Final Pull

7. The Finish

5 . The Final Pull: Up on toes, fully extend your legs. Do not pull with arms or jerk shoulders back. Bar should continue in a vertical path.

6 . The Rack: Super quick explosive movement. Pop feet out quickly to an athletic stance to lower point of gravity. Arm pull is only used to lower body under the bar while your body is in the air. Elbows up. Head level.

7 . The Finish: Stand erect, elbows up, bar resting on the deltoids and collar bone.

Squat Style Clean

Florida is currently the only state which has Olympic weight lifting as a recognized high school sport. This athlete from St. Cloud High School in Florida lifted in the 165 pound class and is utilizing the Squat Style Clean. More weight can be used with this style than the Power Clean. However, athletes do not seem to benefit in increased explosive power when comparing the Squat Clean style versus the Power Clean style.

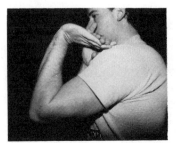

Wrist flexibility exercise

Hold the BFS Wrist Wrap with the velcro strip up with the 4th and 5th fingers and begin wrapping.

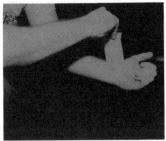

Pull wrist wrap tight and firm around the wrist twice and secure again with the velcro strip.

Wrist Strap: Begin wrapping on the same side of the bar as the thumb grip.

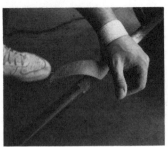

Bring strap around one full revolution.

Grip as shown and strap very tightly.

Robert Washington, from East Carolina University, Power Cleaning with solid rubber bumper plates. Doing Cleans with rubber bumper plates is far superior to regular olympic plates. BFS can even get them in school colors.

BFS Power Clean Standards

Good:	Body weight
Varsity:	175 pounds
All-State:	235 pounds
All-American:	300 pounds
Elite-College:	350 pounds
Stefan:	473 pounds

POWER CLEAN ALTERNATIVES

The Power Clean can be described as a "Quick Lift" because of the quick explosive total body movement required. At least one quick lift should be included as one of the core lifts. Standard and acceptable alternatives to the Power Clean are the Hang Clean and the Power Snatch.

The Hang Clean

The Hang Clean requires the same explosive type movement as the Power Clean. There are two reasons for selecting the Hang Clean as a Core Lift over the Power Clean. First, you may want to switch every 3-6 months for variation to overcome plateaus. Second, the Hang Clean is less stressful to the lower back. An athlete with a sensitive lower back or an athlete with chronic low back problems may be able to do Hang Cleans without aggravation.

The technique of the Hang Clean is virtually the same as the Power Clean. Begin the Hang Clean in the Erect Position as shown in the Power Clean. Next, dip down to the **Middle Pull Position** and then instantly begin the explosive Power Clean movement. Remember to think "Jump" as you start upward. The technique from this point is exactly the same as the Power Clean.

The Power Snatch

Again, the Power Snatch requires the same explosive type movement as the Power Clean. The same two reasons exist for selecting the Power Snatch as a corelift. It adds variation and is less stressful to the lower back because there is less poundage that can be used. Normally, an athlete can Power Snatch between 70-75% of the weight used on a Power Clean.

The technique of the Power Snatch is the same as the Power Clean except the athlete would use a wide grip and the bar is whipped overhead for the finish position.

An athlete may also do a Hang Snatch by doing the same movement as in the Hang Clean and do it for the same reasons.

1. The Start

2. The Beginning Pull

3. The Middle Pull

4. The Erect Position

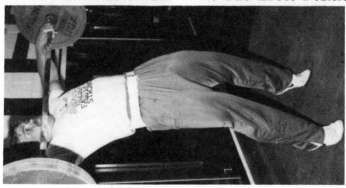

5. The Final Pull

6. The Finish

Stefan Fernholm shown doing a 335 pound Power Snatch. Notice the feet have popped out to help Stefan get under the bar but they are too wide. Feet should only pop out to an Athletic Stance.

Heisman Trophy Winner, Barry Sanders

Lombardi Trophy Winner, Chris Spielman, LB

Outland Trophy Winner, Jason Buck, DT

John Nichols, 1989 NCAA Discus Champ

SEE APPENDIX B FOR ADVANCED GUIDELINES

Ken Patera Cleaning 501 Pounds! (Bruce Klemens Photo)

VII. The Trap Bar

The Trap Bar is a relatively new BFS Core Lift. During the off-season, you would do this lift on Wednesdays with the Power Clean. The Trap Bar is in between a Dead Lift and a Squat with a number of advantages. I used to recommend doing regular Dead Lifts with a spotter, but now I recommend the Trap Bar. Here's why:

The hand grips on the Trap Bar allow the weight on the bar to be in perfect alignment with the athlete's center of gravity. This means a safer exercise, especially with groups of high school athletes. You also do not need a spotter.

Trap Bar workouts are also fast. On one of my first workouts with the Trap Bar, I did 5 sets of 8 reps, going up to 375 pounds. It took much less time than a Squat or Dead Lift workout: only 8 minutes. I was really sore the next day. My Glutes, Hamstrings, and Traps were deeply affected. I could hardly walk. It was just like a heavy parallel squat workout when you haven't squatted for awhile. My lower back felt great. I was impressed.

Al Gerard, who invented the Trap Bar, said, "When you work on my Trap Bar, you should think Squat or Leg Press, not Dead Lift. Although, you will see some big increases on your Dead Lift max, think Squat while using the Trap Bar."

The Trap Bar also lends itself to doing shrugs in a superior way because there is no bar contact with the thighs. Dave Williams, the strength coach at Liberty University says, "The Trap Bar is a tremendous training tool, besides the Dead Lifts and Shrugs our football players also do high pulls from the hang position and upright rows."

The Trap Bar uses regular Olympic plates and the bar is shaped like a diamond in the center. To begin, the athlete steps into the center of the diamond and bends down as in a Power Clean. Make sure the hands are placed squarely in the middle of the grip handles for balance. The hips should

**The Trap Bar An Extraordinary Core Lift. The New
BFS Hex Bar Functions the Same as a Trap Bar.**

Eric Leckner 7-0' Former Utah Jazz Center-Forward

be down, the chest spread and the lower back locked in place. Do the work with the legs as much as possible when lifting up to the erect upright position. To keep back strain down to a minimum, the athlete should bounce the weights slightly on the floor when doing repetitions. Do not come to a dead stop and pause between each rep. As in all lifts, keep your head up and stretch your chin away from your chest. In the Squat, Clean, Snatch, Dead Lift or Trap Bar, if your chin ever touches your chest, you are in deep trouble. Not only is it poor technique, which adversely effects the amount of weight you can lift, it is also very dangerous and could cause an injury to the lower back.

The Trap-Hex Bar only costs $149.00 and can be purchased at our Bigger Faster Stronger office.

THE DEAD LIFT

The Dead Lift with a spotter is recommended to do once or twice per year, especially for football players. The coach and all team members should have a wild max-out party. Everyone shouts, "Go-Go-Go!" as each team member has his turn. The intensity that can be generated can be awesome. We do this at BFS clinics and the average high school football player can do 400 pounds. Our All-State Standard is 500 pounds and the All-American Standard is 600 pounds.

It should be noted that you obviously cannot use a spotter for the Dead Lift in a powerlifting contest and if school records are kept by weight class, I recommend that a spotter also not be used for those records. A spotter usually helps 50-75 pounds, but the real reason to use a spotter is safety. The spotter presses down with one hand on the lower back and hooks the other arm around the lifter's shoulder and chest. The crook of the elbow should be secured against the shoulder while the fist or hand is placed firmly in the middle of the chest. The spotter and lifter should coordinate the lift together. The spotter could say, "one-two-up". As the lift is begun, the spotter pulls up and

Standard Dead Lift Stance—Note Alternate Grip

Sumo-Style Stance—Joe Clifford with 765 lbs.

back while pushing in on the lower back. This is important
for safety. The spotter pulls back to get the weight back on
the lifter's heels. Many times, when high school athletes
Dead Lift by themselves, the weight will shift towards the
toes. When this happens, lower back injuries can occur.
When the weight is shifted back towards the heels, an athlete
can normally Dead Lift in complete safety.

**BFS Clinician, Rick Anderson,
with high school athlete on 600 pound Dead Lift.**

THE STANCE: Use a jumping stance, not a Sumo-
style stance. For an athlete, this is far superior in
developing athletic potential.

Summary

Do the Trap Bar lift on Wednesdays during the off-season as a core lift. Use a jump stance, not a Sumo-style stance. Once or twice a year do the Dead Lift with a spotter and experience a "Max-Out Party". It is recommended to keep the reps down to five or less on all sets.

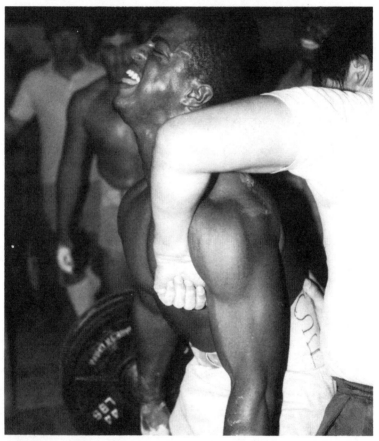

Author, Greg Shepard, spotting a high school athlete at a BFS clinic. I should remove my left hand at this point and let this athlete finish the lift by himself.

Terry Long: History's Strongest Football Player

Terry played tackle at East Carolina University. Terry only weighed 160 pounds in high school and Bench Pressed 135 pounds. He spent two years in the military and began to lift hard. Then, he entered East Carolina and as a senior, he became History's Strongest Football Player. Terry played at 280 pounds, but in the photo we see Terry Dead Lifting 865 pounds in a meet at body weight of 300 pounds. That lift was only 39 pounds off the world's record. Terry's best marks are: Bench-565, Squat-900, Hang Clean-441, 40-4.8.

In the 1980's at 5-11, 280 pounds, Terry became the only lineman under six feet tall to make the NFL. He played for Pittsburgh.

**High School athletes can spot each other
on the Dead Lift.**

* Note stance and grip too wide — get in jump stance

VIII. THE BENCH PRESS

The Bench Press is the most important upper body exercise. It develops overall power in the chest and arms. Some strength coaches leave it out, but I feel Bench Presses with auxiliary exercises make it very important to athletics. The standards are so easily recognizable that there is magic in the numbers of 200-300-400-500 pound benches. I am also smart enough to know that I would never, under any circumstances, ever want to volunteer to get hit by a 400-lb. bench presser.

Bench Presses should be done only twice per week not three times. Do the regular Bench workout on Friday. The Towel Bench or Bench variation should be done on Monday.

Correct Body Position

The legs should be spread wide for a solid base. The legs should also be brought under the knees with the feet firmly placed flat on the floor. Then, by placing your hands on the support standards, push the shoulders down toward the hips. An arch should be present in the lower back with the chest sticking up as high as possible. Even though this position is a little uncomfortable, it gives the best mechanical advantage, and it is also very difficult to illegally arch the hips up from the bench. A common fault of novice lifters is to keep their legs straight and bring a leg off the floor during the Bench Press. This would destroy the vital, firm foundation necessary for a maximum effort.

Poppy Moronta: Virginia Tech 440 Bench
A.Wide Stance B. Feet Flat C. Hips back toward shoulders

Brian Blutreich Benching 405
at Capistrano Valley High. Coach David Elecciri is executing a perfect spot with palms directly under the bar. Brian threw the shot 69-6 1/2 and the Discus 210-8 in high school.

Spacing of Hands and Grip

The Bench Press is the most dangerous lift in the weight room. For this reason, I strongly recommend that the thumbs go around the bar. There is too much danger of the bar slipping and dropping on the throat or face. I know ten lifters who have died bench pressing.

There have been numerous incidents of crushed throats, chins, torn lips, loss of teeth, smashed noses, torn eyebrows, loss of sight, scalped hair and smashed foreheads. Many of these accidents occur at home. Keep your thumbs around the bar. Never lift alone. Always use an alert, smart spotter.

The spacing of the hands affects the position of the elbows and, consequently, affects the muscles and areas developed. A close grip forces the elbows in and results in the triceps being worked more than the chest muscles. A wider grip allows the elbows to be out away from the body. Most champion Bench Pressers use a wider grip. The elbows with this grip should be at a right angle when the bar is touching the chest.

Now, if I were strictly into powerlifting, I'd recommend the wide grip. However, a football player or wrestler does not use his arms in a wide position, but he does use them with the elbows in close. I, therefore, recommend a narrower grip with the elbows in on the bench press to simulate a defensive lineman, linebacker, or a bottom-positioned wrestler. In 1979, the Pittsburgh Steelers had a defensive line who could all Bench Press 450 or more with a narrower, elbows-in grip. It should be noted: as the bar reaches the halfway point, the elbows may be forced out for a stronger lockout.

Techniques

Breathing: Take a deep breath in as the bar comes down. Hold the breath just before the bar touches the chest and halfway through the upward movement. At this point the breath can be let out forcefully. Some lifters make loud

Do Not Arch The Hips

Keep The Bar Even

sounds as the breath is forced out. This keeps everything firm and may also have some psychological benefit, especially on rep work.

Squeezing the Bar: Before a max attempt, the technique of squeezing the bar very tightly can help—in most cases about 5 pounds.

Angle: The bar does not go straight down and straight up, but rather at a slight angle back toward the rack or lifter's face. When this correct groove is found, it makes a lot of difference in pounds. Some refer to this movement as a C Curve.

Looking: If the bar reaches a sticking point, many times just by looking at and concentrating on the right hand, the bar will lock out. Many times I will see bench pressers strain with their eyes closed. This is a bad mistake. The eyes should be open at all times and be focused on a point directly overhead.

Spotting

I like to use one spotter in the middle when the weight is under 300 pounds. A much more even lift-off can be given, and more controlled spotting can be done with one spotter in the middle. With heavier poundages, two spotters are recommended for the lift-off. Since it is good to work out in groups of three or four anyway, it doesn't hurt to have everyone involved in spotting. The principal spotter assists the lifter from behind at the middle of the bar and lifts the bar from the standards to the lifter. He helps the lifter through the "sticking point" if he has trouble with the weight. The two side spotters can be used on each end of the bar. They only touch the bar when the principal spotter calls for help or when the lifter can't lift the bar from his chest.

Dewayne Kingston: 71st High School in North Carolina Demonstrating Wide Grip Bench Press with 325 pounds.

Nick Oniskey: C.B. West High School in Pennsylvania Demonstrating Medium Grip Bench Press with 325 pounds.

BENCH PRESS VARIATIONS

Athletes should have two Bench workouts per week all year round. Three is too many. Benching three times per week will lead to over-training and tendonitis in a great many athletes. More progress can be made over a long period of time, when an athlete benches twice per week.

One of the workouts should be very intensive, while the other should be different. Variations in the Bench will help keep new maxes coming month after month. Our choice for the second workout is the Towel Bench, which is a round cushion made up of three towels rolled up to about a five-inch diameter. The Towel Bench also helps in confidence and helps prevent pain and or injury to the shoulder-joint area.

Other choices for the second workout could be a combination of wide and close-grip Benches, or a light-to-medium regular Bench workout, or a high concentration of heavy dips and tricep push downs.

THE TOWEL BENCH

I recommend Towel Benches for three reasons. First, an athlete gets used to a heavier weight. Normally, fifteen to twenty more pounds can be used on the Towel Bench. This builds more confidence for new levels on the regular bench. Second, it brings variety into the routine. Variety is important as this helps an athlete overcome plateaus. We guarantee that every athlete will break at least 8 personal records per week, if our BFS Set-Rep System is used. Variety is the main reason we can make that guarantee. Third, and most important, Towel Benches will go a long way in preventing what I call "Bench Press Shoulder", a mild to severe pain in the shoulder joints.

As a result of doing many clinics and talking to many coaches and athletes, I became aware of this problem with the Bench Press. It seems that 75 percent of all athletes who Bench Press have "Bench Press Shoulder".

Specifically, this is a dull to sharp pain in the front shoulder-joint area where the upper arm, chest, and shoulder meet. This pain comes from working out too often with too much weight. Typically, an athlete will do benches three times a week with maximum or near maximum poundages. The real stress to this shoulder joint area comes when the bar is one or two inches from the chest. When you think about it, stretching and putting stress on the shoulder joint area three times a week with maximum poundages is bound to cause problems.

To perform a Towel Bench, take 3 towels and fold them in half the skinny way. Lay them on top of each other and roll them up like a sleeping bag. Lay the rolled up towels on the chest and bench with normal technique. I like to bring the bar right into the towels, not just lightly touch, before driving up. Much better yet is our new Towel Bench Pad — they only cost $9.95.

BENCH PRESS STANDARDS

Good	**1 1/2 times body weight**
Varsity	**200 pounds**
All State	**300 pounds**
High School **All-American** .	**350 pounds**
College	**400 pounds**
World Standard **for Greatness** .	**500 pounds**

The value of a 600 pound Bench Press has to be questioned. However, the great champions of size, strength and speed seem to have the ability to Bench Press at least 400 pounds.

Jeroy Robinson, Texas A&M Linebacker does a 470 Close Grip Bench Press.

THE TOWEL BENCH: A great bench variation. Shown is the new Towel Bench Pad.

Soren Tallhem, Swedish Throwing Champion, likes the Neck Bench Press for his Bench Variation. Soren maintains the Neck Bench better duplicates his shot put motion. Soren's best Neck Bench Press is 400 pounds.

Athlete demonstrating **dangerous and improper thumb position.**

IX. Auxiliary Lifts

Auxiliary Lifts are done in addition to the BFS Core Lifts. Less emphasis is placed on auxiliaries. Core Lifts are plugged in the one-per-month-cycle BFS Set-Rep-Rotation System while auxiliary lifts are normally done by doing two sets of 10 reps. If an athlete is training with a small group, the auxiliaries are done after the Core Lifts. Otherwise, a coach would rotate his athletes from Core Lift to Auxiliaries as outlined in the Organization chapter.

Select no more than five Auxiliary Lifts. When you start doing more than that, especially ten or more, then you'll have time and energy problems. You'll find that your athletes will not have enough *time* and *energy* to do Sprinting, Stamina, Flexibility, Plyometric, Agility, and Technique work. Think of the TOTAL PACKAGE. You must not overemphasize one area of training at the expense of another area. Remember, the ultimate objective is to reach one's potential and *win*. Therefore, select only those exercises that will really contribute to your ultimate objective.

Selection of Auxiliary lifts is done as you think of which ones will help you win or prevent specific injury. For example, on a scale of one to ten, how important are neck exercises to a football player or a wrestler? Obviously, very important. However, to a basketball or baseball player, neck exercises are not that important—so you select an auxiliary that is important.

Five Top Auxiliary Lifts

Monday	**Wednesday**	**Friday**
Neck	Neck	Neck
Leg Curl	Heavy Dips	Leg Curl
Leg Extension	Incline	Leg Extension
Glute Ham	Jerk Press	Glute Ham
Power Snatch	Lunges	Straight-Leg D.L.

Our BFS professional staff rated 100 different Auxiliary lifts and came up with the Auxiliary lifts listed above. They fit all sports very well except the Neck Exercise. Basketball players, for example, don't need to work on their neck to win in their sport. Therefore, those athletes involved may leave it out altogether or replace it with another of your choosing.

As discussed in the Organization chapter, your class should be organized just like practice. One third of your class will be doing one Core Lift, one third another Core Lift and the remaining third will be doing Auxiliary Lifts. Then, switch the groups as you divide the total workout into three equal time segments. If you have a total of only 45 minutes of workout time, that means 15 minutes will be devoted to your Auxiliary Lifts. Hence, when five auxiliary exercises are done, you will have three minutes to do each one. Do not allow your kids to stand around. They should always be looking for an open spot.

The following are the BFS Auxiliary Lifts and why they will help you win:

Neck Exercise: Obvious in football and wrestling.
Leg Curls: Develops the hamstrings and strengthens the knee joint area. Helps your speed and prevents injury.
Leg Extensions: Develops the quadriceps and strengthens the knee joint area. Helps prevent knee injuries.
Glute Ham Developer: A superior way to develop the gluteous maximus, gluteous minimus and the entire area of

Neck Harness   **4-Way Neck Machine**

You can also use the buddy system to exercise the neck. For football, wrestling and soccer.

Leg Curls   **Leg Extensions**

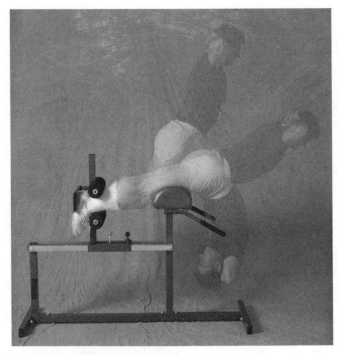

The Glute-Ham Developer

Stefan: Behind-the-Neck-Press
Lead up exercise to Push Press

the buttocks.   It will also strengthen the hamstrings, especially in the lower area. Helps prevent hamstring pulls.
Jerk Press: Place bar behind the neck in a high bar Squat position, squat down slightly and explosively thrust the bar upward. As this is done, split your feet super quickly as you would do in an Olympic style Clean and Jerk. The bar will end up overhead in a locked position. Then stand upright. Do two sets of 5-10 reps. Jerk Presses develop upper body explosiveness, as well as great shoulder strength.
Heavy Dips: Unbelievable in developing powerful triceps. You should have a dip belt for your stronger athletes. When I was doing heavy lifting, I would use five 45-pound plates and do 5 dips - fantastic for offensive linemen, all defensive personnel and shot putters. It is also helpful for jump shots in basketball and all sports who throw an implement or ball.
Incline Press: A favorite auxiliary for many. It develops the upper chest area and aids your Bench Press. It duplicates shot putting and an offensive lineman's pass blocking arm position.
Push Press: Assume the same position as in the Jerk Press and squat down slightly. Now, explosively thrust the bar upward with the legs and arms. Then, explosively pop your feet out from your jump stance and into a half squat position as in a Power Clean (page 121).
Power Snatch: Pages 90-92.
Lunges: This develops power balance. Each leg is forced to work independently from each other. Also, there is no stress on the lower back. You may do this exercise with dumbbells or a regular bar. Develops the hamstrings, quadriceps, and buttocks.
Straight-Leg Dead Lift: Do this with a very light weight. Use no more than 40% of your Parallel Squat max. Do every rep in a slow and controlled manner. Most of your kids will only be using between 55 and 135 pounds. You do this one for speed. It's like magic because you are stretching and strengthening your glutes and hamstrings at

the same time. It is one of the great keys to improving speed.

ADDITIONAL GOOD AUXILIARY LIFTS:

For Football: Hip Sled, Wrist Curls, Lethal Weapon.

For Basketball: Lat Pulls, Tricep Pushdowns, Dumbbell Chest Flies.

For Baseball/Softball: Oblique Twisters with Plate, Wrist Curls, Tricep Pushdowns, Pullovers.

For Tennis/Volleyball: Tricep Pushdowns, Pullovers, Oblique Twisters with Plate.

For Soccer: Lat Pulls.

For Wrestling: Pull-ups, Arm Curls, Rope Climb.

AUXILIARY SETS AND REPS

1. Generally do 2 sets of 10 reps.
2. Exceptions: Jerk Press, Push Press and Power Snatch. Best to do 2 sets of 5 reps.

AUXILIARIES WHICH COULD BE CORE LIFTS

1. Incline Press
2. Power Snatch

Poppy Moronta, Virginia Tech, Performing Push Press with 460 Pounds. The two spotters on the side are absolutely essential. (Photos by Dan Gresh)

Heavy Weighted Dips
by H. S. Senior Brian Harris

**Incline Press: Tim Brown,
Heisman Trophy Winner, Notre Dame**

Stefan doing Straight Leg Dead Lift

You may do from floor or elevate feet for greater stretch.
Keep legs locked.

Seated Shoulder Press   **Milwaukee Buck Fred Roberts**
Lead up to Push Press   **Barbell Lunges**

Greg Shepard Demonstrating Hip Sled

Spread chest, lock-in back, drive hips through like a form tackle, come up on toes.

Stefan: Arm Curls
Football players do
Curls for Girls

Leland Melvin, University
of Richmond. Wrist Curls:
can use Dumbbell or Barbell

All-American Jeff Pegeus:
East Carolina University

Tricep extension or take the weight over the head to the floor, bring it back to chest and then up like a Bench. This is a pullover.

All-American Pitt Panther, Randy Dixon,
doing Dumbbell Inclines. Can also do Dumbell Flys.

Tyrone Thurman, All-American Texas Tech. College Football's Smallest Player. 5-3, 130 lbs Nickname: Smurf. Doing Tricep Extensions

OTHER AUXILIARIES

Step-ups: Great alternative to Lunges

Exercise	Rating for Athletes
Pec Dec	Low
Hack Squat	For Bodybuilders
Leg Sled	Weak Substitute for Squats
Decline	For Bodybuilders
Leg Press	Very Low
Calf Raises	Low
Cable Crossover	For Bodybuilders
Shrugs	Do it with Trap Bar
T-Bar	Substitute for Lat Pull

X. Sets and Reps

The BFS Set-Rep Program virtually eliminates plateaus. You should always be in a position of making progress. No other program can do this. If you have been doing 3 sets of 10 reps, 1 set of 15, 5 sets of 5, you no doubt reach a plateau very quickly. You cannot do the same workout time after time. You must alternate lifts, percentages of maximums, and alternate sets and reps. More complex systems, such as cycle workouts, are better, but you will still eventually hit a plateau. The BFS system allows you to alternate your lifts, sets, and reps in such a way that a specific workout is repeated only every **fifth** week. This system has two simple rules: First, establish your records and, second, break those records. If you follow this system exactly, you will never reach a plateau.

This system has now been used by thousands of athletes. Here is a typical response from Andy Griffin, a highly successful Texas high school football coach: "When is this going to stop? I mean, can they keep setting records like this? My athletes have set so many records these past months, I can't believe it. Thanks!"

Yes, they will. I guarantee 8 new personal records per week for as long as they are in high school.

Ross McQuivey, our 1989 BFS Athlete-of-the-Year said, "The first thing I do in the weight room is look at rep records and set records in my BFS Log Book. I plan on breaking records. I say to myself that I'm going to break this record by five pounds or that I can smash this one. Boy, I'll tell you, it feels so great to break them. I love the feeling after breaking those records. It carries you through the whole day. I feel better about myself and even sleep better."

I recommend that every athlete should have his own BFS Set-Rep Log Book. One Upper-Limit principle is to record everything that is done. How do you know if you are improving if you don't mark down what you've done in the past?

It is an absolute must to record your lifts and using the BFS Log Book is the ideal way to accomplish this. It is by varying your workouts, recording your lifts and planning carefully how to break your records that makes the BFS program special. Breaking records at a phenomenal rate is what makes the BFS program unique. In fact, I guarantee that every athlete will break at least 8 new personal records per week for as long as they are in high school. Plateaus virtually cease to exist.

OVERCOMING PLATEAUS

Everyone experiences plateaus, a leveling off or even a dropping off in performance. Weight training is no exception. People can get frustrated, depressed and ready to quit because of this phenomenon. It is very important to realize this happens to everyone and even more important, to know there are ways to prolong one's upward movement and to *Overcome Plateaus.*

I would like to give a ridiculous example to make a point. A coach says, "Men, we are going to improve our 40-yard dash. We are going to sprint twenty 40-yard dashes every day and I guarantee you will become faster." All the athletes are psyched and do it. Afterwards athletes say, "I'm really tired, this is going to be good for us. Thanks coach." No problem so far, right? Well, what would happen if this exact workout were to be done 5 days a week for 8 weeks? Obviously, by the 8th week the kids would hate it and the 40-yard dash times probably would even get worse. They will have gone through Hans Selye's Stress Syndrome. For some it might take 3 days, while for others weeks. However, everyone will go through it.

Hans Selye developed his Stress Syndrome in 1928 as an explanation of why some people get sick while others remain healthy when being exposed to the same viruses and

bacteria. He found when a person is subjected to any kind
of stress, he will go through all or part of this syndrome. I
have adapted his theory to the BFS Set-Rep System. It
makes sense and it works.

I'd like to explain Selye's Stress Theory by recalling a
swimming experience most everyone has had. A person
comes outside all ready to jump in a non-heated pool. His
friends say, "Come on in, the waters fine once you get used
to it." So he jumps in. Now he is in *Shock* and he wants to
choke his friends, but then he does start to get used to it.
That's *Counter Shock*. Soon he is jumping in and out and
having a great time. This is the *Stage of Resistance*.
Eventually, in a matter of hours, depending on the
temperature of the water, he will start to freeze and even die
if he stays in and this is called the Stage of Exhaustion. This
final stage usually happens very quickly. In two-a-days, for
example, the Stage of Resistance is reached for most by the
fifth or sixth day. The problem is how to prolong the Stage
of Resistance throughout the entire season and not enter into
the Stage of Exhaustion.

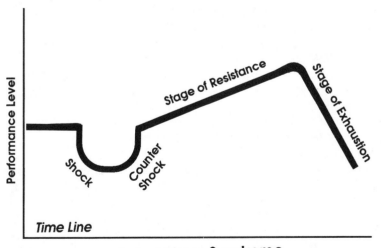

Hans Selye' Stress Syndrome

Selye's Stress Theory can easily he applied to sets and reps in weight training. If an athlete does 3 sets of 10 day after day with the same exercises, the Stage of Exhaustion will rear its ugly head in about four weeks. The same would be true of one set of 8 to 12 or 5 sets of 5 reps.

The trick is to vary your sets, reps, exercises and intensity as much as possible. Every time a variation is inserted into the program, the Stage of Resistance will be prolonged. The BFS Set-Rep System is mass of variation. Everyday is different. Specific workouts are only repeated every fifth week. The system of breaking records as highly motivational which also really helps prolong the Stage of Resistance.

More Ways to Prolong Resistance

1. Use charts for motivation where everyone feels successful.
2. Periodically set dates for competitions against another individual, school or for a new maximum.
3. Use motivational films, stories and people periodically.
4. Use Awards (shirts, certificates, etc.)
5. Vary time, place, days, partners, sequence, intensity and/or diet.
6. Use food supplements. Increase diet, sleep and/or rest.
7. When coming back off a lay-off, forget all past achievements; start all new records.
8. Use one or more of the above guidelines at least once a month. Be smart and sensitive to potential problems.

It should be noted that having a regular routine is in itself an important way to prolong the Stage of Resistance. That's one reason overcoming plateaus is complicated.

However, when entering into a plateau or stage of exhaustion, the tendency is to work harder and increase the intensity of the workout. This usually makes thing worse. More rest, not more work, is most likely needed. Overcoming plateaus and combating stress is as much an art as it is a science. A coach should be sensitive in this area and if great expertise is developed in prolonging the Stage of Resistance, the coach will probably prolong his coaching tenure.

PERIODIZATION OR BFS?

For High Schools, It's No Contest!

The BFS Set-Rep System is perfect for the high school situation. It is superior to the most sophisticated Periodization System. It is superior to the so-called Russian or Bulgarian System. The BFS Set-Rep System flows perfectly from one sport season to the next. It is perfect for a team concept approach. High school athletes will make more progress with greater winning intensity and be more motivated than any other system world-wide. To be sure, these are bold statements, so let's analyze why they are true.

What is Periodization? Phases of training periods divided throughout an annual plan. Some people say: Preparatory, competition and transition phases. These phases are normally broken down into sub-phases and macro or micro cycles. In simple terms; sets, reps, exercises, percentages and training intensities are varied to help an athlete peak at just the right time.

What is the Russian or Bulgarian System? You tell me. Does anybody really have it? Our Swedish BFS Staff member Stefan Fernholm laughs when he remembers hearing Russians snicker at the foolish Americans that think they really have something. We have mountains of research from Russian and East European compendiums. My advice: Let your competition take a Bulgarian weightlifter's routine and use it for a high school football team.

Why is the BFS System Superior? On the surface, periodization which is used by the East Europeans and Russians seems to have great merit. Many top universities espouse periodization. So why shouldn't high schools do it?

Analysis of Various Set-Rep Systems

System	Strength	Weakness	Method of Progression	Ability to Create Intensity	Motivational Factor	Reaching One's Potential
THREE SETS OF 10 REPS	Easy to understand and administer, builds strength base. Good for auxiliary lifts	Plateau will set in very rapidly (6-8 weeks)	When you can do the third set of 10 successfully, move up 5 lbs. next time.	Very difficult to get intense very often, physically and especially mentally	Very Low	No Chance
ONE SET OF 8 TO 12	Easy to understand and administer. Quick workouts. Good for auxiliary lifts.	Plateau out rapidly (6-8 weeks)	Increase poundage when you can do more than 12 reps or get between 8 to 12	Coach needs to be a master motivator. Very difficult.	Very low, rebellion very likely with better athletes	No Chance
THE BFS SYSTEM	No Plateaus. Adaptable to all sports. Self-motivating creates Big Intensity. Easy Transition from in to off season	Needs supervision and coaching. Demands disciplined record keeping.	Continuously BREAK RECORDS anytime with set records and rep records.	Extremely High	Extremely High	Every Chance
TWO SETS OF 25 REPS	Easy to understand and administer builds muscular endurance.	Quick Plateau (4 weeks or less) many high school athletes will quit. Injury factor high.	Get your Sets and Reps: go up next time.	Very difficult to get intense, even once a month.	Extremely Low	No Chance
Period-ization with Various Phases	Adapts extremely well to the individual and one-sport athlete.	A nightmare to implement in high school program with 2 to 3 sport athletes	Sophisticated method based on percentages of maximums. Works best with more mature athlete.	Varies as to phase, sometimes very high	Can be good, although evidence of progression may take time.	Every Chance on Individual Basis
Computer Programs	Easy to show athlete what to do. Plateaus can be postponed. Adaptable to change in strength	Cost, and you cannot adjust during a workout like the BFS program.	Based on input given to computer. Usually step-by-step progression. Keeps overtraining from happening.	Depends on computer input and coaching	Once in a while it can be very good, like on new max day.	Possible

There Are Five Reasons:

1. **Periodization was originally intended for the individual:** Many universities have their athletes train in small groups. Individual workouts are put on a computer printout. High schools have an advantage. They can workout as a team. The football coach can organize the workout like he would a practice. With the BFS system, team and individual intensity levels can reach incredible heights. Periodization systems are much more sporadic when it comes to intensity.

2. **Peaking is a Major problem:** When do you peak? Do you peak for homecoming, the conference championship or the playoffs? In Bulgaria, you would peak for one major contest once a year. In American football, we'd better have some kind of peak every week or we won't have to worry about a playoff peak.

3. **The 2-3 sport athlete:** Universities and Russian/Europeans normally deal with only one-sport athletes. A periodization program done half-way properly in a high school could drive a coach nuts with its complexities. For example, after football, 15 players go into basketball, 20 go out for wrestling and the remaining 30 kids are in an off-season program. Then, in March, 12 of those football players who are out for basketball go out for a spring sport. Seven go out for baseball while five go out for track. The other three basketball-football players join the off-season program. However, the other 30 kids who were in the off-season program have a split. Twenty have decided to enter a spring sport. In the summer, 17 football players also play baseball, while others attend basketball, wrestling and football camps, etc. Wow! Did you get all that? Athletes would be running in and out of phases and cycles all at different times, requiring many different schedules and programs. It would be a nightmare.

   Wouldn't it be nice to have a periodization/cycle type program that beautifully adapted itself to all those situations where the transitions from sport season to sport season required no extra work by the coach. Wouldn't it be nice to see your athletes continually progress throughout every in-season and reach their fullest potential with superior team intensity. That describes our BFS Set-Rep System!

4. **Accurate Maxes?** An athlete has a 175 pound Clean and he's supposed to train with 60% -110 lbs., 70% - 130 lbs., 80% - 150 lbs., etc. Yet, I'll go to a clinic and teach that same athlete about intensity and technique and very typically he will then Clean 225 pounds. So now what? In all probability, much of his training with 110 and 130 pounds for a 8-week periodization cycle was unproductive.

5. **Progress Is Too Slow:** The BFS Set-Rep System provides intensity filled, challenging and motivating training sessions. Computers don't allow for daily variances in strength. The BFS System corrects itself on a set by set basis during the actual workout. You don't have to wait for long periods of time to break a record. On the BFS System you break records every workout. Periodization can hold high school teams back, while our BFS System propels teams forward week after week at break-neck speed.

We've borrowed a lot from periodization and Russian/European systems. All we have done is package it into a system that works amazingly well for high school athletes involved in team sports. While taking into consideration their unique time and logistic constraints. Let your competition try to sort out all the research and come up with a periodization program. Let your competition copy a Russian weightlifter's system. Let your competition use the university's program and scramble to adapt it to the high school situation.

THE BFS WORKOUT

The lifting part of the program consists of a 3-day workout week. If you lift more times than that, you will probably neglect or underemphasize other important training areas like flexibility, agility, plyometrics and speed training.

The BFS Rotational Set-Rep System

WEEK I: 3 x 3 after Warm-ups. This is an easy week. On the last set, do 3 or more: An All-Out Effort!

WEEK II: 5 x 5 or if you only have 45 minutes of class time cut it down to 3 X 5. 5 X 5 is extremely difficult. It is brutal. On the last set, it's 5 or more. Again, an All-Out Effort!

WEEK III: 5-4-3-2-1 or if time is a problem 5-3-1. This is of medium difficulty. On the last set, do one or more. If you use our BFS Set-Rep Logs, you try to break as many rep records as possible on any last set.

WEEK IV: Establish another set record and more rep records. Do 10-8-6 on the Bench, Towel Bench, Box Squat and Squat, and 4-4-2 on the Clean and Dead Lift or Trap Bar Lift. **Important Concept:** Do six or more reps or two or more reps on the last set depending on the core lift.

WEEK V, etc.: Start over. Do more than Week I and try to break some more rep records.

MONDAY: BOX SQUATS—First set, 145 pounds x 3 reps. Now for the second set, you may either go up in poundage, stay the same or go down. Let's say you do 175 pounds for the second set and 205 for the third set. **Important Concept:** on the final set, you should do 3 *or more* reps; up to 10 reps, if you can. Don't worry if this first workout seems too easy and you aren't tired. You want to make sure the spotting and lifting techniques are learned.

TOWEL BENCH: Since most athletes know their max on the bench, take 70% of your max for your first set. For example, if your max is 200 pounds, begin with 140 pounds for 3 reps on your first set. If you've never done benches before, use 70% of your body weight or 105 pounds whichever is the least. If this is too much weight for 3 reps, use 60% or even 50% of your bodyweight. For your second set, you may go up, stay the same or go down. Do 3 or more reps on the final set but on this first workout select a weight you can do 10 times. We want, if possible, to establish your set record and *all* rep records.

Now Record What You've Done

Establishing Set Records

Record your set workout. It might look like this:

$$145 + 175 + 205 = 525$$
$$140 + 150 + 150 = 440$$

The total amount of weight lifted is your set record. In the example above, the Box Squat set record is 525 pounds and the Towel Bench set record is 440 pounds.

Establishing Rep Records

Let's say you did 10 reps at 205 on the Box Squat and 10 reps on the Towel Bench on the final set. Record your Box Squat and Towel Bench rep record. Simply mark in the weight lifted for the correct number of reps and mark in the date in the upper right hand box.

You will notice that all the rep records are the same at this time. Don't worry about this. These numbers will change rapidly as you break your rep records. This will normally happen every workout.

3 X 3 SET RECORDS

BOX SQUAT			TOWEL BENCH		
1	145	TOTAL		1	140	TOTAL	
2	175		525	2	150		440
3	205	DATE	2/3	3	150	DATE	2/3

REP RECORDS

BOX SQUAT		TOWEL BENCH	
REP	Establish Records	REP	Establish Records
MAX	205 [2/3]	MAX	150 [2/3]
2	205 [2/3]	2	150 [2/3]
3	205 [2/3]	3	150 [2/3]
4	205 [2/3]	4	150 [2/3]
5	205 [2/3]	5	150 [2/3]
6	205 [2/3]	6	150 [2/3]
8	205 [2/3]	8	150 [2/3]
10	205 [2/3]	10	150 [2/3]

WEDNESDAY: CLEAN—Do the 3 x 3 workout. Use 70% of your maximum. If you've never cleaned before, use 70% of your body weight or 105 pounds whichever is the least. Use the same procedure for the second and third set (as in Monday's workout) and record your efforts as outlined on the previous page. On the final set, you should do 3 **or more** reps up to 5 reps. Try to get 5 reps.
TRAP BAR: Do the 3 x 3 workout. Start with 145 pounds or your bodyweight whichever is the least. Follow the same procedure and again record your efforts. Again, on the final set, you should do 3 **or more** reps up to 5 reps.

FRIDAY: BENCH PRESS—Do the 3 x 3 workout. Use the same poundage and procedure as in Monday's Towel Bench workout.
SQUAT—Do the 3 x 3 workout and use the same procedure as Monday's Box Squat workout.

THE SECOND WEEK: 5 sets of 5 reps (5 x 5). This is a brutal and long workout. You may wish to cut down to 3 sets of 5 because of time or energy especially on the Trap Bar and Clean day. Select your poundages as in the first week. Record your efforts. **Important Concept:** You should do 5 **or more** reps on the last set except when doing the Clean or Trap Bar.

THE THIRD WEEK: (5-4-3-2-1). This is not quite as hard as 5 x 5 but you still may wish to cut this down to 5-3-1 because of time or energy. In the example on the next page, 165 was done for 5 reps, 170 for 4 reps, 175 for 3 reps, etc. Record your efforts. You will establish you 5-4-3-2-1 set records and you should be breaking some rep records as illustrated below. **Important Concept:** You should do one or more reps on the last set.

THE FOURTH WEEK: Follow the system for Week IV as explained on page 137. In addition, you will notice the rep records go to only 5 reps on the Clean and the Dead Lift.

AN EXAMPLE OF
RECORDING THE TOWEL BENCH

5 X 5			5-4-3-2-1		
5	145	**TOTAL** 765	5	165	**TOTAL** 875
5	150		4	170	
5	155	**DATE** 2/10	3	175	**DATE** 2/17
5	160	**WEIGHT** ** 166	2	180	**WEIGHT** ** 167
5	155*		1	185 ***	

*   Got six reps when trying for 5 or
       more reps
* *   Record your body weight here
       As you get bigger you will get
       stronger
* * *   Got two reps, for example, on this
       last set

REP RECORDS

REP	Estab. Records	1st Break	2nd Break
MAX	2/3 A. 150	2/10 B. 160	2/17 C. 185
2	2/3 A. 150	2/10 B. 160	2/17 C. 185
3	2/3 A. 150	2/10 B. 160	2/17 C. 175
4	2/3 A. 150	2/10 B. 160	2/17 C. 170
5	2/3 A. 150	2/10 B. 160	2/17 C. 165
6	2/3 A. 150	2/10 B. 155	
8	2/3 A. 150		
10	2/3 A. 150		

A. Established Records in 3 x 3 Week
B. Broken Records in 5 x 5 Week
C. Broken Records in 5-4-3-2-1 Week

Doing extra reps on these two lifts could cause an injury, especially to the lower back. As fatigue sets in, chances for muscle spasms and incorrect lifting techniques increase.

THE FIFTH WEEK: Now the fun of the BFS System moves into high gear. From now on, every time you come into the weight room, you've got a challenge and an objective. You should try to break as many set and rep records as possible. You begin the fifth week by again doing the 3 x 3 workout. You will notice on the previous months example, a total of 440 was achieved on the Towel Bench. **Your objective is to simply do more!**

An Example of the Fifth Week
Towel Bench

3 x 3 SET RECORD

BOX SQUAT		
1	140	T O T A L
2	150	440
3	150	D A T E 2/3
1	160	T O T A L
2	170	510
3	180	D A T E 3/3

Look at what happened! The set record was smashed by 70 pounds! In addition, a new 3 rep record was attained (Refer to the example on the previous page). 180 pounds should be recorded under the third Break column along with the 3/3 date.

*Many athletes like to try to break their 10 rep records after doing 3 x 3, since this is an easy week. This is called a "Burnout" set.

THE SIXTH WEEK: Break your 5 x 5 set record and as many rep records as you can!

THE SEVENTH WEEK: Break your 5-4-3-2-1 set record and as many rep records as you can!

THE EIGHTH WEEK: Again concentrate on breaking your Set Record and Rep Records!

If you are trying for a new 6 rep max, and you still have power to spare when you get to the sixth rep: **Don't Stop!** Try to squeeze out as many reps as possible — up to 10. **Go for it!** Again, if you are trying to break a 2 rep max but have power for more reps: **Do it! BE INTENSE!** Remember, each additional rep is a **New** record! **Want to win? Break a record!**

Now keep rotating your workouts in this 4-week cycle. You can expect to break 8 or more records per week or 400 per year for as long as you want. There are 60 possible records to break. Each of the six core lifts has 3 set records (3 x 3, 5 x 5, 5-4-3-2-1); that's 18 possible set records. The Bench Press, Towel Bench, Squat and Box Squat each have 8 rep records, while the Trap Bar Dead Lift and the Clean each have 5 rep records. That's a total of 42 possible rep records. That's why it is easy to break so many records. Remember we are not concerned with only breaking a 1 rep max, but all kinds of rep records. We know, for example, if we break a 3 rep record that our max will also soon go up. What would happen if you broke 8 personal records per week for one year? It kind of boggles the mind doesn't it? **The Sky is The Limit!!**

HELPFUL HINTS:
1.   *Or more* means the number of reps up to ten on the Bench, Towel Bench, Squat and Box Squat and up to 5 reps on the Clean and Trap Bar.
2.   Dothan High School in Alabama has a bell at each station. When an athlete is going for a record the bell is rung. It really seems to help the intensity.
3.   Many coaches are using teachers aides to assist the athletes in recording.
4.   Changing the sequence of the lifts can help shake a plateau (Do the Bench first, not Squat, for example).

THE FINER POINTS:

A. Warm-ups: If you lift over 200, you definitely need warm-up sets. Usually these sets can be done with 5 reps. The following table is your guideline to warm-ups:

Your Set Routine Begins With	Warm-Up With
Less than 200	0-1 set
200-295	1-2 sets
300-395	2-3 sets
400-495	3-4 sets
500-595	4-5 sets

EXAMPLES:
3 x 3 with 275 pounds (Warm-up with 195 & 235)
5 x 5 with 330 pounds (Warm-up with 235 & 295)
5-4-3-2-1 with 450 pounds (Warm-up with 235, 325 & 415)

B. Missing a Rep: Sometimes you may miss a rep. For example, you're trying to do 3 x 3 with 275 and on the last set you can only do 2 reps. You have 2 options.
 1. Rest and try again with the same or a lighter weight.
 2. Penalize yourself 5 pounds per 100 pounds on the bar.

For example, in the above situation you're penalized 10 pounds, so add 275 + 275 + 265 for your total. If you're lifting in the 500-pound range, your penalty would be 25 pounds for missing one rep and 50 pounds for missing two reps.

Penalty Table

Range	Penalty	Range	Penalty
100 – 195	5 pounds	400 – 495	20 pounds
200 – 295	10 pounds	500 – 595	25 pounds
300 – 395	15 pounds	600 – 695	30 pounds

C. Adjusting: The BFS system gives you the flexibility in adjusting poundages, as you progress through your workout. For example, your 3 x 3 set record is 1095 pounds. So you do your first set with 370 pounds and it's easy. For your second set, you select 390 pounds and it's super tough. Therefore, on your third set, you bring it back down to 370 pounds. Your new set record total is 1130 pounds.

D. When to Start Over: You should start your records over after a layoff of four or more weeks, a major sickness or a big drop in weight. Also, after 2-A-Days.

E. 75 Total Records: There are 60 records up for grabs plus 15 more if you count Auxiliaries and Performance Records (Dot Drill, Sit and Reach, 40-20, VJ and SLJ).

WHAT ABOUT COLLEGE OR PROS?

The BFS Set-Rep System is perfect for any athlete who's primary goal is to develop into a bigger, faster, stronger athlete.

READ YOUR BODY
AND MAKE
A GREAT DECISION!

WANT TO WIN?
BREAK A RECORD!

XI. In-Season Training

BFS In-Season
Program: All Sports

<u>DAY #1</u>	<u>DAY #2</u>
SQUAT	CLEAN
BENCH	BOX SQUAT
TRAP BAR or S.L.D.L.	TOWEL BENCH

One of our Upper Limit Training Guidelines is consistency. It is an absolute necessity to train In-Season in **All Sports**. No matter what sport, all athletes will do two workouts per week. Day #1 is the most physically demanding and, therefore, should be done farthest away from the contest as possible. Day #2 lifts can be done all-out with extremely fast recuperation. Therefore, an athlete can do these lifts the day before the contest, if necessary!

Football could be as follows:
Monday, Day #1; Thursday, Day #2; Friday, Game.

Basketball could be as follows:
Monday, Day #2; Tuesday, Game; Wednesday, Day #1; Friday, Game; or Tuesday, Game; Wednesday, Day #2; Friday, Game; Saturday, Day #1.

Each core lift takes only 10 minutes. Each day takes only 30 minutes. We're only asking one hour per week to have spectacular results. Limited auxiliaries can be done as time and energy permits. The best time of day to do an In-Season workout is before lunch, not before or after practice.

The Basic BFS
In-Season Program

1. Train Twice Per Week
2. Train in the Morning
3. Each Session takes 30 Minutes
4. Do the Basic BFS Core Lifts and Only about Two Auxiliary Lifts.
5. Do Only Three Big Sets. Just Follow the BFS Set-Rep Program!
6. Progress! Don't be Satisfied with maintaining.

Okay, you are now beginning the football season. What do you do with the weights? If you said, "Wait until the off-season," you get a dandelion. You've just got to find time to weight train.

Let's say you Benched 250 pounds right before you put the pads on in August. If you don't train at all, you will be Benching 220 pounds by the first of November. That's right when you want to be strong. If you do the BFS in-season training program, you'll most likely be Benching 280 pounds. If you are used to training in the off-season, and you don't train in-season, I guarantee you'll be mentally down because of a perceived weakness at playoff time. Conversely, if you do train in-season, you will be mentally up for the playoffs. The bottom line is simple: You can't afford not to take the time and weight train.

Train Twice Per Week: Once is not enough to make progress and three times seems to be too draining during the in-season. With the exercises in the BFS Program, you may workout the day before the game with positive results.

Train In The Morning: If at all possible, train in the morning before school or in a class before lunch. There are disadvantages when athletes weight train just prior to or just after football practice. I'd rather get up a half hour earlier to lift than try to lift before or after practice. You'll get better results.

Each Session Takes 30 Minutes: If you take more than this time, I think you'll run into trouble. Remember your objective is to win the football game. There are so many things to focus on during the season which take a lot of time and energy, you simply cannot afford to spend many hours in the weight room. A total of one hour during the week is sufficient. The amazing thing is the amount of progress you can make with this concept.

Do the Basic BFS Core Lifts: You still want to keep your Parallel Squat, Bench and Clean progressing throughout the season. You just can't let those go. You can skip a lot of auxiliary exercises. The beauty of doing the Box Squat in-season is the recovery time which is almost immediate. That's why you can Box Squat on Thursday and play a game on Friday. To keep the stress factor down, you might want to keep the poundage on the Box Squat within about 100 pounds of the Parallel Squat.

The Towel Bench is also great to do in-season, because it keeps the stress level down while allowing for some great progress to be made on the Bench. The stress to the shoulder joint area is also much less than the regular Bench Press. Therefore, this is the lift you do on Wednesday or Thursday before the game. The Straight Leg Dead Lifts should be done with light weights (this means no more than 40% of your Parallel Squat max). Most high school athletes will, therefore, be doing only between 55 and 135 pounds. Your objective is to get a good hamstring and glute stretch while also building strength in this area. Remember, this exercise is a key to improving speed. Also, remember that you need only to do two sets of ten reps with the Straight Leg Dead Lift. You would not plug this exercise into the normal BFS Set-Rep routine.

My suggestion for the two football auxiliaries would be a neck exercise and dips. Dips are done for tricep power which helps all linemen and defensive players. The neck exercise is done for obvious reasons. However, you may have another exercise you feel will help you win a football game. If you can justify it, then do it.

Do Only Three Big Sets: Just follow our BFS Set-Rep System. Week Number One: 3 x 3, Week Number Two: 3 x 5, Week Number Three: 5-3-1, Week Number Four: 10-8-6, or in the case of the Trap Bar or Cleans, doing 4-4-2. Then, of course, on Week Number Five you repeat Week Number One's workout of 3 x 3 but challenge yourself to do more. Next, you will repeat Week Number Two's workout the same way and so on. Hopefully, you will be able to get in three full cycles during the season.

Progress!: Most colleges try to maintain. What you hope is that your competition will also adopt that philosophy. The philosophy of maintaining in college is acceptable, but it is loaded with big problems at the high school level. First of all, the college athlete is more fully mature and at a greater strength level. The college athlete may be benching 400 pounds and be happy with maintaining that level during the season. However, the 16-year-old who is benching 200 pounds is still maturing and can easily gain strength during the season. Don't sell yourself short!

Second, a college athlete normally plays only one sport and in January he is ready for the off-season. But what about that 16-year-old? What if he also plays basketball or wrestles? What if he goes out for track or baseball in the spring? What are you going to do—maintain all year?

Let your competition do that. You should go for it during the season. Don't be satisfied with maintaining. Get going! It's fun to get stronger. You'll play better, feel better and be more confident.

Special Note: Mark Eaton, center for the Utah Jazz, broke 275 personal records in-season during his rookie year on the BFS program. Mark later became an NBA All-Star and two-time Defensive Player-of-the-Year.

THE STORY OF THE THREE JOES

Joe One's Story

Joe One's football coach said, "We've got to practice, have meetings and watch game films. We just don't have time to get in a workout." So as a result, Joe One lost most of his strength that he built up over the summer. When it came to basketball, Joe's coach said, "Well, we have two games per week plus practices. If football can't lift in-season, we certainly can't." Joe One's baseball coach said, "Weights will screw you up, so we ain't doin' nothin'." Poor Joe One. At the end of his freshman year, he was about the same level of strength as his 8th grade year. This same scenario was repeated all four years. At graduation ceremonies, Joe One's coaches looked at Joe One and said, "He was a good athlete. It's too bad he wasn't bigger, faster and stronger. Why don't we ever get some mature looking athletes?" In-Season, Baby, In-Season!

Joe One's Strength Level

Joe Two's Story

Joe Two's football coach went to hear a major college strength coach talk about In-Season. "What we want to do is MAINTAIN!" So that's what they did during Joe Two's football, basketball, and baseball seasons all four years. Poor Joe Two. He spent all his life maintaining. The high school coaches didn't stop to think that the major college situation was different. At that level you only play one sport and the more mature college athlete is satisfied with maintaining his 500 squat, 400 bench and 300 clean over one sport season. However, at the high school level, the big majority of athletes play two or more sports. High school sophomores may have a 250 squat, 175 bench, and a 160 clean. We don't want to maintain these lifts. To set up a maintenance program in high school is to set up a program of failure. You will **NEVER** reach your potential.

Joe Two's Strength Level

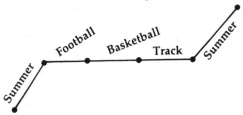

Joe Three's Story
Joe Three's football coach does the BFS In-Season program and follows the Set-Rep system. Gains were not as much as in the off-season, but clearly significant gains were made throughout each sport season. Since the In-Season program is the same for all sports, a smooth transition was easily made from one sport season to the next. Joe Three stuck to his program faithfully all four years. Joe Three broke an average of 400 personal records each year and reached his potential. His lifts went off the chart!

Joe Three's Strength Level

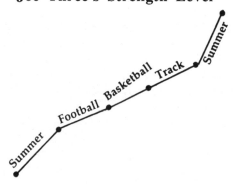

ADDITIONAL TIPS

If you are using our BFS Set Rep Log Books, do not lift during Two-A-Days. Your kids are worn down and exhausted mentally and physically. There is way too much stress to add a lifting program.

Put the old book in a file after the Summer. That is the last year's book. Get a new book and start all over with new records after Two-A-Days. Don't worry about the past. Start easy. Establish all new set and rep records. Build yourself again and soon you'll be doing more than the old book. Then, if you go into another sport, just keep going. If you go into an off-season mode, then you can really turn up the intensity juice.

Karl Malone of the Utah Jazz during his 1997 NBA MVP Season doing Box Squats with BFS Vice President, Rick Anderson.

NBA Defensive Player-of-the-Year Mark Eaton being spotted by 7-0 Eric Leckner, both former Utah Jazz players.

"You've got to train In-Season"

In our last season (1997) as strength coaches for the Utah Jazz, if a player missed an in-season workout it could cost him $35,000.

XII. Organization

A. NUMBER OF ATHLETES ÷ 3

Take the number of athletes or students and divide by three. You want 3 groups. One for core lift #1, one for core lift #2 and the other group for auxiliaries. For example, let's say we have 48 people. That would give us 16 people per group.

B. NUMBER PER GROUP ÷ 4

Now take that number and divide by four. We divide by four to give us the number of people per station. We want the lifter plus 3 spotters. This method also helps us determine what equipment is needed for our situation. In our example, we need four squat stations, four bench stations plus auxiliaries. On Wednesday, you would replace the squats and benches with the trap bar and cleans, if you were following the BFS program.

C. TOTAL TIME ÷ 3

Take the total lifting time available and divide by three. Many high school programs are done during school time and dressing—shower time takes away from actual available time. In our example below, we have only 45 total minutes which gives us 15 minutes per area. Each group would then rotate from area to area every 15 minutes. The Coach can blow a whistle or yell "switch" to begin this rotation process.

D. TIME - AUXILIARIES

Finally, take the number of auxiliary exercises and divide into fifteen. This gives us an average of 3 minutes per auxiliary exercise. In our example, 16 people should be rotating freely between the five auxiliary exercises. There should be no standing around. The coach or teacher's aid may want to inform the auxiliary group at each 3 minute interval.

Example: **48 Athletes ÷ 3 = 16 Per Group**
16 ÷ 4 = 4 Stations
45 Minutes ÷ 3 = 15 Minutes
15 Minutes ÷ 5 Auxiliaries = 3 Minutes

JUST LIKE PRACTICE

A great way to organize a high school or college weight room is to handle it just like a football practice or like a practice from another team sport. Let your competition prescribe a workout and sit at a desk reading a newspaper.

Require the Same Discipline: Athletes should be on time and have the feeling that it's football practice in the weight room. Athletes should be attentive, hustling and team oriented. Let your competition make their weight training session a social hour.

Instill a Team Concept Approach: Make gains as a team. Take team pride in individual records. You could have contests between defense and offense, juniors and seniors, your team and another team, etc. A coach must be active just like a team practice, constantly motivating and teaching. Let your competition make workouts dull and without team pride.

Organize Time and Total Program Efficiently: Wouldn't it be great if the opposing football coach spent all of his practice time on offense and did absolutely nothing with defense or the kicking game? Let your competition work only on weights or concentrate largely on the upper body or bodybuilding. With the BFS Total Program, you will work each important area with just the right amount of time. You will work on flexibility and agility everyday. You will lift three times per week, concentrating on the legs and hips with total body lifting movements like the Squat and Power Clean. You will work on Speed and Plyometric Training twice per week in the off-season. Time is also set aside to work on technique skills by position and sport. Some time should be set aside (5 minutes) on Tuesdays and Thursdays to discuss subjects such as nutrition, rest and strategy. A short motivational story could be given once a week. An ideal way to give a motivational story is to share stories from the BFS Journal or BFS story videos.

Too Much To Do? Do Some Things Outside Class! Does a good QB go out and throw with his receivers on his own? Sure he does. Why not extend this concept to your training program? Let your competition stretch for 15 of the 42 minute physical education class period. Let your competition get frustrated and exclaim: "We can't get to it. There isn't enough time!"

Give your athletes a chance to be excellent, a chance to reach their potential. If your team is truly committed to winning, most of them will stretch and do their agility drills outside class time. All a coach has to do is test on Tuesdays and Thursdays and the results will verify the athlete's commitment. Some Plyometric, Speed and Technique work can also be done on their own. Signing commitment contracts or goal cards can be of great benefit in making your success happen.

Require Disciplined Spotting and Technique: A football coach wouldn't say, "Okay, you eleven guys are the scout team. Do anything you want." Let your competition be that way in the weight room. But you always have spotters who encourage their teammates and pull out the best in them. Every athlete should be keenly aware of the coaching techniques of every lift and accept the responsibility of being a coach while they are spotting.

It's Better to Modify the Program Intelligently, Than to Compromise Discipline and Organization: For example, one of the workouts in our 4-week cycle is to do 5 sets of 5 while another is to do a 5-4-3-2-1 workout. In a 42 minute Physical Education period, that many sets can't be done. Therefore, we recommend doing 3 sets of 5 and 5-3-1 for those respective workouts. It's perfect and very little is actually lost in the way of physical development. Now, there is time to do it right. Be creative in your use of time and your equipment.

Don't Scrimmage with the Kids: Every coach should experience lifting, but there are too many weaknesses when a coach gets into his own training during the athlete's workout time. Although athletes respect a coach who keeps in shape, it is just too difficult to teach and motivate properly, if you're busy lifting. Once in a while, it could be a great learning situation if a coach demonstrated things like intensity, poundage and technique, provided the coach has that capability.

Luther Elliss, Detroit Lions
Preparation is the Key

XIII. Coordinating All Athletic Programs

I have received many letters from high school football coaches complaining some athletes just get a good start in a weight program, only to have to quit lifting to play basketball, baseball, track or tennis. All coaches should be concerned about the total development of the athlete and the athletic program. All coaches must work together. A school cannot have a top notch athletic program when one coach says one thing and another coach from another sport says something different.

I would encourage each school to have a meeting with all coaches and administrators to discuss a workable plan for all concerned. After a plan has been agreed upon, then stick to it as a unified coaching philosophy. A baseball coach does not want a football coach telling an athlete to lift weights for football during the baseball season, even though it may actually help the athlete. There must be mutual agreement, cooperation and understanding.

The following points are suggestions to ponder for coaches of all sports:

A. The foundation of strength and power for all athletes is centered in the hips and legs. All coaches from all sports should want their athletes to have stronger hips and legs. It can make improvements in such areas as running, jumping and injury prevention. What coach would **not** want those improvements?

Sometimes coaches are worried about muscle soreness or becoming muscle bound, thus losing a basketball touch or baseball timing. Squats will not affect this at all. Soreness or tiredness for practice can certainly be alleviated by doing box squats.

B. Strength can be lost over a period of weeks. Any coach who has worked his team hard in an off-season strength program can lose any advantage by that eighth or ninth game, if the weight training is not continued.

If it takes 12 weeks to attain a certain strength level, it will take about 12 weeks to return to the previous strength level. However, some athletes who train regularly notice a difference in only one week of missed workouts.

Strength can be maintained fairly well with one workout a week, but a 3-sport athlete does not want to maintain his strength level all year round. The obvious solution is to have all athletes from all sports use the BFS In-Season Program. Then an athlete can continue on the same program from sport season to sport season without interruption. The following recommendations are important for all high school programs to consider:

Recommendations
1. All coaches should agree to implement the BFS Core Program.
2. All coaches should agree to use the BFS Super Set-Rep Program for the Core Program.
3. Each coach is then free to choose any auxiliary exercises or methods to augment his particular sport.
4. All coaches need to contribute and give support to the supervision, maintenance, and finances of the weight room facility.
5. All coaches should agree to use the BFS in-season philosophy and program.

When all coaches agree to the above recommendations, the athlete really benefits. There is no confusion or mistrust. The athlete can progress with his training and development smoothly from one sport season to the next. Schools which have adopted this plan report a greater harmony between coaches, with the athletes more willing to participate in more than one sport. With this increased spirit and willingness to cooperate, the coaches feel that coaching is certainly more fun, and the wins come more frequently.

XIV. Agility/Dot Drill

The first thing athletes should do before any activity is the BFS Dot Drill. It only takes about a minute. Let your competition do jumping jacks or not warm-up at all. You need to work up a little sweat and get the blood temperature elevated before exercising. Therefore, you might as well do something constructive and measurable. The BFS Dot Drill is perfect. It is an agility/quick foot drill which will produce great results with individual and team pride. Do it before lifting, sprinting, plyometrics or stretching. A coach should time his athletes about twice a month and record the progress and results.

The Dot Drill will be hard at first. It is tiring and you may appear clumsy. However, if you'll do this six times a week, in a very short time improvement will come rapidly. You can have quick feet in a month or two.

Each athlete should set two goals. The first is to do it 6 times per week and, secondly, on how fast he wants to go. The Dot Drill is done by Mark Eaton with Coach Shepard in 60 seconds after a weight training session on Video Cassette.

Dot Drill Standards

	Lineman Type Athlete	Skill Athlete
Good:	65 seconds	60 seconds
Great:	60 seconds	55 seconds
All-State:	55 seconds	50 seconds
All American:	45 seconds	40 seconds

High School Boys Record: Michael Brown 33.37 seconds
Poplar Bluff, Missouri
High School Girls Record: Kristian Meyers 37.77 seconds
Poplar Bluff, Missouri

Dot Drill Diagram

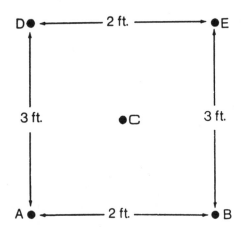

Five dots are placed on the floor. It works best if a 3"
round dot is painted on the floor. Some coaches paint many
stations for larger groups. An athlete at home can use
anything approved by his parents to mark his dots. There
are five separate dot drills. Each drill is done a total of six
times.

  I. Up and Back
     A. Start at one end with feet on A and B.
     B. Now jump quickly to C; with both feet then to D
        and E.
     C. Now come back the same way.
     D. Repeat 5 more times.
 II. Right Foot
     A Your feet from up-and-back should be on dots A
       and B. Now go to dot C with your right foot.
     B. Now go in order: Dot E, D, C, A, B.
     C. Repeat 5 more times.

III. Left Foot

    A. You will end the right foot drill on Dot B. Now go to dot C with your left foot.

    B. Now go in order: Dot E, D, C, A, B.

    C. Repeat 5 more times.

IV. Both Feet

    A. You will end the left foot drill on Dot B. Now go to C with both feet.

    B. Now go in order with both feet: Dot E, D, C, A, B.

    C. Repeat 5 more times.

V. Turn Around

    A. You will end the both feet drill on Dot B. Now go to C with both feet.

    B. Now go to dots D and E with both feet as in the up and back (Drill #1).

    C. Now quickly jump and turn 180 degrees to your right and face the other way. You should still be on dots D and E.

    D. Hit C with both feet and then A and B with feet split.

    E. Now turn quickly again with a 180 degree spin to the left with your feet still on A and B.

    F. Repeat 5 more times.

A simple way to think when doing the right foot, left foot and both feet drills is **IN** (In to the middle - C), **OUT** (Out to E), **ACROSS** (Across to D), **IN** (In to the Middle - C), **OUT** (Out to A) and **ACROSS** (Across to B).

Dan Santhouse, Widener University
American Record Holder BFS Dot Drill: 36.6 seconds

XV. Flexibility

A stretching program should never be used solely for a warm-up for other activities. It is an exercise regimen itself like lifting and running. A stretching program should be done to increase flexibility and range of motion. It must be worked at daily both in the off-season and the in-season. Flexibility exercises entails work, sweat and concentration of exact and proper position. The vast majority of schools and athletes can make big improvements in their flexibility program.
    Stretching is done for the following reasons:

1. To improve speed.
2. To increase joint range of motion.
3. To improve performance.
4. To decrease injury possibilities.
5. To decrease seriousness of injury occurrence.
6. To improve jumping ability.

We can improve the performance of a thrower by increasing the range of motion. If a pitcher can get his arm back a little farther, he will throw harder and faster. If a discus thrower can get his arm and shoulder back two inches farther, it might produce an improvement of 10 feet. If an athlete can improve his flexibility in the hip flexor area so that his stride length is 2 inches greater, that alone may improve a 40 yard dash time by 2 tenths of a second.
    There are 3 main methods of flexibility training. First, the most common method is called ballistic. This is where an athlete bobs or bounces. Do not do this method. It is dangerous. Second, is the static method, where an athlete will do a slow controlled stretch. Third, is the PNF method or Proprioceptive Neuromuscular Facilitation. See why they call it PNF! The PNF method requires a partner and the

athlete actually goes in the opposite direction against his partners resistance. PNF is probably the best method, provided a good partner is available; but that can be a real challenge.

BFS 1-2-3-4 FLEXIBILITY PROGRAM

The BFS Program uses the static method. This method is great because you do not have to find a knowledgeable partner. Since flexibility training must be done everyday, year round, the static method seems to be the best choice because the athlete is free to stretch anytime and anyplace.

We have created a stretching program which takes less than 10 minutes per session. It thoroughly stretches every major area of the body, especially the trunk, hips and legs. It's as easy as 1-2-3-4. These numbers are keys to help everyone understand and remember the program.

The BFS 1-2-3-4 Flexibility Program is perfect for any level of competition. It's a state-of-the-art method especially designed for speed. And because it's designed for speed, it is perfect for all sports. The whole school or university should use the same program; that's what makes it so beautiful. The three-sport athlete who plays football, basketball and baseball, for example, does the same 1-2-3-4 BFS Flexibility Program. It's perfect.

It only takes 10 minutes and it's easy to understand. After the program is learned, athletes can stretch anytime, anyplace, and anywhere without a partner. That's why we recommend the static method over the PNF partner method. It is too hard to find a good partner consistently in a high school, college or pro situation.

Each exercise should be held for a minimum of 10 seconds, 3 repetitions each, or 30 seconds for 1 repetition. The stretch should not be done with a bounce, but worked in a slow and controlled manner. Stretch everyday, work with intensity, and remember to do the BFS Dot Drill first.

One on the Bench

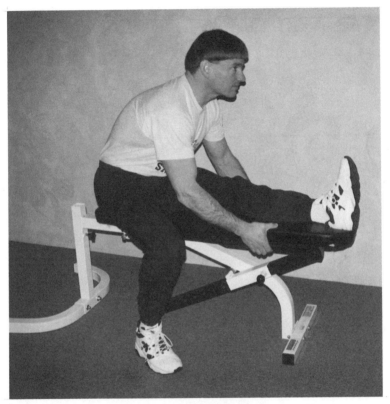

Hamstring Stretch:

This is the best ever Hamstring Stretch. Left leg is locked at knee. Left foot straight up and bring toes back. Pull upper body forward with eyes straight ahead. Do not put nose on knee. Do not hang heel over the end of the bench.

STRETCH FOR SPEED . . .

Two in the Air

A. Latisimus Stretch:
Cross your hands and raise
your arms above your head
and as far back as possible.

B. Pectoral Stretch:
Cross your hands behind
your back, raise your arms
up and back. Do not lean
over.

AND JUMPING POWER!

Three on the Wall

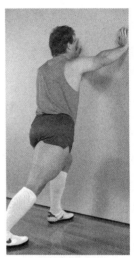 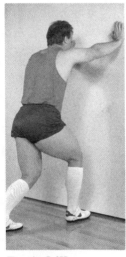 

A. Calf Stretch: Keep flat on ground, with hands on wall, move hips forward and down. Back foot and toes should be straight, then switch. Look straight ahead. Look like a sprinter.

B. Achilles Stretch: Same as preceding but with slightly bent knee. Slowly squat down thereby increasing the pressure on the Achilles tendon, then switch after 30 seconds. Lift back heel off floor about an inch.

C. Quadriceps Stretch: With one hand on the wall, grab one ankle from the outside and pull leg up and away from buttocks. Knee should be at a 90° angle, then switch. *Important:* The knee should be pulled straight back and *never* out to the side.

Four Minutes on the Floor

A. Groin Stretch: Sit with feet together, grab ankles *not* feet, pull in and press down with elbows on the thighs.

B. Adductor Stretch: With feet as far apart as possible, grab ankles or feet and slowly pull the torso toward the floor.

C. Gluteus Maximus Stretch:

Twist torso with opposite arm, thereby achieving a stretch in the gluteus maximus. Press knee across the down leg firmly with elbow, then switch after 30 seconds.

D. Hip Flexor Stretch:

Place front foot two feet in front of back knee so that the front lower leg is straight up and down. Place hands on knee and force hips forward and especially down to achieve stretch in anterior hip area. Keep head and back upright, then switch after 30 seconds.

Special Note: This is the *most* important stretch you can do. This will increase your stride length but it must be done *exactly* as shown. If you bend over or put your elbows on your knee, you will be wasting your time.

E. Abdominal Stretch: Lay flat on the floor, put hands on floor—shoulder width apart, extend elbows thus creating an arch in the lower back. Relax.

Administering the Sit and Reach Test

The sit and reach test measures flexibility in the back of the legs and in the lower back. The test is done by sitting on the floor with legs together (putting legs against a board or a partner's hand will help keep you from moving). Reach as far as possible and hold for 3 seconds. Use a yard stick by placing it with the 6 inch mark at heels and the 1 inch mark closest to the athlete. Reach as far as possible, then check results.

	Male	Female
Excellent	6 inches past heels	8 inches past heels
Good	2 inches past heels	4 inches past heels
Fair	-2 inches short of heels	0 inches at heels
Poor	-6 inches short of heels	-4 inches short of heels

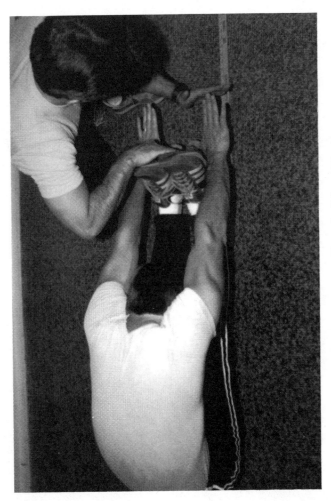

Sit and Reach Flexibility Test

OTHER HELPFUL HINTS

A. If you can't do one on the bench, do this Figure Four Hamstring Stretch.

B. If you can't reach forward and grab your toes on the Adductor Stretch, do as shown.

C. Another view of the Achilles Stretch.

D. Another view of the Quad Stretch. Every joint is safe.

XVI. Speed and Plyometrics

Speed and Plyometrics should be done on Tuesdays and Thursdays during the off-season. Speed and Plyometric workouts should also be done twice per week in-season and should be part of the normal practice schedule.

The BFS Dot Drill

The first thing athletes should do is the BFS Dot Drill. It is an agility/quick-foot drill designed as a warm-up. The drill is described in detail in Chapter XIV.

Stretching - Flexibility

After the BFS Dot Drill, all athletes can begin the BFS 1-2-3-4 Flexibility Program. If the athletes are stretching on their own on M-W-F weight training days, this is an excellent time to check on the technique of each flexibility exercise. A coach can also find out who's really been emphasizing flexibility at home. Once a month, the Sit and Reach test should be administered to monitor flexibility progress. After doing the BFS Dot Drill and 1-2-3-4 Flexibility Programs, each athlete will be warm, pliable and ready for Speed and Plyometric training. The time elapsed is now only about 12 minutes.

Speed Training

Athletes should be tested for speed twice per month either on a 40 or 20 yard sprint. Times should be recorded and progress charted. Give athletes one trial run at 75-90% speed and then give three timed sprints. Record the best of the three times.

Sprint training workouts on Tuesdays and Thursdays last about ten minutes. Five of those minutes should be concentrating on technique. If you use the BFS 8-point Sprint Technique System, you will be successful with form. Concentrate on one form weakness at a time. Whether it is head, eye, back, arm, leg or foot plant position; only work on one technique at a time. A great way to know what specifically to work on is to use video analysis. Athletes really like viewing themselves and it really heightens their awareness of proper sprinting technique.

The remaining five minutes should be devoted to ten all-out quality sprints from 10 to 50 yards. About 30 seconds rest should be given between sprints.

When the weather is bad, do not stop sprinting. Let your competition do that. In Minnesota that would mean avoiding sprints for six months. Replace the 40 yard sprint with 20 yard sprints indoors. There is about a two-second difference. Therefore, a 3.0 twenty is equivalent to a 5.0 forty.

Carl Lewis: He ran 9.92 at the Seoul Olympics for a new American record for 100 meters. The Gold Medal was awarded to Lewis after Ben Johnson tested positive for Steroids. Lewis stated that he ran as fast as he could. Not true—Lewis made four critical errors and probably could have run 9.87. He turned his head three times to look at Johnson—that's three errors. When you turn your head, you can't relax and be as fluid. The fourth error was to let up two to three yards before the finish line. Many youngsters are looking for Steroids to get faster. Follow the program below and you won't need Steroids.

Eleven Guaranteed Ways to Improve Speed

1. Sprint train twice per week, minimum.
2. Do ten 10-50 yard sprints.
3. Get timed twice per month (record and chart all times).
4. Sprint all-year round. In areas with bad weather, run the twenty-yard dash for time. A 3.0 twenty is about the same as a 5.0 forty.
5. Use video analysis of each athlete. Extremely valuable!
6. Flexibility training six times per week. Must be done correctly to improve speed.
7. Plyometrics twice per week, minimum.
8. Parallel Squat: If you Squat, but don't go parallel, YOU WILL NOT IMPROVE SPEED maximally. Parallels must be done, period!
9. Straight-Leg Dead Lift: This builds and stretches the glutes and hamstrings at the same time, critical to speed improvement. Use 40 percent of Parallel Squat max. Two or three sets of 10 reps.
10. Teach the BFS 8-point Sprint Technique System.
11. Power Clean: This will give you an explosive start.

BFS 8 POINT SPRINT TECHNIQUE SYSTEM

1. **HEAD**—head should be **upright**.
2. **EYES**—eyes should be fixed looking **straight** ahead.
3. **TOES**—toes pointed straight ahead.

4. **BACK**—back should be upright and slightly **arched**.
5. **SHOULDERS**—shoulders should **rotate** vigorously with elbows fixed in a 90 degree angle.
6. **WRISTS**—wrists should simulate a **whip** action as the shoulders rotate back.
7. **FEET**—feet should make the initial **plant** directly under the hips and not out in front of the body.

8. **FORWARD LEG**—the initial leg action is to lift forward, not up. The lower leg should **hang** before planting with the foot and toes up as pictured.
9. **BACK KNEE**—on the follow through, or end-of-the-leg drive, the back knee should fully **extend** as pictured.

THE START

Let your competition start from a football stance when getting timed on a forty. I guarantee that no college scout or pro scout makes a note that times are from a track stance or a football stance. All they do is mark down your time so you might as well do it right.

Learn the modified BFS track stance. The above photos show Kevin Devine, the NFL's fastest player.

Hands: Thumb and first finger should be on the starting line. Weight should be supported by finger tips.

Feet: A rule of thumb is that one foot is back 4 to 6 inches from the line while the other foot is back an additional twelve inches.

Head: Keep it down. When it is up you will tighten up.

Phase I: Look at left photo. The back knee is down. Total body is relaxed. You are now "On your mark".

Phase II: Look at right photo. You are now "Getting Set". Raise your hips higher than shoulders. Shift weight as far forward as possible. The shoulders should be way out

in front of the hands. Even though this is uncomfortable, you have great forward momentum for a super start.

Phase III: "Go!" Kevin Devine, who is with the Jacksonville Jaguars, used the modified BFS track stance at the NFL combine and ran a 4.2 forty. Going into the 1998-99 season, Kevin is Pro Football's Fastest Player.

In the modified BFS track stance one arm comes way up on "set". On "go" this arm punches forward with great power and simultaneously the back leg will do the same. Kevin's left arm and right leg explode forward at the same time.

You will stay low. Extend back leg completely. Keep arms at right angle with extreme vigorous arm movement.

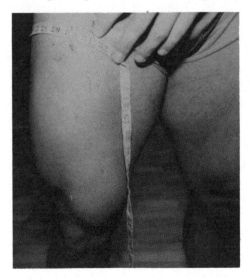

Stefan's massive 31-inch thighs. Super strength, super size, super flexibility, super form, equal a 4.25 forty at 270 pounds.

PLYOMETRIC TRAINING

The BFS Plyometric Program also takes ten minutes. Begin by taking ten quality vertical jumps. Do the vertical jumps by a wall or basketball standard. Mentally measure the first jump and then try to improve with each successive jump. A minimum of 15 seconds should be taken between vertical jumps. Vertical jumps should be tested once a month.

The second phase of our program is to do three sets of three successive standing long jumps. High School standards are as follows: Fair–22 feet, Good–25 feet, Great–28 feet. Both the Vertical Jump and the Standing Long Jump should be tested once a month.

Plyometric Box Jumping is the third phase. Assuming you have boxes, begin by doing five jumps from a 20-inch box and just land in a hit position. Next, jump in the same manner, but this time recoil straight up as quickly as possible. On the next series, jump from one box, to the floor to the next box and repeat 5 times. Now you are ready to get after it. Follow the same procedure; but now do it as rapidly as possible. You should have four to five boxes each about 21 inches high. As you become more advanced, you can raise the height of the last box. A good jump for the last box is 36 to 40 inches.

A fourth phase is to jump on a box from a stand. It will create interest and enthusiasm for plyometrics. You may wish to test a Standing Box Jump once a month.

The final phase can be a series of plyometric bounding drills. All these phases may sound like a lot to do in just ten minutes, but if you are organized, it's amazing the amount of work that can be done. Divide a class into two main groups: one group will work on speed, while the other will work on plyometrics. Divide the speed group in half with one group working technique and the other working sprints. The plyometric group can also be divided into two groups. Half of these athletes can be doing Bounding, Vertical Jumps and Standing Long Jumps. The other half then works on Box

Jumping. It can be a tremendously productive period which will pay great dividends.

Any remaining time left can be devoted to a fun activity, motivational period or learning-lecture period on any topic such as nutrition. The more wisely this time is used, the better you'll be.

GO FOR IT!

PHASE ONE

Vertical Jumps

Stefan has put his ear on the backboard from a stand

JUST JUMP OR RUN

This high-tech device accutately measures an athlete's Vertical Jump and any speed distance. It is quick, easy and versatile. Call 1-800-628-9737 for details.

**Stefan dunking a basketball from a stand.
Stefan is 6'–1 1/2", 270 pounds.**

Denver Bronco strength and conditioning coach, Al Miller, demonstrating the vertical jump test. Make a mark against the wall and measure. Then you chalk your finger tips and make a mark. Stefan jumped to 10-6 on this jump. He is on the way down.

PHASE TWO: Stefan has a Standing Long Jump of 11-3 and three successive at 32-6.

**Beginning Position for Vertical Jump
or Standing Long Jump.**

Notice how low Stefan gets. Notice his head and arm
position. It takes a lot of strength and flexibility to get into
this position.

PHASE THREE

Plyometric Box Jumping

The first part of the BFS Plyometric Box Jumping Program utilizes just one box. It is absolutely essential to step off the box. Never, never jump off a box unless you're doing a series of jumps and even then, you step off the first box. The athlete begins this first exercise by stepping off the box and landing in a hit or ready position as illustrated. Repeat this jump five times. Except in extreme cases, all your athletes should be able to easily complete this exercise.

The second exercise is to step off the box, land as before and then immediately and explosively jump straight up. Repeat this exercise five times. The third exercise utilizes two boxes. Place the second box 2 1/2 to 3 feet from the first. Now, step off the first, land and explosively jump on top of the second box. Again, repeat this exercise five times.

CLASS ORGANIZATION
To streamline a class, lay out your series of boxes. The athletes line up behind all 5 boxes. Everyone goes through the line for exercise one, etc.

My son, Matt as an 8th grader, jumping as rapidly as possible through a Box Jump Course. He was able to jump onto a 38-inch Box on the last jump. This completes the Plyometric Box Jumping Phase.

PHASE FOUR

Standing Box Jump

Box Jumping for height can be a great part of your plyometric program and total conditioning program. The concept is similar in going for a max in the weight room with the same benefits.

Box Jumping is great to do as it bridges the gap between strength and explosive power. It is great to Squat 500 pounds, but that alone does not insure explosive power. Box Jumping can help the muscular system contract more quickly and with greater force. The effect of Box Jumping is similar to the overload principle in weight training. As you gradually increase the resistance or the weight on the bar you will get stronger. Likewise, when you gradually increase the height of your plyometric boxes, you will increase your explosive power and jumping ability.

You can measure the increases and improvements in jumping ability in several ways. The most common way is to measure one's vertical jump. You can also measure an athlete's standing long jump, either for one jump or three successive jumps. Another way is to have an athlete jump up on a box. However, the benefits and the mental aspects are different than those of the vertical jump and standing long jump.

The average high school athlete with some training should be able to jump up on a 36-inch box with your elite athletes being able to jump up to 48 inches. My son in the 8th grade (5-7 1/2, 132 pounds) jumped to a 38-inch height. I couldn't stop him smiling.

I've seen a lot of great mental things take place as the height of the boxes have gradually been raised. A super big benefit is the self concept and confidence factor. You'll get statements like, "Wow! I never thought I could do that!" As far as I'm concerned, that makes Box Jumping worth the effort with that benefit alone.

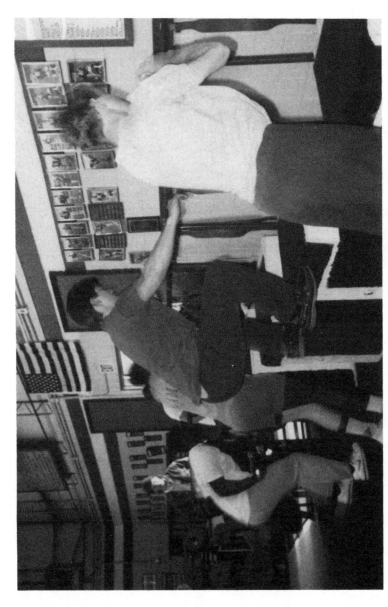

Athletes at Statesboro High School in Georgia doing Standing Box Jumps.

Jumpin' Jeroy Robinson LB, Texas A & M 6-2, 240 pounds.

Jeroy Robinson going 54 inches!

PHASE FIVE

Plyometric Bounding

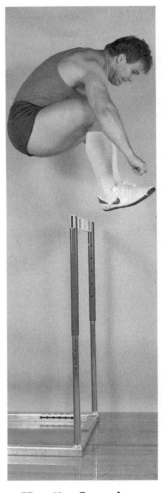

Hurdle Jumping   **Side Hops**

Bound for Speed, Height or Distance

Bounding For Height

Skip Bounding For Speed

PLYOMETRIC SUMMARY

As we become more sophisticated and scientific in our total training program, we learn that plyometrics can have great value. An athlete who works super hard in the weight room, neglecting all other forms of training, is not going to reach his potential. Plyometrics can add the icing on the cake in the speed, jumping and explosiveness department. For the lineman who is 6'4", 270 pounds and benches 450, squats 600, VJ's 24 and runs only 5.0, something is missing. Plyometrics can move the VJ to 30 and improve the 40 to a respectable 4.7. For the running back who runs 4.6 and has average lateral movement, plyometrics can make the difference between good and great.

Frank Costello, in his book "Bounding To The Top," states, "The athlete stores kinetic energy while descending and converts it to potential energy for the concentric contraction required to respond immediately. The myostatic or stretch reflex, makes this reaction possible." Stefan Fernholm states, "Plyometrics have played a major role in getting my 40 yard dash down to 4.25 and my vertical jump to 39 inches at a bodyweight of 270 pounds."

Simply put, plyometric training involves maximum explosive contractions as quickly as possible. Your feet spend as little contact time as possible with the ground or floor. When you jump up, do so with maximum effort. When you bound for height or distance, it's all out. YOU ARE GOING TO TEACH YOUR BODY HOW TO USE IT'S STRENGTH. YOU ARE GOING TO BECOME EXPLOSIVE!

BFS Clinician Jim Brown coaching Matt Shepard on the Power Clean. When this photo was taken, Matt had just graduated from the BFS Readiness Program after his seventh grade year.

MONDAY	WEDNESDAY	FRIDAY
Box Squat	Power Clean	Parallel Squat
Towel Bench	Straight Legs	Bench Press
Auxiliaries	Auxiliaries	Auxiliaries

XVII. The BFS Readiness Program

The Bigger Faster Stronger Readiness Program has been designed for those not yet ready to engage in heavy Power Weight Training utilized by more mature athletes. After a person goes through the BFS Readiness Program, he or she will then graduate to the BFS Regular Program of serious Power Weight Training using free weights. This chapter will provide the athlete with a program of where to start, how to do the exercises, how to progress, how to coordinate other athletic activities into a total program and, finally, how to graduate.

Who Can Use The BFS Readiness Program?

A. Junior High Boys and Girls: Athletes or general physical education students in the **7th Grade** may begin this program. We realize that some orthopedic surgeons may say this to too early to start any kind of weight training. They might say because the bones have not completely hardened, a problem might occur. However, after careful study, thought and observation of young athletes who do weight train, we feel the benefits far outweigh any possible risks.

First of all, we are in the business of helping athletes and people reach their potential; and without weight training this is virtually impossible. A recent study on 7th graders weight training has drawn preliminary conclusions that no interference of bone growth resulted from weight training. Dr. Mel Hayashi, a noted orthopedic surgeon from Thousand Oaks, California, states, "The BFS Readiness Program should provide great benefits to the junior high athlete. I have no concerns as long as the athlete has good technique."Dr. Hayashi has been a chief orthopedic surgeon at the past Olympic Games and has been a chief resident at the Mayo Clinic. Many strength coaches of major universities throughout the nation have been asked when an athlete should start weight training. The vast majority responded: "In Junior High." The Eastern Bloc countries start their athletes weight training at the age of 12. In addition, we know weight training is one of the greatest ways to build self-confidence and self-esteem. A seventh grader can receive just as much satisfaction going from 85 pounds to 100 pounds on his bench as can a 12th grader going from 285 to 300 pounds. However, we also believe strict supervision is a must along with the teaching of proper technique to make the BFS Readiness Program work in the Junior High.

B. High School Women Athletes: Some women go right into the weight room and lift right with the guys. They are not afraid or intimidated. Even though they use less weight, they match the men set for set and rep for rep. However, it has been our experience that a majority of high school age women would be better served in large groups by starting their weight training with the BFS Readiness Program.

C. High School Male Athletes: If an athlete cannot squat to parallel 145 pounds for 10 reps with good form, then we advise those male athletes to start with the BFS Readiness Program. In September this may mean as many as 50% of 9th graders, 10-20% of 10th graders and 5% of upper-classmen.

D. Rehabilitation: The severely injured athlete may find the BFS Readiness Program of great benefit as he rehabilitates.

E. Mothers and Fathers: Many parents would find the BFS Readiness Program a great way to get started on a free weight program with the added benefit of progressing on the same program with their son or daughter.

The Readiness Program in the Junior High

The BFS Readiness Program can produce spectacular results in any junior high school. It can be implemented in a physical education class in conjunction with other activities or as an entity unto itself. It can really be surprising just how fast seventh graders can learn and profit from this program.

Weight Training: Teach and stress the technique of the BFS Core Lifts with just the 45-pound bar. A two- or three-day-per-week cycle may be used. I actually prefer two workouts per week, especially in the beginning. It's very easy to get three core lifts done in a 40-minute physical education class. On the first day, do Box Squats, Towel Benches, and Power Cleans. On the second workout day, do Parallel Squats, Bench Presses, and Straight-Leg-Dead-Lifts. If you have enough time, do auxiliary exercises.

The unique concept of the BFS Readiness Program is the criteria for increasing poundage. Most programs allow poundage to be increased when the last set is done successfully. In our program, the athlete must be able to do not only the prescribed number of sets and reps successfully, but he must also do each set and rep with perfect technique. In our BFS Readiness Program Instruction Manual, easy-to-follow guidelines on how to judge perfect technique are presented. When the technique of the correct number of sets and reps has been judged to be perfect, then the athlete may increase the poundage by five pounds for the workout the following week. This system is really amazing for producing great technique in young kids.

Graduation from the BFS Readiness Program occurs when the athlete can Parallel Squat 145 pounds for two sets of 10 reps, Bench Press 105 pounds (or 90 percent of body weight, whichever is less) for two sets of 10 reps. If you really get after it, about one out of five boys will graduate by the end of the seventh grade year. After graduation, the athlete would then use the Standard BFS Program. If the emphasis continues throughout the junior high years, many athletes will be able to Bench 200, Parallel Squat 300, and Power Clean 175 before they enter high school.

Flexibility: I coached my son's eighth grade football team. The whole team did the 9 1/2-minute BFS 1-2-3-4 Flexibility Program. The parents knew I expected them to do their flexibility exercises on a daily basis. Most of the kids did it on their own every day at home. All I had to do was teach it and check on them once in a while. If kids are given a chance to be upper-limit, it's amazing the high number that will respond.

Agility: Again, my team did the BFS Dot Drill every day on their own. My son did it in 47 seconds, and most of my 31 players did it in under 60 seconds. If you haven't seen the BFS Dot Drill, I can tell you—to see a 13-year-old whip through the BFS Dot Drill in 50 seconds is really impressive.

Speed and Plyometrics: You can teach kids at any age how to run correctly. You want an edge? Teach seventh graders how to run: Less than 1 percent of our nation's seventh graders have had this seemingly basic opportunity.

Teach kids how to jump. My son helped me with a clinic in Georgia. He demonstrated Plyometrics and the high school Senior basketball players were amazed when Matt jumped from a 20-inch box to another 20-inch box, then to another, and then finally popped up on a 38-inch desk. I was even surprised.

Matt said, "Dad, that's nothing."

The Seniors were reluctant to try until a 13-year-old showed them how.

ANSWERS TO QUESTIONS

Question No. 1: When Can We Start The BFS Flexibility Program?

I taught my 3rd grade daughter our flexibility program. She had it mastered in 15 minutes and began teaching the neighborhood kids. There is absolutely no reason why the

BFS flexibility program can't be taught to all athletes in junior high. If I were the head football coach at a high school, I would have all the little league teams do the flexibility program, even if it went down into the 4th grade level. Wouldn't it be nice to have every athlete come into high school with great flexibility with a 10 minute daily flexibility habit already formed? This means injury prevention and this means speed! In our country, no one does flexibility training properly at early ages. Any coach that can influence the right people to install the BFS flexibility program at the junior high and grade school levels will most certainly have an edge, besides providing a great service.

Question No. 2: When Can We Start Plyometrics?
    We generally do not teach athletes at any level in this country just how to jump. All we do when we test an athlete on a vertical jump is say, "Jump as high as you can!" Coaches, there are definite techniques to be mastered to reach a maximum. We can and should teach grade school and junior high athletes the techniques of the vertical and standing long jumps.
    As for plyometric drills, I can see no reason why basic plyometric drills cannot be incorporated in the total junior high conditioning program. Two 10 minute sessions per week on plyometrics can pay big dividends by the time these athletes come into the high school program.

Question No. 3: When Can We Start Teaching the BFS Sprint Technique System?
    I don't believe you can start too soon! The longer an athlete is allowed to run incorrectly, the harder it will be to unlearn bad habits and to learn correct technique.
    As I worked with NBA hopefuls at try-out camp for the Utah Jazz and players for the Sacramento Kings, I asked them about their previous work with flexibility, plyometrics and sprint training. It was zilch. Zero! NBA players are usually quite poor in flexibility. LaSalle Thompson of the

Kings was an exception. I asked them if they'd like to have more flexibility and be taught how to run. Of course, they all agreed. I also asked them if they would have liked to have been taught these techniques when they were in the 7th grade. Of course, they all agreed.

Question No. 4: How is the Readiness Program different than the high school program?

There is really very little difference. The 7th grader can do the same flexibility program, the same agilities, the same beginning plyometrics and exactly the same sprint technique system. The only real difference is in the lifting program; although, the same core lifts are done and with the same concept in the selection of auxiliary exercises.

Question No. 5: What can be expected?

If the BFS Readiness Program is utilized by upper-limit coaches, then great things will be accomplished. I can promise that a high school with an enrollment of 1,000 can expect 25 athletes will come from the junior high each year with these abilities: a minimum 300 pound parallel squat with great form, a minimum 200 pound bench and a minimum 175 pound clean with great form. They will also possess great flexibility, plyometric abilities and correct running form. With these abilities come great side benefits, such as, self confidence, great work habits and a winning attitude. The one thing that does amaze me is the great number of schools who will again this year do nothing. We have the technology available. Let's use it! Get the edge!

The BFS Readiness Weight Training Program

A. How To Start

Start with just the 45 pound Olympic Bar on EACH CORE LIFT!

Do not worry if this amount of weight is very light and does not seem challenging.

We are always going to test for two things. First, can you do the two sets of ten or five reps and second, can you do each rep and each set with great technique. Therefore, we really want you to work on PERFECT TECHNIQUE, especially at first.

If 45 pounds is too heavy (which might be the case on the Hang Clean or the Bench Press) start with less. Do not feel bad if you have to start with less. I don't care where you START, only where you FINISH!

B. How To Progress

Two things must happen to progress. You must be able to complete your two sets of ten or five reps and be able to do each rep of each set with PERFECT TECHNIQUE. When these two things happen, then you may go up 5 pounds the next week you do the same lift. Now record the date of your successful workout.

All serious weight trained athletes keep records. You should do the same. You will have pride and satisfaction as you work up in poundage towards graduation.

If you cannot do the two sets of ten or five reps or do them with perfect technique, you must then keep repeating the same weight until you can.

We have a BFS Readiness Program Record Book or Record Card. Every athlete should have the book or the card. Books are $2.25 each. Cards are only fifty cents. (Must order at least 25). Write or call to order.

C. How to Judge Technique

A coach, parent or training partner should judge your technique. If you train alone, then obviously you will have to judge yourself. I want to encourage you to train with someone; if at all possible. There are three reasons why: it is more motivating, you'll have a spotter and, third, you'll have a judge.

I will now go through each lift and give three judging rules on each lift. If the lifter breaks any one of the three rules during any set, he may not progress next week.

The Bench and the Towel Bench: 2 Sets of 10 Reps

1. Touch Your Chest! If the bar doesn't touch your chest, or the towel, it doesn't count.

2. Uneven Extension! A little bit is OK. However, we do not want one arm going up way before the other arm. Also, look for uneven elbows at the bottom position. Sometimes one elbow will be by the chest, while the other is way out. Don't count it! Force the athlete to do it right.

3. No Arching! If you get in a wide stance, with feet underneath and shoulders forced towards the hips, it is hard to arch (lifting hips up from bench). We feel, especially for the young lifter, this is an important rule to follow as it will give an athlete better chest development.

The Box Squat: 2 Sets of 10 Reps

1. The Lower Back! It must be "locked in". It must not be out.

2. Sit and Pause! You must actually sit on the box and rock back slightly before you drive forward and up. If you just touch and come up, the technique doesn't count.

3. Drive up on Toes! At the finish of the lift, you must come up on your toes as you would during a jump.

The Squat: 2 Sets of 10 Reps

1. The Lower Back! Same as Box Squat.

2. Proper Depth! You must go down until the top of the thigh is at least parallel with the floor. For many beginning lifters, this will be very difficult. If problems do arise, always go back to the low power position.

3. Stance, Knees and Toes! Your stance should look like an athlete's stance. Not narrow or real wide. Watch the toes, a 45° angle is too much. Also, watch the knees. If they come way in on the way up, do not count the lift.

The Power Clean: 2 Sets of 5 Reps.
    1. The Lower Back! In the starting position the lower back should be "locked in".
    2. Start slow, then jump with the bar close to the body. Elbows high with chin away from chest.
    3. Rack the bar to deltoids properly and be in an athletic position.

The Straight Leg Dead Lift: 2 Sets of 10 Reps
    1. No technique requirement, but always go slow and controlled.
    2. Maximum poundage should be 55 pounds.

D. Organization

    a. Time: The BFS Readiness Program takes only 45 minutes Three Times Per Week.

    b. Athletes Per Bar: A maximum of 5 athletes per bar. This allows for a lifter with 3 spotters and one athlete getting ready. Rotate in order.

    c. Physical Education Class: A class could be divided into three groups in the following manner:

Group I
Core Lifts

Group II
Auxiliary Lift

Group III
Agility–Running–Skill

    Each group then rotates every 15 minutes for a total class time of 45 minutes.

d. Equipment Needed: (15 athletes)

Olympic Bench Press: Approx. cost	**$ 199.00**
Squat Rack:	**349.00**
Squat Box:	**49.00**
Three Economy 300 LB. Sets	**477.00**
BFS Training Plates:	**59.00**
	$ 1,133.00

*Cost goes up about $150.00 for each additional five athletes. The above equipment suggestions are for heavy duty equipment meant for years of constant use. Equipment for home use would be less expensive. You may call our Toll Free number 1-800-628-9737 for additional help. SEE APPENDIX A FOR NEW READINESS EQUIPMENT IDEAS.

E. Graduation!

Graduation is based on your performance—not age. This is as it should be. Some people mature faster than others and some learn technique faster. Graduation requirements somewhat favor the bigger and heavier athlete. You will see below a male athlete must do 2 sets of 10 reps with 145 pounds on the squat. Since everyone starts with 45 pounds and goes up at a maximum rate of 5 pounds a week, it will take a minimum of 20 weeks to graduate.

We justify this philosophy, as graduation means the athlete is now ready to begin the regular BFS program. This regular BFS program requires a much more strenuous mature frame. The total BFS program will allow everyone to reach their potential soon enough. Graduation requirements are based on three lifts: the squat, bench and hang clean. An athlete must pass all three lifts to graduate. The box squat, towel bench and straight leg dead lifts are not tested for graduation requirements. However, they are just as important as the others.

GRADUATION REQUIREMENTS

Event	Male	Female
SQUAT	145 lbs.	105 lbs.
2 sets of 10 reps		
BENCH	105 or	95 or
2 sets of 10 reps	90% of body weight	90% of body weight
POWER CLEAN	105 or	95 or
2 sets of 5 reps	90% of body weight	90% of body weight

F. Awards

We feel some kind of award for graduation is very appropriate. It will make graduation special and develop pride of accomplishment.

Awards can be like our BFS Certificate of Achievement or awards like ribbons, medals, shirts or simply the athlete's name on a chart. Give an award for each event passed.

Matt Shepard graduated at the end of his seventh grade year and won the National Olympic Weight Lifting title in the 123-lb. class (for 12-13 year olds), while also being a three-sport athlete.

Start with just the bar on all Core Lifts, even the Box Squat. Do 2 sets of 10 reps.

Poor Technique has no place in the BFS Readiness Program.

**The Towel Bench and the Regular Bench are Core
Lifts.   Do 2 Sets of 10 Reps.**

**POWER CLEAN: Do 2 Sets of 5 Reps.
USE BFS TRAINING PLATES.**

Start with the bar. Be Consistent and. . .

soon you'll graduate!

XVIII. Nutrition

I believe you must eat well to perform well. By performing well, I mean performing your best. I have come to realize that the majority of high school athletes really don't eat very well. Some of the reasons could be more working mothers, more broken homes, more eating at fast-food places, more quick grocery stores, and more effective advertising to eat poorly. More and more athletes (kids) have to fix meals by themselves. And often they are given money to eat out on their own instead of a well prepared, healthy meal. It's common for fast food chains to give special deals on a "hamburger, fries, and soft drink." meal. Convenience stores entice kids with video games and the junkiest of junk food. Therefore, more emphasis on eating right needs to take place.

The BFS Nutrition Plan has been in effect for many years with great results. We rate our meals on a scale of 0-10. The system is simple for kids to understand. Breakfast, lunch, dinner, and snacks are each rated. A maximum of 40 points can be earned daily.

Any good food from one of the basic food groups is given two points: Dairy products like milk, cheese, and eggs, meat products such as beef, poultry, and fish, bread and cereal group items and fruits and vegetables are each given 2 points. A huge amount of any one item is given a bonus point (5 eggs receive 3 points).

French fries receive zero points. The maximum points for any one meal or snacks is 10. A salad or sandwich which has everything gets a maximum of 5 points. Water with a meal is 2 points. Pop, candy, donuts, pastries, coffee, tea, or alcoholic beverages get 0.

Below are some examples:

	JOHN	pts.	MARY	pts.	BILL	pts.
Breakfast	2 eggs juice 2 milks bacon toast	10	grapefruit toast poached egg skim milk	8	none	0
Lunch	2 big sandwiches 3 milks apple cookies	10	yogurt water celery apple	8	coke fries	0
Dinner	roast beef peas salad milk orange	10	salad skim milk orange	9	pizza coke	3
Snacks	milk bananas ice cream	6	apple water carrots	6	cookies coke	0
TOTAL	POINTS	36	POINTS	31	POINTS	3

The BFS Nutritional Rating Chart is as follows:

30-40 points: Great
25-29 points: Good
20-24 points: Fair

15-19 points: Poor
10-14 points: Very Poor
5-9 points: Drastic
0-4 points: Death

I feel that if an athlete won't get at least 25 points per day, he probably should have a food supplement and take a multiple vitamin. Seventeen points is the national average. John and Mary should have a nutritionally sound diet. It should also be noted that Mary's diet is non-fattening, even though she earned 30 points. Bill actually raised his hand during a clinic and said he wanted to get Bigger Faster and Stronger. Yet he didn't realize how bad his diet was until it was closely examined. Bill said he didn't have time to fix breakfast, the school lunch was no good, and Mom left a pizza in the freezer and cookies for a snack. If Bill would fix himself cereal, milk, toast, and juice for breakfast, eat the school lunch, drink milk for dinner with some fruit, and have milk, juice, and a banana for snacks in addition to what he ate, it would up his point total to the 30-point level. The beauty of this system is that Bill doesn't have to do any cooking. He just has to follow the plan and add up his points.

The second part of the BFS nutrition plan is the motivation of setting and meeting goals. At a BFS clinic, the first goal we set on our way to becoming champions is to obtain 30 nutritional points daily. This means that each individual is dedicated and totally committed to getting 30 points every day. Coaches put on their goal card: "30 (5)". This means that each coach on the staff will be committed to asking five different kids daily how they're doing on their 30 points. In 30 days the players should have formed great eating habits; which should be paying big dividends not only physically but academically as well.

Gaining weight: there are two basic ways to gain weight. Both ways are contingent upon consuming more calories than are expended. Many athletes expend 5,000 or more calories daily. Therefore, a huge amount must be eaten in order to gain weight.

The first way to gain weight is to eat a big 30 points, never miss a workout, especially squats, and have a big snack after dinner. The snack should be something like two big meat and cheese sandwiches with two glasses of milk with each sandwich.

The second way is to take a weight gain protein supplement. It should be the BFS Super Weight Gain supplement or an equivalent. Ours has 18 vitamins and minerals along with all the essential Amino Acids. In fact, it has 18 free amino acids, including L-Carnitine.

All food supplements should be mixed in a blender. Bananas, fruit, ice cream, etc., may and should be added for extra flavor and calories. It is important to weigh every day and record this on a daily basis. If weight isn't gained after two or three days, then more calories must be consumed. As long as the total BFS program is followed, the weight gains will be desirable.

CREATINE

The body actually produces it's own store of Creatine. The amino acids Arginine and Glycine are synthesized into Creatine by the liver and kidneys. 95% of the Creatine produced is transported to muscle cells, where it is used in manufacturing the energy-producing molecule Adenosine Triphosphate (ATP). The levels of Creatine available to muscle fiber determines the amount of ATP produced. When Creatine stores in the body are depleted from physical exertion, the level of ATP diminishes causing muscle fatigue and increased levels of lactic acid.

By supplementing the diet with Creatine Monohydrate, the body's store of Creatine is increased along with the production of ATP. Ingested Creatine Monohydrate enters the bloodstream making its way to the cells of muscle tissue. Sufficient intake literally "saturates" the muscles with Creatine providing increased strength and faster recovery time from intense physical training.

The benefits of taking Creatine Monohydrate can be seen quickly, often within a few days. Athletes can expect a marked improvement in power and endurance from the addition of the amazing compound. For example, an athlete involved in weight training may find the number of repetitions at a given weight increase in number. In addition, Creatine Monohydrate can help increase muscle size. The cells of muscle tissue are made of approximately 70% water. When the muscle cells absorb Creatine, they also take in water. This process, called "Cell Volumnizing" or "Cellular Hydration", allows the muscle to increase in mass. During cell volumnizing the water is stored in the muscle cell and is not to be confused with water retention where water is stored outside the cells. Scientific research supports the theory that as cell volumnizing is increased, the rate of protein metabolism is also increased leading to faster muscular development.

SUMMARY

Every athlete should have 30 Nutritional Points on a daily basis. Do not spend a lot of money on Nutritional Food Supplements. The only extras that should be given consideration are Weight Gain Food Supplements and Creatine.

Remember, the real key is intensity, consistency and a great natural diet.

THE REAL TRUTH ABOUT FAT

We are eating much less fat than 20 years ago but obesity has jumped 30% in the last decade. Type II diabetes has tripled in this same time period. Strokes and coronary heart disease are also rising. Fat is not the problem but most people think it is. We have replaced fat with carbohydrates which is really starch and sugar. We as a nation, have adopted the USDA food pyramid which means a high carbohydrate, low-fat diet. However, it should seem obvious, this high complex carbohydrate, low-fat diet plan has failed.

Food is composed of three macro nutrients: carbohydrates, protein and fat. Meats are mostly protein and fat while plants are mostly carbohydrates. It is very difficult to cut out one macro nutrient. The reasonable position in the past has been to eat less meat, eggs and dairy products and replace those with grains, fruits, vegetables and fat-free snacks. Americans have cut back on protein in order to eliminate fats.

The bad news is that eating more carbohydrates stimulates your body to <u>store more fat</u>, so many people get more fat. Carbohydrates can stimulate profound metabolic hormonal changes. Surprisingly, dietary fat doesn't do much to make you fat.

Eating carbohydrates, even those non-fat foods with carbohydrates, causes a rapid increase in the hormone called <u>insulin</u> and decrease in its opposing hormone called <u>glucagon</u>. Even complex carbohydrates stimulate this same kind of a response.

All carbohydrates are basically sugar. Starches are made up of sugar molecules. All carbohydrates are converted sugar. If you were on a 2,200 calorie per day diet and followed the USDA food pyramid of 60% carbohydrates, your body would have to contend metabolically with two cups of sugar per day. Low fat/high carbohydrate people who do lose weight will also lose muscle. The high protein/lower carbohydrate people will lose weight more easily and quickly usually with no or little loss of muscle.

Insulin is released by your pancreas. Elevated insulin levels can cause monster health problems. The main job of insulin is to regulate blood sugar levels and it should be considered the master hormone for all metabolism. It influences every cell in the body. When excess insulin is produced, it creates havoc on the body which can cause all kinds of medical disorders.

People think that cholesterol is all bad but if we don't get enough cholesterol, our body will make it because its critically important to human health. Normally, 20% of your body's cholesterol comes from diet while the other 80% is produced by your own body, mostly by your liver. Insulin disrupts production of healthy cholesterol.

Therefore, diet can only control 20% of your cholesterol but if you regulate your insulin, you can control the 80% produced by your body.

People respond to elevated insulin levels differently. Some people deal with it effectively and experience no adverse effects. However, 75% of our nation's adult population cannot deal effectively with elevated insulin levels. More teenagers than ever before are also having difficulties. This state or condition is known as Hyperinsulinemia which can be described as an excessive level of insulin in the blood.

To deal with the effects of Hyperinsulinemia which could be high blood pressure, high cholesterol and/or high triglycerides, many doctors prescribe drugs which affect the ability of the liver to produce cholesterol. However, many times this creates other health problems. The good news is that the BFS Nutrition Plan can control the body's insulin production without the use of drugs.

Genetics play a big factor in the way insulin can adversely affect your system. One individual could have diabetes, another heart problems, sleep apnea or even gout. About 74% of Americans are over-fat so it looks like there is a connection with the 75% of adults who have Hyperinsulinemia to one degree or another.

When we eat too much carbohydrates our insulin level goes up and it drives sugar and fat into the fat cells to be stored. Insulin's job is to also prevent the stored fat from leaving the fat cell.

Fat cells are little balloon-like cell structures whose job is to store calories in the form of fat. These little cells can get smaller or bigger but if more goes in than comes out, you will have fat problems. Obesity is simply the accumulation of too much excess body fat. Obesity causes the fat cells to store more fat.

Glucagon is also made in the pancreas. It is the counter-regulatory hormone. Glucagon works the opposite of insulin in virtually every way.

Glucagon retrieves fat out of the fat cells for energy and at the same time it blocks entry of fat into the fat cells. Normally there is a balance between the rising and falling of insulin and glucagon. However, if you have elevated insulin levels you will be continually storing fat because glucagon cannot do its job. Therefore, people with Hyperinsulinemia continually store and accumulate fat. The right food can keep insulin from rising and thus allow glucagon to do its job.

IMPLICATIONS
FOR THE COACH

The implications of this nutrition plan are enormous for any coach at any level. You, in a very real sense, can now become a nutritional guru of sorts. You can wisely counsel your athletes, students and community. You can help yourself if your are one of the 75% who have Hyperinsulinemia. You can have safe levels of triglycerides, blood sugar, cholesterol and blood pressure. You can lose fat and inches while maintaining or increasing your lean muscle tissue. And, you can now do this on a diet you can not only live with but enjoy.

You will have to do a paradigm shift in thinking. For example, you may have said things, like I have, "It's not the potato, it is all the butter and sour cream." That statement is incorrect. Actually it is the potato that is bad not the butter.

In addition, I believe a high-protein, low-carbohydrate

diet will not adversely affect your kidneys as long as you start out with normal kidney function.

THE NITTY GRITTY

You will have to be very smart and on guard all the time to be successful on this nutrition plan. Think of proteins and fats as time bombs that can blast away fat, triglycerides and cholesterol problems. But, supreme caution, red-alert! Carbohydrates can trigger these same time bombs to make you fat and create some serious health problems.

Here is what I mean; lets say you eat three eggs and some ham for breakfast, the protein-fat time bombs will work for you. However, if you add orange juice and toast (carbohydrates), these same time bombs will blow up in your face. Listen carefully, if you add carbohydrates to some fat intake, insulin will take that fat right to the fat cells and keep it there. If you don't add the carbohydrates, glucagon will ignore the fat you've just eaten and go get your stored fat.

The Fat You Eat Will Only Turn Lethal If You Add Carbohydrates

Lets examine a typical dinner: a meat of some kind, and a tossed green salad. No problem, but, if you add a potato or fries, you are in trouble. The high carbohydrate content of the potato creates a release of insulin which sets off the fat time bomb which was in the meat. Leave the potato alone! If you say, "well, I used only low-fat margarine on my potato," you just flunked. Begin reading this section again from the beginning. Instead of the potato, I like to have low-fat cottage cheese, olives and even some hard cheese.

Let us now take a fast food favorite: double cheeseburger, fries and a coke and super size it. The fries, coke and bun make the fat in the meat and cheese race to your fat cells. Drink water not coke or sodas. Have another double cheeseburger instead of the fries. Finally, throw away at least half the buns. Eat. Enjoy. Let glucagon go suck out the fat in your fat cells.

IMPLICATIONS FOR THE ATHLETE

Let's face it. If you have a tendency to be over-fat as a teenager, it won't get any easier as you get older. Believe me, it gets tougher. Now is the time to change your habits. Now is the time to eat correctly. You, not your parents, will be mostly responsible for the success of this change.

A lean, muscular athlete will perform better than an over-fat athlete if all other conditions are equal. You will run faster, jump higher and have more agility if you are not over-fat. The beauty of this nutrition plan (never call it a diet) is that you can gain significant strength while you are losing fat. Diets where you count calories and are eating mostly carbohydrates will usually make you weaker as you lose weight. This happens because you will also lose lean muscle tissue which is bad for an athlete.

Wrestlers should benefit enormously from this plan. Too many wrestlers starve themselves on a low calorie/high carbohydrate diet. This is incredibly bad. This plan should keep you healthy and strong throughout the season while losing unwanted fat. Just think about it. Your competition probably will continue to do stupid dietary things. This will give you a chance to beat an older, more talented and/or more experienced opponent.

A STEP-BY-STEP PLAN

I thought it might be helpful to give a step-by-step graduated plan. Some of you may wish to jump right in like I did and do everything. Others may wish to try Step One and see how that goes and then move to Step Two, etc.

STEP ONE: Drink water for every meal and during the day. You should drink 64 ounces. You may wish to drink something else but it should have no carbohydrates. Soda Pop should be completely out, although a limited number of diet sodas are permissible.

Rick Huegli, the University of Washington Strength Coach says, "We could and should do more about nutrition but one thing I have done is to require every football player to bring a bottle of water with them to workout. Water is the best and easiest change an athlete can make in his nutrition."

STEP TWO: If you eat anything after 7:00 p.m., eat low-carbohydrate food. You might try beef jerky. It is important to let glucagon do its thing for as long as possible.

STEP THREE: Replace potatoes and corn with cottage cheese, cheese and/or an extra salad. One potato has 33 grams of carbohydrates and only 4 grams of protein while one serving of low fat-cottage cheese has 13 grams of protein and only 6 grams of carbohydrates. This difference is significant in lowering insulin and raising your glucagon level.

STEP FOUR: Eat breakfasts with a minimum of 40 grams of protein and a maximum of 10 grams of carbohydrates with water to drink. For example, you might eat three eggs (carbs 3, fats 15, proteins 21) two slices of ham (carbs 0, fats 4, protein 18) and one serving of cottage cheese (carbs 6, fats 2, protein 13). This would give you a total of 9 grams of carbs, 21 grams of fat and 52 grams of protein.

Contrast this with one bowl of shredded wheat, one cup of non-fat milk and one glass of orange juice. This breakfast has a total of 82 grams of carbs, 1 gram of fat and 15 grams of protein.

Ninety-nine point nine percent of the population would think the shredded wheat breakfast would be vastly superior in losing fat and lowering cholesterol. However, because the insulin level is raised, that 1 gram of fat in the shredded wheat breakfast will be taken to the fat cells and kept there. Then, during lunch, you'll add some more.

Even though there is 21 grams of fat in the ham and eggs breakfast, the glucagon will keep this fat from entering the fat cells and even take fat out while you are waiting for lunch.

STEP FIVE: Start the Phase One Power Protein Nutrition Program. Have a minimum of 100 grams of protein per day (A little less if you weigh less than 150 pounds or if you are a woman). Eat a maximum of 40 grams of carbohydrates.

It is recommended you also take a good daily vitamin supplement and (4) 99 mg tablets of potassium each day to help deal with any fluid loss. It is recommended that if you are taking any prescription medications (especially for high blood pressure) you must consult your physician or pharmacist before you begin taking potassium supplements.

STEP SIX: Start the Phase Two program after about one month. At this point, you can increase your carbohydrates to 100 grams per day.

REMEMBER: You never count calories! Only grams of carbohydrates and protein.

FIVE LETHAL FOODS
1. Coke or Sodas
2. French Fries
3. Potato Chips
4. Donuts
5. Candy

Information for this "Truth About Fat" section was drawn from the books listed below and Dr. Greg Shepard's own experience.

BOOKS TO READ

1. Dr. Atkins' New Diet Revolution
   Robert C. Atkins, M.D.
   1992 -1995 Published by M. Evans & Company

2. The Carbohydrate Addict's Diet
   Rachael F. Heller, M.A., M.Ph., Ph.D.
   Richard F. Heller, M.S., Ph.D.
   1991 Published by Dutton

3. Protein Power
   Michael R. Eades, M.D.
   Mary Dan Eades, M.D.
   1996 Published by Bantam Books

4. The Zone
   Barry Sears, Ph.D.
   1995 Published by Harper Collins

XIX. Anabolic Steroids

I am unalterably opposed to anabolic steroid use by any athlete, bodybuilder or competitive lifter. Anabolic steroids should be banned because they are downright dangerous. In fact, there are about 70 health reasons not to take steroids. These reasons should be enough to scare any clear-thinking individual to death. Severe heart and liver problems are a real possibility. Sexual dysfunction in both males and females is prevalent. Acne, which can lead to facial scarring, seems minor when compared to life-threatening steroid complications. "Roid rages" are a not-so-cute way of describing mood changes which have led to violence and even murder.

Anabolic steroids should be banned primarily because they present a very real danger to one's health; and secondarily, because of the so-called illegal advantage steroids are supposed to give in competition.

I believe that calling steroids "performance enhancing" is, for many athletes and sports, incorrect. Steroids are even debilitating to performance. However, everyone from athletes, to doctors, to the general public has automatically assumed that steroids create a tremendous advantage. That's the Great Steroid Myth.

I have written about this subject in several publications. I have since come up with 13 facts or statements which support my claim.

Steroids are not performance enhancing. Taking steroids decreases your chances of winning while creating enormous potential health problems at the same time.

Let us now examine these 13 facts and statements.

I. Bodybuilders, Powerlifters and Athletes From Main Stream Sports are Not the Same

Bodybuilders don't run, jump or score goals. Powerlifters are interested in only three things: the Bench, Squat, and Dead Lift. Training programs for athletes, bodybuilders and powerlifters are as different as night and day. Steroids are purchased illegally many times through older bodybuilders. Why would any athlete take advice from someone who stands and flexes?

II. Steroids = Roller Coaster Ride

Most people, at first, get a great high and a great rush of quick strength, because of the increased testosterone intake. However, it sends a message to the brain which tells the body to stop producing it's own testosterone. Therefore, when you stop taking steroids, you crash down hard. It's not unlike other kinds of drugs. So you're way up on your bench one day and way down the next. When you're down on strength, you become depressed. This is right out of the text book.

III. Steroids Build up Tolerances — 20 Milligrams can Escalate to 500 Milligrams

Many people get crazy and escalate their dosage. They mix different kinds of steroids and inject themselves. Again, this is not unlike addictions of other kinds.

IV. Super Great Gains Can be Made with Intelligence, Intensity and Persistence

Many people don't even train when they are on the juice.

V. Uncontrolled Aggressiveness is BAD!
Many people on steroids enjoy physical confrontations. But, you say, isn't that good for football? Well, yes, but only up to a point. You must have a controlled psyche. When you're out of control, you make mistakes or you can get thrown out of the game. This obviously contributes to losing, not winning. Hey, if I've spent hundreds of hours training with natural intensity, and then someone tries to take my position from me or to take my win from me, they're going to be in for one heck of a fight. I don't need steroids for aggressiveness. I paid my dues.

VI. Intensity can be Made Awesome by Teammates and Coaches.

VII. Fast Workout Recovery can be Made by Intelligent Variation and Selection of Exercises.

VIII. The Stress of Getting Caught
Most people sneak and hide their steroid abuse, go miles away from home to get their steroids and needles. They certainly don't want their parents to know. Upper Limit athletes don't sneak or hide. Sneaking around is just a bad precedent to set for yourself.

IX. Steroids Don't Help Agility, Flexibility or Technique, etc.
Training to reach your potential as an athlete is very complex. Steroid users many times place too much importance on size and strength and forget about many other areas that are necessary in winning.

X. Steroids are a Crutch Theory
If an athlete looks to steroids to help him get through a

crucial situation, he becomes a loser. If it's 4th and one and he doesn't look inside for something extra, but has the feeling of "where's my pill", then obviously the <u>user becomes a loser.</u>

XI. Strength and the Diminishing Return Theory
The stronger an athlete becomes, the less important extra strength becomes. It is ridiculous to assume that a lineman who benches 450 is superior to a lineman who only benches 415 pounds. Analyze your weaknesses. If you are slow, decrease your time in the weight room and increase your time on plyometrics, flexibility and speed techniques.

XII. The Best Don't Do It!
The vast majority of athletes are not on steroids. It is a myth that an athlete has to take steroids to compete.

XIII. Tendon and Ligament Injuries
There are studies which indicate that steroid users suffer from a greater incidence of tendon and ligament injuries than do non-steroid athlete.

SHOULD WE TEST FOR STEROIDS IN HIGH SCHOOL?

Argument For

We have to do something. We can't stand idly by and watch our youth destroy their lives. For heaven's sake, kids are dying, committing crime and creating enormous health risks for themselves. Steroid use among high school students is increasing rapidly. It is time to take a stand.

Athletes who are caught with steroids in their system should be suspended for at least one sport season. Athletes need to learn that taking steroids will not be tolerated. We don't need to test everybody, just random testing of a few. This would keep the costs down and yet send a powerful message that needs to be sent. We don't want to extensively punish the high school abuser, but we do need to put a stop to it by a mandatory educational process during rehabilitation and counseling. Those that complain about a few dollars should ask themselves, "what's a kid's life worth?" Think about it!

Argument Against

We should do something, but testing high school students is not the answer. It opens up a mass of legal entanglements. Testing minors at random or testing minors because we think they may be on steroids is risky business from a legal standpoint. Much of the steroid abuse comes from non-athletes. What are we going to do, random test the whole high school?

Testing is costly, even random testing to a few once a year is costly. As the BFS survey indicates, some schools are at high risk and some are at low risk. The money spent on testing could be spent better elsewhere especially at low risk schools. Let's spend money, if in fact we do have extra money, on positive steps rather than the negative solution of testing. Education, better facilities, increased curriculum and responsible supervision in weight training are what we need; certainly not testing!

BFS NATIONWIDE SURVEY

Twenty-three hundred athletes who attended BFS clinics from coast-to-coast participated in this suvey on steroids. These athletes, the majority of which were football players, were divided into the following groups: Seniors, Juniors, Sophomores, Freshmen, 8th grade and younger, and women. They were asked the following three questions: First, have you ever seen anyone inject themselves with steroids; Second, have you ever seen anyone swallow a steroid pill; Third, do you know for sure, absolutely, for sure, any high school athlete who is presently taking steroids.

The three questions were carefully formulated as to be non-threatening in order to get honest responses. We did not want to ask an athlete directly if he was on steroids or not. We do believe that athletes are usually exposed to steroids first by watching someone take them. Normally, an athlete does not walk into a gym and get injected on the first day. We wanted to find out what the exposure level was for steroids among high school athletes. Some results were expected, while other results may break new ground.

First as expected, the older the athlete—the more likely his exposure. About 10 percent of high school junior male athletes had seen someone inject or swallow a steroid compared to about 4 percent of the freshman male athletes. Second, high school women athletes had virtually no exposure to steroids. Apparently, male athletes don't want girls to see them swallow or inject themselves with steroids. Third, exposure to seeing others inject themselves or swallow a steroid pill was nearly the same. This was not expected, since swallowing a pill is easier than injecting a steroid.

As the results of our suvey began to come in, a pattern emerged which should be carefully considered. First, a large high school in Phoenix startled us by having 17 of 34 junior football players who had actually seen someone inject themselves with steroids. Upon further evaluation, it was discovered that most of the lifting by the athletes was not done at school, but at a local nearby muscle-gym. Phoenix has been a hotbed of powerlifting for two decades and many older lifters are really into heavy training. These high school athletes were witnessing steroid injections at this gym. It was extremely rare to have steroids taken at school. Steroids are taken at home or in a muscle-gym. Second, a medium size high school in a smaller North Carolina town had 46 out of 46 juniors who had never seen anyone inject themselves with steroids. There was no muscle-gym in the town and the high school had a fine weight training facility. The football coach ran the program and the athletes lifted weights during regular school hours.

As we analyzed the school situation compared with the answers to our three questions, we developed a system of dividing high schools into groups. some high schools are at extremely high risk for steroid abuse, while other have virtually no risk. The chart rating schools illustrates these two extremes. Obviously, you may interpolate between them.

If you are a big city high school with a Muscle-Gym nearby, you'd better have a great weight room supervised by active, motivated coaches during class time. If you don't, you are almost assured of an alarming steroid abuse problem. In defense of Muscle-Gyms, Powerlifters and Bodybuilders, there are, of course, many who try to be a great example and influence on high school athletes. Unfortunately, however, the vast majority of steroid deals are made at these gyms.

RATE YOUR SCHOOL

Extreme Steroid Risk	**Virtually No Risk**
I. Big City High School	I. Smaller Town High School
II. Muscle-Gym Nearby	II. No Muscle-Gym in Vicinity
III. Adverse Powerlifting and/or Bodybuilding Influence.	III. No Adverse Powerlifting and/or Bodybuilding Influence
IV. No Weight Training Facilities	IV. Have a Great Weight Room
V. No Class Time Allotted for Weight Training	V. Weight Training—Body Building part of Curriculum
VI. Weight Room run by Non-Coaches.	VI. Weight Room Supervised by School Coaches.

Rating System Developed from BFS Survey

The Best Don't Do It!

Barry Sanders, the 1988 Heisman Trophy winner; Parallel Squats 556, Benches 360, Power Cleans 365 and has a Vertical Jump of 40 inches. Barry said, "Coach Shepard, I will promise on my life that I've never even touched a drop of alcohol."

XX.   Standards

It is very important to know what your athletes are doing, what they are trying to strive for, and why they are doing what they are doing. Personally, I could not work and sacrifice for hours in the weight room and not know exactly where I stood in relation to my strength. Machines cannot even come close to the free Olympic bar in determining standards of strength. The following is a table of standards for each lift.

	Squat	Bench	Dead Lift	Cleans
Good	1 1/2 x body wt.	body weight	2 x body wt.	body wt.
Great	2 x body wt.	1 1/4 x body wt.	2 1/2 x body wt.	1 1/8 x body wt.
Super	2 1/2 x body wt.	1 1/2 x body wt.	3 x body wt.	1 1/4 x body wt.
Varsity Level H.S.	300	200	400	175
H. S. All State	400	300	500	235
H. S. AllAmerican	500	350	600	300
College-Pro Level	500	400	600	300
World Standard Big Men	600	500	700	350
Women Good H. S.	145	105	235	105
Women All-State	235	145	325	145

Competitive Lifting is Fun!
(Bruce Klemens Photo)

XXI. Competitive Lifting Meets

There are two forms of recognized competitive lifting: Powerlifting and Olympic Weightlifting. Meets can be very motivating and give you something to work for in the off-season. Meets can also test your competitive will. Powerlifting consists of three lifts: the Squat, the Bench and the Dead Lift. Olympic Weightlifting consists of two lifts: the Snatch, the Clean, and the Jerk. Weight classes are almost the same except for the heavyweight class.

POWERLIFTING

I have used Powerlifting for my athletes involved in high school sports many times. For me, it worked out well and helped us win in football. Our kids not only believed they were strong, but they knew without question they were strong because of the Powerlifting meet.

My last coaching stint was in 1978 in Salt Lake City at Granger High School. We won four straight State Powerlifting Championships and one Regional Adult Championship in Denver. In that meet, one adult lifter remarked, "You mean we got beat by a bunch of high school kids?"

One of my kids at Granger High School set a near World's Teenage Squat Record with a 725 pound effort. Lynn Perkes, a football player from Madison High School in Idaho where I coached from 1973 to 1975, did set a National Teenage Squat Record. Lynn, at a body weight of 119, squatted 380 pounds. Both these meets were held in Little Rock, Arkansas.

I would suggest before you enter a Powerlifting meet that you consult with an experienced Powerlifter for the rules because things are quite different than lifting at school.

Another word of caution. Remember, you are lifting to help your sport. You should not ever become so caught up in powerlifting that you quit a sport like football. You can powerlift forever. You only get one shot at high school sports. Finally, stay away from steroids. Many lifters at these meets are on them and also sell them. Take in the good—reject the bad—and enjoy the meet.

OLYMPIC LIFTING! IT'S FUN!

I strongly recommend that all coaches get involved in Olympic Weightlifting. It's a fun and challenging sport. The Olympic Lifts also help build an athlete's explosive power. Don't be intimidated by the Snatch and Clean and Jerk. An athlete can compete very well on the Snatch by doing a Power Snatch. You don't have to drop down with your butt one inch from the floor. A Power Snatch is similar to a Power Clean in many respects. The Clean and Jerk is even easier. Just do a Power Clean like most athletes are already doing. Then dip, launch the bar upward, split the feet explosively, and you have the Jerk part of it.

Hardly anybody Olympic Lifts anymore, so you don't have to do much to get national recognition. For example, a 16-year-old, 165-pound athlete can be ranked in the top 25 in the nation with a 135-pound Snatch and a 200-pound Clean and Jerk. If an athlete weighs over 181, its even easier! Just Snatch 135 and Clean and Jerk 170 pounds.

What you read is not a misprint. It's that easy. What it means is that every high school has the capacity of having every member of a ten-man team ranked in the top 25 nationally. Obviously, that can do wonders for your program, not to mention the increased self-concept improvement for the individual.

HOW TO GET STARTED

The United States Weightlifting Federation is a great source of information on getting started in Olympic Lifting competition. Their address is as follows: One Olympic Plaza, Colorado Springs, Colorado 80909. Phone: (719) 578-4508.

The U.S. Weightlifting Federation provides the following services:

1. Club Coach Courses: They have various sites and dates throughout the country to certify and qualify coaches. They have different levels of certification. This process also helps in qualifying judges.

2. The Weightlifting U.S.A. Magazine: Subscription is $20.00 per year for six issues. Write or call the above address.

3. You can attend meets. The magazine has a listing of all meets.

4. They sponsor one big meet per year: The Junior Nationals. The weight classes in Kilos are as follows: 46, 50, 54, 59, 64, 70, 76, 83, 91, 99, 108, and 108+. In pounds: 101, 110, 119, 130, 141, 154, 167, 183, 200, 218, 238, 238-plus. There are different age groups from 12-19+. The competition is open to both boys and girls who compete separately.

Coach Paul Dick, a football coach at Churchville-Chili High School in the Rochester, New York area, sent me a video of one of his 15-year old players. His name was David Harvey-Bowen. David blew me away with his 340 Power Clean. He was awesome. I called Dragomir Cioroslan, the U.S. Weightlifting Coach and told him about David. I got Paul Dick all excited and featured David in our BFS Journal. Five months later David set six national records at the Junior National meet in 1996. Coach Dick tells me that David is ready to Power Clean 380 pounds and Power Snatch 300 pounds. The competition is giving David another way to express himself and should open other kinds of doors besides football.

XXII. Motivation From BFS

There are two kinds of motivation: Intrinsic and extrinsic. Intrinsic means coming from within. It is the deepest and most powerful form of motivation. When an athlete himself resolves to commit everything to being the best, and then is motivated enough to follow through without reservation, then you really have something.

An athlete recently remarked to me, " Coach, do I have to do this exercise?" I responded, "No, of course not, but I thought you wanted to be Upper Limit." You see I could have said, "Get your lazy butt over there and do it." The athlete responded the way I wanted and even better, it was his decision. After he did the exercise he commented, "Thanks Coach, I had a great workout."

If coaching were all science, we'd just have to read a manual and push a button. Fortunately, it is more an art; because a coach often represents the most powerful adult in a young athlete's life. That is why positive reinforcement is so much better than negative reinforcement.

Extrinsic motivation means coming from outside the person. It could be a simple pat on the back or an "A" on a report card. Coaches have charts, award decals and give trophies for outstanding achievement. These are all examples of extrinsic motivation.

These forms of extrinsic motivation are fine; but a coach must never forget to always steer extrinsic motivation to motivate athletes intrinsically.

MOTIVATIONAL IDEAS

1. **Use Charts**
   A. BFS Motivation Charts (For Lifting Progress)
   B. BFS Speed and Plyometric Charts

2. **Posters**
   A. BFS Standard Posters Showing the Core Lifts
   B. Upper Limit Posters: Full color posters of Stefan demonstrating the total BFS Program

3. **Videos:**
   A. Tom
   B. Eight Fantastic Stories
   C. The Core Program
   D. Flexibility and Nutrition
   E. Sets and Reps - Auxiliary Lifts
   F. Readiness Program
   G. Beyond Man's Upper Limits starring Stefan

4. **Shirts and Hats**
   A. BFS has their own
   B. School Logo and Color

5. **Post the stories from our BFS Journal on your weight room wall**

6. **BFS Clinics: Probably the Ultimate in team and individual motivation**

7. **Use the BFS Set-Rep Log. It is self motivating.**

8. **When appropriate, use the Readiness Program Log Book.**

For complete information on these motivational products and services and a BFS Journal send $2.00 to:

Bigger Faster Stronger
805 West 2400 South
Salt Lake City, UT 84119
801-974-0460
Or call toll-free: 1-800-628-9737

ABOUT BFS

BFS stands for Bigger Faster Stronger. It was founded as a business in 1976 by Coach Greg Shepard and since that time has maintained steady growth. In 1976 Coach Shepard started with an idea, a book, and one movie. Now the total BFS Program offers a large variety of products and services. The BFS motto is "Dedicated to Helping Athletes Succeed."

Dr. Shepard feels that BFS has the responsibility of experiencing and finding out about everything related to the strength and conditioning of athletes. Information found through research is assimilated and either added to the total BFS program or discarded. He is proud to assert that no other company or entity has paid for advertising or endorsements that would in any way be in conflict with BFS concepts.

Rick Anderson and Bob Rowbotham have been Executive Vice-Presidents of BFS since 1980. They have been a tremendous asset to the growth and development of BFS. Over one thousand BFS clinics have been held nationwide, and tens of thousands of athletes, coaches, and schools have been aided by the BFS philosophy and concepts.

It is the intent of BFS to continually update products and improve service in order to "..*Help* Athletes Succeed".

Rick Anderson BFS Vice-President

Bob Rowbotham BFS Vice-President

APPENDIX A

READINESS EQUIPMENT IDEAS

We have designed several patent pending products which make complex lifts like the Power Clean and Snatch easy and safe for all athletes, especially Junior High age boys & girls.

1. **Training Plates**: They are the same size as an Olympic 45 lb. Plate but weigh only 5 pounds each. Their cost is just $59 per pair.

2. **BFS Bumper Plates**: 10, 25, 35, and 45 lb. plates available in most all of the school colors. They are all the same diameter as a regular Olympic Plate. The cost for the 10 Pound Bumpers is $125 per pair.

3. **Special Bars**: Our Aluma-Lite bar looks and functions like a 45 lb. Olympic Bar, but it weighs only 15 pounds! Cost: $119

Ultra-Lite Bar: Also functions like a normal Olympic Bar and weighs 30 pounds. Cost: $69

APPENDIX B

I demonstrate two advanced coaching secrets for Power Clean/Snatch transfer at every BFS clinic. I gather all the coaches around a Power Clean platform. I state, "I will do one rep with bad technique and then one with good technique. I will repeat this sequence three times. Your job is to figure out what I am doing wrong."

This first secret can mean 20-50 pounds on a maximum attempt. This mistake is very common with athletes whose technique seems quite good to most coaches. Only about three coaches out of 100 will notice this mistake. That's why I call it a secret. Then, when I tell them what it is and repeat the mistake it becomes quite obvious.

The first mistake is dipping the chin for just an instant before the rack phase of the Clean. Keep the chin up throughout the entire lift. It is best to focus the eyes on a point high on a wall. Coaches, before you teach this secret to your athletes, watch them Clean. You will be amazed as to how common a mistake this is, especially with your better athletes.

The second advanced coaching secret is even harder to discover. It is rare to find even one coach out of 100 to guess correctly the mistake after my demonstration. I have been to Top Ten Division I football schools who really emphasize the Clean. One school in particular was making this mistake with all their athletes. If you make this mistake, the ability to transfer explosiveness to jumping power is completely lost.

You discover the first mistake by watching the chin. The second mistake can be discovered by zeroing in on the knees. After a coach has taught an athlete reasonable technique, then you can become a great coach by watching the chin and knees.

It really is simple with the knees. They should completely and fully extend exactly like the knees would do on a maximum force vertical jump. Most athletes do not do this. Most athlete's knees are bent throughout the entire lift. Do *not* mistake quickness for good technique. Just because the feet come off the platform does not mean a great jump

Stefan demonstrating jump phase of the Clean. Photo at left shows Stefan, 6-1 270 lbs., jumping. He put his ear on the backboard from a stand at a BFS Clinic. Notice the body similarity between the two photos. We use the overload principle by getting into a jump position with weight and then jump. Can we transfer? Of course!

has been executed. Do *not* take your eyes off the knees. It is easy to be tricked into thinking everything is fine when in reality it is disastrous.

I did a BFS clinic for a great high school football team. They had an All-State junior running back. Everyone was in awe at his strength and technique on the Clean. He could take 275 pounds and rack the bar in a low squat position just like an Olympic Lifter.

I shook my head and told the kid he had huge problems. You see, when an athlete Squat Cleans, he will invariably concentrate on getting into a quick low squat position rather than fully concentrating on the jump phase. Very little transfer was taking place with his technique.

I told him to Power Clean the weight and not Squat Clean it. He thought for sure he wouldn't be able to do as much. I laughed to myself because I knew what was going to happen.

We concentrated on a fully extended jump. Boy, was he surprised. In 15 minutes this 200 pound junior running back Power Cleaned 300 pounds!

Power Clean/Snatches can be done very safely. Wonderful transfer can take place to all Power Sports. Huge improvement can be made in a short time. EXPECT A MIRACLE!

APPENDIX C

**A Fantastic Sport Specific Football Machine
Shown with Detroit Lion Luther Elliss**

THE LETHAL WEAPON
Now Only $995

- Use as an auxiliary exercise
- Teach football skills in the weight room
- Teach players how to deliver a football blow
  from a perfect power position

**For Additional Information
Call BFS at 1-800-628-9737**

APPENDIX D
The BFS Athletic Achievement Computer System

Report Options available on the MAIN MENU are:
• Individual Ironman Rankings
• Individual Power Rankings
• Individual Ironman, Power and Overall Rankings
• Team/Grade Ironman and Power Rankings
• Current Top 10 Rankings
• All Time Top 10 Rankings for Your School
• Name and Address Listings

You may select a single athlete to print a report for, or select *several* athletes by any or all of the following criteria:
• Grade
• Period
• Sport
• Position

Individual Ironman Rankings - This report shows an athlete's standings in the Squat, Bench, Dead Lift, and Power Clean. The report also lists some recommendations for the athlete in areas that he or she may need improvement.

Individual Power Rankings - This report shows an athlete's standings in the 20 & 40 yard dash, Dot Drill, Vertical Jump, Long Jump, and Sit & Reach. There are also recommendations for each area in which the athlete may need improvement.

Individual Ironman, Power and Overall Rankings - This report shows an athlete's standing in all events and then lists his or her ranking by grade and also over-all school ranking in each category. There are also recommendations for improvement.

Team/Grade Ironman and Power Rankings - This report prints the average rankings for all the athletes selected. This means you can get an average of your 9th grade football players, and compare that to an average for 10th grade players. Or compare third period to fourth period. You may choose any other combination of sport, position, grade and period.

Current Top 10 Rankings - This report shows the best ten scores for each lift and event. The record will report only the scores of those athletes, either male or female, who are presently enrolled in the school. You may select either grade, period, sport, or sex with this report.

All Time Top 10 Rankings - This report shows the top 10 scores in each of the events requested, however, the list will include athletes who may have already graduated, or left the school for other reasons.

Name and Address Listings - This report shows the athletes you select, along with their address, phone number, ID number, grade, period, sport and position. The list will be either 12 or 13 entries, depending on the size of the entry.

Appendix E

"Beat The Computer"
The Best Computer Training System in the World!

Prints out the complete BFS Set Rep workout with weight, Sets & Reps for each athlete based on their own records! Then, they try to Beat the Computer on the last set!

Complete System only $249
For further information on BFS Computer Systems
Call 1-800-628-9737

MOTIVATIONAL GUIDELINES

SLOGAN:
A NEW DAY—A NEW GLORY

MOTTO: 11

FIVE POWER AXIOMS FOR SUCCESS

1. Team must establish *team goal.* It must come from them. Win State Championship!
2. Team must establish a *work ethic* plan.
   On a scale of one to ten: Our team works at an 11 pace.
3. Team must be *focused* on team goal.
   Keep your eye single to the glory of *winning* the State Championship.
4. Team must realize a *personal destiny.*
   We must play the song we came on earth to play.
   Let us not die with our music still in us.
5. Team must commit to *helping each other* in reaching their fullest potential in *mind, body and spirit.*

TRAINING CREED

The human body is a marvel created with wondrous intricacies and unfathomable complexities. When your body is overloaded, as in weight training exercises, it adapts, builds, and grows to make itself ready for tomorrow.

After another workout, this process of adapting, building and growing repeats itself to prepare for even greater loads. Then as you progressively and wisely add more and more weight and stress, your body will surge to even greater heights.

This miraculous process can be like a snowball propelling itself down a giant mountain. You will start seeing improvement in every phase of training. Everyday will be exciting as you see all your lifts improve along with greater speed and jumping abilities.

Positive energy will flow through your entire system both physically and mentally. Your positive energy will be contagious. You will feed this energy to your teammates and your teammates will feed you. It's as if no one can stop you or your team.

No amount of money can buy these dramatic changes. No one can give you progressive improvement. You must earn these things yourself through your own sweat and hard work. You must always keep your eyes on your goals, never wavering. When this is done, you will exude more self confidence. You will believe in yourself.

Winning and meeting challenges will take on whole new perspectives. Your attitudes toward school, family and life will see dramatic changes because you will look for what is possible rather than reasons for failure.

Ride the High Places and you will soar to the Upper Limit of your potential. Your body was created to "Expect A Miracle."

But, of course, Loyola was fighting against the Reformation that had produced his beloved Puritans. He therefore attacks Loyola on the grounds that the authority Loyola served was a sham and defines "Jesuitism" as the practice of sustaining the pretense of authority in institutions that no longer possess it. Although he names the practice after the Jesuits, the pamphlet is, in fact, an attack on the Church of England, the chief practitioner of Jesuitism in Victorian England. Much as he fears anarchy, Carlyle takes the side of the *sansculottes,* because they intended to reinstate the authority that had vanished from the churches of Rome and England. *Latter-Day Pamphlets* expresses the anger and frustration of a man who, expecting apocalyptic revolution to produce epic society, had in 1848 seen revolution debased from tragedy to farce.

The contradictory impulses of "The Negro Question" and *Latter-Day Pamphlets* also emerge in Carlyle's attitude toward his own authority. At certain moments, his inflated sense of authority makes him capable of imagining himself ruling England as a Cromwell, while at other moments his doubts about the authority of literature lead him to question the entire enterprise of writing social criticism. On the one hand, as Mill recognized when reading "The Negro Question," Carlyle was now writing as if he possessed transcendental authority: "The author issues his opinions, or rather ordinances, under imposing auspices; no less than those of the 'immortal gods.' 'The Powers,' 'the Destinies,' announce through him, not only what *will* be, but what *shall* be done" (*Essays on Equality*, 87).[69] But Mill did not seem to realize that Carlyle's exaggerated claims to authority may have been intended to cover up his anxiety that he lacked any authority at all. When *Latter-Day Pamphlets* attacks English literature for failing to transform the heroic actions of the English into a written epic, it implicitly draws attention to Carlyle's failure in regard to Cromwell (281–82, 322–27). If the *Latter-Day Pamphlets* express his anger at his contemporaries for failing to discover a Cromwell, they also express anger at himself for failing to convince them that they need one.

Mill's response to Carlyle's persistent command that the poor work must have hit home: "I do not include under the name labour," wrote Mill, "such work, if work it be called, as is done by writers and afforders of 'guidance,' an occupation which, let alone the vanity of the thing, cannot be called by the same name with the real labour, the exhausting, stiffening, stupefying toil of many kinds of agricultural and manufacturing labourers" (*Essays on Equality*, 91; see August, xxvi–xxvii). Is writing, even writing social criticism, work?

Carlyle himself had long been apprehensive that it was not, that speech or writing could never become action but always displaced and deferred it, and he dedicated one pamphlet, "Stump-Orator," to this question. Perhaps recalling how as a young student he had aspired to achieve "glory in literature," he now rues an educational establishment that entices young men into the literary profession by telling them that they will "astonish mankind" (172). "[T]here never was a talent even for real Literature," he replies, "but was primarily a talent for something infinitely better of the silent kind," while defending himself against Mill's charge by claiming that no other profession is open to men of talent (212; see 190–91). In the conclusion of "Stump-Orator," Carlyle virtually acknowledges that his time has passed, that his opportunity to become a heroic Cromwell has been wasted in his enslavement to literature. He leaves the future to the young: they "are in the happy case to learn to *be* something and to *do* something, instead of eloquently talking about what has been and was done and may be! The old are what they are, and will not alter; our hope is in you" (213).[70] Carlyle, age fifty-five, clearly includes himself among the old who can only talk eloquently about "what has been" (Abbot Samson, Oliver Cromwell) or "what may be" (a green flowery world). If the author of *Latter-Day Pamphlets* always seems to be on the attack, it may be because he believes, at bottom, that his words are impotent.

In moving to London in 1834, Carlyle had hoped to "commune" with fellow souls, but by the time he wrote *Latter-Day Pamphlets* he felt cut off from almost everyone. Whereas *The French Revolution* established his authority, "The Negro Question" and *Latter-Day Pamphlets* expressed his suspicion that his authority was specious and served in turn to undermine that authority in the minds of the reading public. His relationship with Mill, whom he met rarely in the 1840s and almost never afterward, is exemplary. Just one decade after writing the rave review of *The French Revolution* that confirmed Carlyle's reputation as a major writer, Mill felt compelled to rebut publicly the views Carlyle put forth in "The Repeal of the Union" and "The Negro Question." Carlyle later regarded the period following the publication of *Latter-Day Pamphlets* as a time when even friends whose political views were much closer to his own than Mill's, friends like Forster and Spedding, "fell away . . . into terror and surprise;—as indeed everybody did" (*Rem.*, 126; Spedding, 753; see *NLM*, 2:14). As he at least half intended, "The Negro Question" and *Latter-Day Pamphlets* drove away those who were not of his faith; but instead of leaving behind a saving remnant, this strategy left him virtually alone. For the next fifteen years, he abandoned the attempt to address his contemporaries about the problems of the day and, turning inward, meditated on the authority of fathers and the careers of their sons.

FIVE

The Return of the Father: 1851–1865

THE YEAR THAT *Latter-Day Pamphlets* appeared, 1850, marked the end of thirteen years of economic and political disturbance and the beginning of a period of economic prosperity and political calm that endured until new appeals for reform, culminating in the Reform Bill of 1867, again disturbed the nation. Apart from a few months in 1851, during which he wrote *The Life of John Sterling*, Carlyle was occupied during most of this period with the writing of *Frederick the Great*. Neither work directly addressed the political issues of the day as *Chartism, Past and Present,* and *Latter-Day Pamphlets* had done, but they continued to explore the problem of authority by returning to the relationship between father and son that had preoccupied him in his early career. In *The Life of John Sterling*, Carlyle plays the role of father attempting to conceive a literary son; in *Frederick the Great*, he envisions a son seeking to obtain the authority of the father.

Fathering the Literary Son: *The Life of John Sterling*

In writing *The Life of John Sterling*, Carlyle was authoring the myth of Sterling's literary career just as in life he had attempted to father Sterling as a literary son. *John Sterling* rewrites the career paradigm that Carlyle had created in the 1820s. Like *Sartor Resartus*, the biography is in three parts and traces the hero's discovery of his literary vocation. Both Teufelsdröckh and Sterling are political radicals who reject a religious career in favor of a literary one. But, while *Sartor Resartus* ends just as Teufelsdröckh is about to author a "new mythus," *The Life of John Sterling* shows what happens when the author actually tries to create the new mythus: he fails.

Carlyle uses the life of Sterling to explore his own dilemma, arguing both that the literary career is the only one open to men of talent and that it does not satisfy the need for action. He seems to be choosing between making a final attempt to assume an active role in the political arena and withdrawing from it altogether, as literature could not be effective. Writing to his influential friend Harriet Baring of his "disgust with [the] trade," he wondered if he should "squeeze into Parlt. itself, and there speak *Pamphlets*, hot, and hot, right from the heart" (Wilson, 5:7).[1] "Throughout the 1840s," Kaplan concludes, "the prospect of becoming a man of action, a public actor rather than a private thinker, had attracted him strongly. . . . Given his friendship with Bingham Baring and his relationship with Peel, the possibility of a new career in public service was more than wishful thinking" (361). Although Carlyle hoped that the Northcote-Trevelyan Report (1854) would lead to the appointment of civil servants by merit, he also continued to complain that, like Burns and Sterling, he was excluded from government by his class origins, that "Fate . . . allowed [him] no other" profession (Wilson, 5:121–22).[2] As in *Latter-Day Pamphlets*, he argues that because the major professions are not open to earnest young men like Sterling—who is best suited for a public life as a member of Parliament—they are forced to make a living in literature (*LJS*, 39–42). In *The Life of John Sterling*, he writes an apologia for the nineteenth-century man of letters.

In *Sartor Resartus*, Carlyle had projected an image of himself as the rebellious son who rejects his father's faith but then attempts to recuperate the transcendental through literature. In place of his religious father, James Carlyle, he had adopted a literary godfather, Goethe. With the "Reminiscence of James Carlyle," Carlyle turned from fiction to history, rejecting the transcendentalism of Goethe and the Germans in favor of his father's preference for the "real." *On Heroes and Hero-Worship* had further deemphasized the importance of literature by excluding Goethe and replacing him with men of letters who could not create a new mythus. *The Life of John Sterling* consolidates this process by replacing the earlier triad of Thomas Carlyle/son, James Carlyle/father, Goethe/godfather with the triad of Sterling/son, Thomas Carlyle/father, Coleridge/godfather. Carlyle's satiric portrait of Coleridge and "transcendental moonshine" is a displaced repudiation of the German transcendentalism of Goethe, who had influenced the young Carlyle just as Coleridge had influenced Sterling. The Carlyle of *The Life of John Sterling*, moreover, is no longer a rebellious son, but the father who leads Sterling back to reality, reenacting the moment when he had submitted to the law of the father after writing the "Reminiscence of James Carlyle."

The first half of *The Life of John Sterling* closely parallels the narrative pattern of *Sartor Resartus* and Carlyle's career paradigm. Carlyle, like the Editor of *Sartor*, had known the subject of his biography personally and uses his letters and writings to compose the narrative of his life. Like Teufelsdröckh, Sterling "renounce[s]" the law and finds himself unable to discover a suitable profession (*LJS*, 40; see 38). Teufelsdröckh believes that he has recovered paradise in the heavenly love of Blumine, whom he compares to the "moon," but then learns that his discovery is a mere "calenture" (*SR*, 139, 147); Sterling falls for Coleridge's "transcendental *moon*shine" only to discover that Coleridge's teachings are "fatal delusion[s]" and "fatamorganas" (*LJS*, 60; emphasis added). Teufelsdröckh is a radical *sansculotte* who travels to Paris at the time of the 1830 revolt; in the same year, Sterling allies himself with the philosophic radicals and becomes involved in an abortive Spanish rebellion. Like Teufelsdröckh, he wanders endlessly in search of health and, after the Spanish debacle, which ended in the execution of the rebels, reaches the conclusion that his radicalism is a "Philosophy of Denial," an Everlasting No (*LJS*, 90). In response to this crisis, Sterling, like Teufelsdröckh, who mounts the "higher sunlit slopes" of the "Everlasting Yea" and becomes an author, discovers that "his true sacred hill" is literature (*SR*, 184; *LJS*, 266).[3]

The second half of *The Life of John Sterling* represents what might be regarded as a continuation of *Sartor Resartus*, in which Teufelsdröckh fails to become a paternal authority and to author a new mythus. Instead of producing a *Palingenesia*, Sterling produces only a meager quantity of essays, poems, and tales, which are almost entirely ignored by the public. This is in keeping with Carlyle's abandonment of the transcendental aspirations of *Sartor* after the death of his father. Yet although Carlyle had abandoned these transcendental aspirations, he had continued to hope that he might become a literary father. Even though Sterling fails to become a father, he becomes a model for literary sons, those who might recognize Carlyle's authority and enable him to become a father himself.

Carlyle depicts his relationship with Sterling as the relationship of father and son, of hero and hero-worshipper. Sterling plays the role of audience for Carlyle's writings, their relationship beginning with an exchange of letters on *Sartor Resartus*. Although, in their first exchanges, Sterling shows his inclination to adopt an independent critical position, Carlyle soon is able to regard him as his ideal reader, a son who finds in him the kind of father that he wants to be. By 1840, Sterling is Carlyle's most approving reader, telling him that he considers the *Miscellaneous Essays* "*the* book of the last 25 years in England" and publishing the "first generous human recognition" of his work (Tuell, 309; *LJS*, 191; see *CL*, 11:191–92). *The Life of John Sterling* both describes how Carlyle attempted to father Sterling's career by persuading him to give up religion, or at least the Church of England, in favor of literature, and shapes the narrative of Sterling's career itself so as to make it fulfill this desire.

Carlyle wrote his narrative to correct Julius Hare's biography, which, Carlyle claims, misleadingly represents Sterling "as a clergyman merely" (3). Because Hare views Sterling from the point of view of Christian orthodoxy, he inevitably represents Sterling's career as a "defeat of faith," whereas Carlyle wishes to argue that his abandonment of conventional Christianity enabled him to become in the end a "victorious believer" (5, 6).[4] Carlyle begins his narrative by insisting that Sterling's interest in organized religion and theological issues ended when he resigned his curacy in 1835, shortly before they first met, that "during eight months and no more had he any special relation to the Church" (3). However, recent studies have established that, although health prevented Sterling from retaining his curacy, he still considered himself a clergyman and a follower of Coleridge when he met Carlyle in 1835 and that he sustained his connection with the church until at least 1839. Only in 1840, when he published defenses of Strauss and Carlyle, did he part with his more orthodox friends, and, even so, he continued to interest himself in theological issues.[5]

Carlyle shaped the biography by pushing back to 1835–37 the date of Sterling's conversion to literature and by suppressing evidence of his continuing interest in theology. As Carlyle prepared to write by rereading Sterling's *Essays and Tales*, he was already looking for signs of heterodoxy, insisting in a comment written in the margin of the book that "This man must soon leave the Church" (Tuell, 344). Even before Sterling takes up religion, Carlyle is insisting that his only "solid fruit lie[s] in Literature" (74). As early as 1837, just two years after Sterling had given up his curacy, Carlyle claims, "he began to look on Literature as his real employment," he "felt more and more as if authentically consecrated to the same," and he learned to look at "Literature as his work in the world" (144, 152, 157). Nonetheless, the evidence of Sterling's continuing interest in religion and his indecision about his vocation force Carlyle to push back the date of Sterling's conversion, and, in discussing 1841, he finds it necessary to assert that "Literature was still his constant pursuit" and that "we now hear nothing more" of Strauss and church matters (221, 222). In order to compensate for these difficulties, he gives prominence to those letters and episodes that emphasize his influence on Sterling and Sterling's literary interests. He reprints only those portions of Sterling's critique of *Sartor Resartus* that bear on its artistry, suppressing "several pages on 'Personal God'" and quotes Sterling's assurance that his "thoughts have . . . been running more on History and Poetry than on Theology and Philosophy" (116, 139; see 138).[6]

At this point, Carlyle's shaping of Sterling's career in the biography nearly merges with his attempt to shape Sterling's career in life. Finding Sterling intelligent and earnest, Carlyle was respectful of his orthodoxy but encouraged every sign that he was abandoning theology for literature: "One of the announcements you made me was as welcome as any other: that you were rather *quitting* Philosophy and Theology. I predict that you will quit them more and more" (*CL*, 9:117–18). Carlyle makes it clear that he had actively striven to shape Sterling's beliefs, countering Sterling's concern about his "pantheism" with "flippant heterodoxy" and discouraging religious discussion by resolving to "suppress" all conversations "on the Origin of Evil" as "wholly fruitless and worthless" (*LJS*, 124, 130–31). He even went so far as to encourage Sterling to stop using the title "Reverend" on the title pages of his books (*CL*, 12:6, 322). Most importantly, he persuaded Sterling of the importance of Goethe. At first, Sterling had regarded Goethe as too pagan, but Carlyle convinced him of Goethe's higher spirituality by describing how his mentor had "save[d]" him from "destruction" and provided him with a higher kind of faith (*CL*, 9:380, n. 12, 381; *LJS*, 147). Even though by 1840 Carlyle had himself lost some of his enthusiasm for Goethe, his letters to Sterling made belief in this literary father an article of faith (*CL*, 11:216–17, 13:321–22, 14:24, 73). Sterling relented, and he was soon following in Carlyle's footsteps as a translator and critic of German literature.

Carlyle tries to counteract the tendency toward transcendentalism implicit in his insistence on the value of Goethe and literature by attempting to persuade Sterling, at the same time, that prose is superior to poetry. Carlyle makes the same objections to poetry and aestheticism that he had made to Coleridgean moonshine, criticizing Sterling's letters on Italian art as "nebulous" and suppressing his aesthetic appreciations as capitulations to the century's "windy gospels" of "Art" (175, 174; see 164). Carlyle's caricature of Coleridge, like that in his letters of 1824, condemns him because his poetic speculations draw his followers into an endless circuit of desire for the transcendent and prevent them from achieving closure in action.[7] Carlyle argues, accordingly, that in an era of "revolutionary overturnings" prose alone achieves closure by producing something outside of itself, by doing battle: only the "Intelligible word of command, not musical psalmody and fiddling [i.e., poetry], is possible in this fell storm of battle" (196).

Yet, although Carlyle converts Sterling from religion to literature in the first half of the biography, he cannot, in the second half, convert him from poetry to prose. When, at the beginning of 1837, Carlyle encouraged Sterling to switch from theology to "poetry and history," his emphasis was on the latter, for by the end of the year he was discouraging him from writing verses (*CL*, 9:379). While Carlyle advised all poets of his acquaintance, except possibly Tennyson, to adopt prose, he seems to have hoped that he might really succeed with Sterling, and he persisted in his advice for at least five years.[8] Yet, although *The Life of John Sterling* represents Sterling as asking the question "Write in Poetry; write in Prose?" the question is really Carlyle's (195). At first, Sterling tries to satisfy his new friend, reporting in 1837, for example, that his new writings for Blackwood are "prose, nay extremely prose" (147). But, in spite of Carlyle's harsh criticisms and advice to the contrary, he persists in writing verse (*CL*, 12:320–22, 14:21–25; *LJS*, 250). Finally, acknowledging that Sterling is becoming "set more and more toward Poetry" and that "With or without encouragement, he [is] resolute to persevere," Carlyle concedes that "if a man *write* in metre, this sure enough was the way to try doing it" and in retrospect decides that he ought to have been more definite in affirming Sterling's poetic vocation (204, 250, 216–17; see *CL*, 13:132).[9]

The question turns out to be not "prose or poetry" but whether Sterling was a "true son" who accepted Carlyle's authority or a "mutinous rebel" who denied it (264). Sterling lives in an era of revolution when sons do not respect the authority of their fathers. Instead of being a disciple who conforms to authority as he might have in an era of faith, Sterling is a rebellious son—a "Radical," and an "emblem" of the era of revolution—who cannot make himself submit to his literary father (36, 5–6, 267). He criticizes *Sartor Resartus*, persists in his Coleridgean transcendentalism and in writing verse, even doubts the heroism of Cromwell. Like Teufelsdröckh, the young colt who breaks his constraining neck-halter, Sterling is an escaped "Arab courser . . . Roaming at full gallop over the heaths" (40). The emphasis on wasted energy, however, suggests that Sterling is more like Farmer Hodge's emancipated horse in *Latter-Day Pamphlets* than the coltish Teufelsdröckh of *Sartor Resartus*. Indeed, Carlyle would have Sterling, like the emancipated slave, brought under the law of the father, "trained to saddle and harness" (40). Whereas in *Sartor Resartus* Carlyle focuses on the son's need to rebel and turn to literature as a means of recapturing the transcendental idyll from which he has been sundered by the father, in *The Life of John Sterling* the rebellious son becomes a past self for whom his present self lays down the paternal law. Yet, just as Carlyle's literary persuasion was unable to lay down the law for blacks and Celts, so it cannot constrain Sterling to submit to his authority and give up poetry.

Born of the era of revolution, Sterling remains an eternal wanderer. He cannot achieve closure by writing a myth that enables action; he is, like Childe Roland, fit only to "fail" with his fellow questers. Whereas Teufelsdröckh's wanderings presumably end when he becomes an author, Sterling's continue, even increase, after he is converted to literature; his five major "peregrinities" are emblems of his restless, "nomadic" character: "He could take no rest, he had never learned that art; he was, as we often reproached him, fatally incapable of sitting still" (155, 26; see 30, 40, 91, 92, 96, 102, 104, 121, 133, 134, 184, 266; *CL*, 8:50). The relationship between ill-health and wandering in *The Life of Schiller*, as well as that between ill-health and self-consciousness in "Characteristics," now manifest themselves in the life of Sterling, whose "bodily disease was the expression, under physical conditions, of the too vehement life which . . . incessantly struggled within him" (155).

Yet Carlyle ultimately concludes that Sterling is not a "mutinous rebel," that he is both "filial" and "submissive," because in this "Talking Era . . . the anarchic, nomadic, entirely aerial" career of "Literature" is the "only one completely suited" to him (264, 43). His decision to write poetry is not an evasion of the call to battle, but the only possible form of action for a man of his sensibility: he is finally a "victorious doer" because life's "battle shaped itself for" him "chiefly in the poetic form" (6, 222). Sterling must wander endlessly because, even though he can stop being a rebellious son, he cannot become an authoritative father. Like Carlyle, he discovers that literature is no more capable of escaping the endless circuit of desire than is Coleridgean religion. In his final effort to conform to the law of his literary father, Sterling attempts in his last work, *Cœur-de-Lion*, to write a Homeric epic, but this work is left incomplete at his death, literally without closure (255).

Instead of blaming himself for directing Sterling into the fruitless pursuit of literature, Carlyle condemns Coleridge for leading him into the "deserts" of theology and failing to bring him to "new firm lands of Faith beyond" (60). Yet, as Clough was to charge (perhaps with this passage in mind), Carlyle was equally guilty of leading a younger generation "into the desert and . . . [leaving] them there," no longer sons but not yet fathers (Hale, 46). If Carlyle could still claim to recall his preexistence in paradise, the doubly belated literary son could only recall the wanderings of exile. If Carlyle could in a limited way engender progeny like Sterling, Sterling could not accomplish even that; his writings all fall "dead-born" (250). Yet the Sterling of this biography is an avatar of Carlyle, not the Carlyle who believed he could become a procreative father, but the Carlyle who so often felt his works were born dead.

The Life of John Sterling also expresses the irony that, whereas Carlyle had sought to father a king, to shape Peel in the image of Cromwell, he had only succeeded in fathering a man of letters, shaping Sterling in his own image. A heroic soul born in the nineteenth century, it suggests, will not possess the vigor of the Puritan general, but will instead suffer the debility of the man of letters too enfeebled by consumption to perform the duties of a parish curate. Whereas Carlyle had once hoped that heroism could be recovered by replacing the hero as man of letters with the hero as king, he now seems to conclude that only the diminished heroism of the man of letters is any longer possible. In the end, *The Life of John Sterling* is not just an apologia for the man of letters but an elegy for heroism.

The rhetoric of *The Life of John Sterling* signals Carlyle's withdrawal from public controversy. Instead of the angry prophet addressing a fallen nation, here he is a melancholy memoirist recalling and defending a beloved friend. Whereas in his previous works he had debated with his audience, *The Life of John Sterling* excludes its readers: all of the conversation is between Carlyle and Sterling (106, 124, 252). Undoubtedly because it was a much "gentler business" than "The Negro Question" and *Latter-Day Pamphlets*, because he did not have an antagonistic relation with the man he wrote of, Carlyle found the book easier to write than those more controversial works (Sadler, 286; see Kaplan, 372, *Rem.*, 127). The reviewers immediately noticed the change in tone and praised its calm, its tenderness, its freedom from "rant, eccentricity, and extravagance" (Dixon, 1088; see 1090).[10]

Although Carlyle isolated himself from his audience by avoiding a direct engagement with them, he also continued to isolate himself by attacking their most cherished beliefs. The religious reviews, recognizing that in spite of its milder tone *The Life of John Sterling* took up the attack on the Church of England and orthodox Christianity where "Jesuitism" had left off, were "in a terrible humour" with him (*LL*, 2:97). In *The Life of John Sterling*, they claimed, Carlyle had finally revealed himself as a demon—a "Mephistopheles," a "Satan," a "Herod"—who delighted in leading an innocent young clergyman into the paths of heterodoxy (*North British Quarterly*, 245; *Christian Observer and Advocate*, in Seigel, *Critical Heritage*, 403, 405).[11] Carlyle concluded that the "review newspaper and world [were] all dead against" him, that "though no one hates" him "nearly *everybody* of late takes [him] on the wrong side, and proves unconsciously unjust to" him (*LL*, 2:139–40). Indeed, his "Heterodoxy" probably cost him a government pension and election as rector of the University of Glasgow.[12]

Although he frequently took up his pen in the early 1850s to address the religious and political questions of the day, his writings all led to the same issue as the manuscript known as "Spiritual Optics."[13] This manuscript does not mention *The Life of John Sterling* or the controversy it aroused, but it clearly refers to it when Carlyle asks "Why . . . men shriek so over creeds?" But he makes little headway toward producing an effective reply; instead of producing an effective response to his critics, he gets locked up in the contradiction between his beliefs that cultural values are relative and that they are transcendental. Finding himself at a dead end, he abruptly concludes, "alas, not a word of this is coming rightly from my heart; nor is it tending (naturally) toward any good or even perceptible goal whatever!" In another manuscript, he again finds himself drawn to contemporary subjects, even though he was writing history—"modern Dundases with their appointments

to India . . . the Pig-Iron interests . . . the reduced whiskey interests"—
he concludes that it is "much better . . . that we say nothing. *Altum
Silentium*" (Tarr, "The Guises," 19).[14] Instead of trying to make himself heard over what he thought of as the Babelian din of London,
he sought isolation from it by having a soundproof room constructed
at the top of his house and withdrawing into the world of Frederick
the Great.

Frederick the Great was not admired by all, but it created still less
controversy than *The Life of John Sterling*. Indeed, during the thirteen
years that he worked on *Frederick*, Carlyle managed to avoid almost
all public controversy.[15] As a prodigy of scholarship and a heroic act
of writing, it helped to restore Carlyle's reputation as a historian and
man of letters. Those who had parted with Carlyle could not be won
back by it, but those who wished to think well of the hallowed man of
letters could do so. If in 1854 he was found too heterodox to be elected
rector of the University of Glasgow, by 1866, after the appearance of
Frederick, he was elected, by a huge margin, rector of the University of
Edinburgh.

The Son as Father: Frederick's Art of War

Frederick the Great, like Carlyle, finds himself divided between com-
pliance with the law ordained by his natural father, Friedrich Wilhelm,
and the desire to pursue the interest in art and literature validated
by his spiritual father, Voltaire. So the triad of son, father, and godfather—Carlyle, James Carlyle, and Goethe—this time becomes Frederick, Friedrich Wilhelm, and Voltaire. Like all sons, Carlyle and
Frederick seek to become paternal authorities themselves. Carlyle, de-
barred from assuming the authority of James Carlyle, had attempted
to obtain the literary authority of Goethe. But, since his allegiance to
literature was also a rebellion against the authority of his father, it constantly undermined itself. The impossibility of achieving his father's
authority through writing, manifested in his insistence in *Latter-Day
Pamphlets* and *The Life of John Sterling* that the man of letters is excluded from political action, led him to project himself into the figure
of Frederick, whose father forces him to abandon his desire to write
in order to lead a life of military action.

Carlyle ascribes the same characteristics to Friedrich Wilhelm that
he had ascribed to his father in the "Reminiscence of James Car-

lyle," his father's "inflexible authority" becoming the "unquestioned authority" of Frederick Wilhelm (*FG*, 1:348). Friedrich Wilhelm possesses the same combination of qualities—"simplicity," preference for silence, disdain for art and speculation—that made James Carlyle an unselfconscious believer. Friedrich Wilhelm's rustic simplicity manifests itself in his love for the "Spartan Hyperborean" hunting lodge at Wusterhausen that he prefers to his palaces at Potsdam and Berlin. Disdaining talk, he holds "Tabagies"—"Tobacco-Parliaments," not speech-making parliaments—that consist mainly of silent smoking. Finally, he distrusts literature and speculation, turning Jakob Gundling, his only literary courtier, into a "Court-Fool" and banishing the philosopher Christian Wolff from his domains (2:80–93). Finally, he is, like James Carlyle, a man of action, a builder or "Aedile."[16]

Like Carlyle, Frederick is born into a world that contains not only the rustic idyll of Wusterhausen but the French culture that his father had attempted to banish from Brandenburg when he assumed the throne (1:334ff.). Consequently, the narrative of *Frederick the Great* develops in terms of a dialectic between German culture, identified with Friedrich Wilhelm, and French culture, identified with Voltaire and the *philosophes:* between masculinity (the "centre" of German culture is "Papa") and femininity (Frederick's mother and sister are francophiles), between Lutheran orthodoxy and freethinking heterodoxy, the Spartan and the Athenian, the "solid" and the "unsolid" (1:319–34, 385). The "proud spirit" of young Frederick inevitably comes into conflict with the "iron laws" of his father, and although Friedrich Wilhelm thinks "[t]his Fritz ought to fashion himself according to his Father's pattern . . . it cannot be. It is the new generation come. . . . A perennial controversy in human life; coeval with the genealogies of men" (1:427). Like Teufelsdröckh and John Sterling, the "fiery young Arab" colt Frederick "break[s] harness" and, rebelling against his father's "imprison[ing]" military discipline, combs out his hair "like a cockatoo, the foolish French fop, instead of conforming to the Army-regulation" and takes to "verses, story-books, flute-playing" (3:11, 2:189, 1:422). Like Carlyle, he becomes unorthodox and develops dyspepsia, the physical correlative of the modern condition of doubt (see also Adrian). When Friedrich Wilhelm discovers his son "unlawful[ly]" playing music and wearing French costumes, he ferrets out "contraband" Latin texts, banishes "illicit French Books," and "ruthlessly" shears his son's cockatoo locks (2:188, 1:422). Unable to bear any longer the beatings his father metes out when he discovers these "effeminate" practices, Frederick tries to flee Prussia (1:393). Friedrich Wilhelm discovers the plot, executes Frederick's close friend Hans Hermann von Katte for treason, and only absolves his son from the same fate when he promises to "quit his French literatures and pernicious practices, one and all" (2:352). Frederick's attempt to flee Prussia is his "Everlasting No"; just as Sterling's remorse at the death of Boyle in the Spanish rebellion leads to a religious conversion, so Frederick achieves an Everlasting Yea of sorts after witnessing the execution of Katte. He now learns to "love this rugged Father," and before long he is performing his duties like "Papa's second self" (3:29, 150).

Yet Friedrich Wilhelm's repression only makes Frederick's "French" or literary self emerge all the more powerfully. Frederick obtains a private residence at Reinsberg where he is free to pursue his artistic pursuits, and it is at this period of his life that he first corresponds with his new "Intellectual Father," Voltaire (5:271). As Carlyle had regarded Goethe and the Germans as the new priesthood and the authors of the new liturgy, so Frederick regards Voltaire as "Preacher, Prophet, and Priest," the bearer of the "new 'Gospel'" (3:193, 192). Although Frederick outwardly obeys his father, he has not really accepted his beliefs, and in his relations with Friedrich Wilhelm he becomes "calculat[ing], reticent . . . half-sincere" (2:373). He pretends, for example, to dislike the woman Friedrich Wilhelm has chosen for him to marry so that he will appear all the more submissive when he accepts her. Because Frederick submits to the superior power but not to the superior belief of Friedrich Wilhelm, the conclusion of the first half of the history does not so much resolve the conflict of father and son as polarize the conflicting French and German "elements" in the hunting-lodge at Wusterhausen and the art projects of Reinsberg.[17]

When Frederick takes the throne in the second half of the history, his contemporaries justifiably wonder whether he will indeed be a second Friedrich Wilhelm or whether he will reign as an enlightened philosopher-king.[18] Once his father dies, and physical compulsion disappears, it would seem that he is free to follow his own desires. Indeed, although he surprises his contemporaries by expanding his army, he does initially dedicate himself to the arts in homage to the "Muses." But the second half of the history will demonstrate that Friedrich Wilhelm's authority was more than simple strength or power, that he remains "the supreme ultimate Interpreter, and grand living codex, of the Laws," and that his laws have the authority of the "Laws of this Universe" (2:72, 119; see 1:340, 434, 2:72, 326). Frederick cannot obtain authority through rebellion but only through submitting to the law as laid down by his father. By the end of the first year of his reign, he is at war and begins to discover that "Bellona [will be] his companion for long years henceforth, instead of Minerva and the Muses, as he had been anticipating" (3:413).[19] Indeed, Frederick, who wages three major wars, outdoes his father, who fought only one, becoming in the process more like Friedrich Wilhelm than Friedrich Wilhelm himself.

But, while Frederick's first war teaches him the value of his father's virtues—he wins, not through his own efforts, but because he has inherited a well-prepared army from his father—he has not yet learned the limitations of the arts and still clings to his literary father, Voltaire. In order to depict the final triumph of war over art, Carlyle presents Voltaire's visit to Berlin in 1750–52 as a mock tragedy. During the ten years' peace following the Silesian wars, Frederick attempts to revive his artistic projects, in part by convincing Voltaire to take up residence in Berlin, but, although Frederick imagines that he can still dedicate himself to the Muses, his experience of war has made that project impossible. Frederick eventually perceives that while *he* has been "battling for his existence," Voltaire has been growing "great by 'Farces of the Fair,'" and he quickly grows impatient when his literary father gets embroiled in a series of ridiculous adventures culminating in the controversy of the "Infinitely Little" (5:267, 348). The latter episode, which soon comes to represent the pettiness of the intellectuals involved (one cannot help but recall the Lilliputian debate between the Big-endians and the Little-endians), generates the mock-tragic denouement of Voltaire's visit. Voltaire might win the intellectual debate, but, as the real issue is power, he is destined to lose, for he has made the mistake of attacking Maupertius, the president of Frederick's royal academy. The farce ends when the king, who cannot accept being embarrassed in this manner, has Voltaire arrested and forces him to depart from Berlin in disgrace.[20] Just as Friedrich Wilhelm had banished French courtiers when he assumed the throne, Frederick, now truly become his father's "second self," banishes Voltaire's French frivolity from his court (1:334–35). "Voltaire at Potsdam is a failure," Carlyle reports, and, "happily," the "Life to the Muses" is "extremely disappointing" (5:380, 205).

In *Frederick the Great*, the literary man has become the opposite of what he had been in Carlyle's writings of the 1830s. Whereas Carlyle's literary father, Goethe, had recaptured the transcendental, Sterling's literary father, Coleridge, produces only transcendental moonshine, and Frederick's literary father, Voltaire, is a skeptic, belonging to the "Anarchic Republic . . . of Letters," who makes the transcendental inaccessible (4:396; see 1:11, 270, 8:217–18). In his depiction of Voltaire, Carlyle inverts his earlier representations of authorial creativity. Whereas Teufelsdröckh was to become a Goethe-like author whose *Palingenesia* would bring about the phoenix rebirth of society, Voltaire is a "Phœnix douched"; instead of realizing ideals, he produces the anarchy of revolution, "Realised Voltairism" (5:294, 3:177).[21] Whereas Carlyle depicted the Germans as conveyors of a new religious spirit, he depicts Voltaire's "spiritual[ity]" as mere wit (*esprit*), and his writings as "Gundlingiana," the antics of a court jester (3:177, 8:218).

When Frederick banishes Voltaire, he finally recognizes that his own "swift-handed, valiant, *steel*-bright kind of soul . . . [is] very likely for a King's . . . not likely for a Poet's" (3:238). Except as historical documents, his writings have lost all interest; he emerges as a hero precisely because he is the one man of action in a "Writing Era" (1:11). It is not by imitating Voltaire, the author of farces, that Frederick becomes "Vater Fritz," but by imitating Friedrich Wilhelm, one of "the Authors of Prussia" (4:366).

In the figure of Frederick the Great, Carlyle completes his vision of the author as creator of a new paradise in the image of the God of Genesis. Carlyle's first project that dealt with Frederick—a translation of a text describing Frederick's interest in draining swamps and the profits to be obtained thereby—was an extension of his growing obsession with land reclamation (see *NL*, 2:141). In *Frederick the Great*, where Carlyle proceeded to represent Frederick as the author of Prussia, Frederick inherits the authority to create Prussia from the "fathers" who, from the year 928 to the accession of Friedrich Wilhelm in 1713, began the process of separating land and water "into two firmaments" through the territorial expansion of Brandenburg by war, purchase, colonization, and land reclamation (2:51; see 1:78, 96, 131, 176, 250, 293, 309, 341, 3:313, 4:47, 5:308, 8:254, 305, 306).

Battle, both literal and figurative, is Carlyle's principal metaphor for the work of creating the Prussian nation. Whereas the wars of the eighteenth century are otherwise indicative of its "anarchic" tendencies, Frederick's battles, like those of his ancestors, are "pitched fight[s] . . . against anarchy" which, like his land reclamation projects, turn land to human use (1:72). His wars not only aim to suppress the "inveterate ineffective war[s]" of the era but to produce order by acquiring the lands that constitute the new Prussian state. This at least partially accounts for the lavish attention Carlyle devotes to the geographical details of Frederick's battles. He made a journey to Germany exclusively to examine the twelve major battle sites, and in the history he provides detailed narratives and maps of the armies' positions and maneuvers, indicating the specific relationship of the battles to the physical geography of the land (see Brooks). The creation of a culture is no longer for Carlyle a matter of "spirituality," for the ideal has become associated with Voltaire and Gundlingiana; instead it is a matter of physical force, of military drill, forced labor, and agricultural production.

Yet, while Frederick authors an epic nation, Carlyle fails, as he acknowledges from the start, to "disimprison" the "imprisoned Epic" of Frederick the Great so that it can transform his own anarchic era as Frederick, at least temporarily, transformed Germany in the eighteenth century (1:17). Carlyle, aged sixty when he got under way with the history, recognized that *Frederick the Great* was the "last of [its] kind," a last desperate search for epic closure (Marrs, 719; see Kaplan, 397). This search stretched out the process of writing the history far beyond his expectations but never brought him to the termination he desired.

While in *The French Revolution* Carlyle had written an epic history of a people who could not author an epic myth, in *Frederick the Great* he authored a non-epic history of the creation of an epic nation. The following passages, each representing the spread of rumor, illustrate the differences between the two histories:

> Not so, however, does neighbouring Saint-Antoine look on [the repair of the castle of Vincennes]: Saint-Antoine to whom these peaked turrets and grim donjons, all-too near her own dark dwelling, are of themselves an offence. Was not Vincennes a kind of minor Bastille? Great Diderot and Philosophes have lain in durance here; great Mirabeau, in disastrous eclipse, for forty-two months. And now when the old Bastille has become a dancing-ground (had any one the mirth to dance), and its stones are getting built into the Pont Louis-Seize, does this minor, comparative insignificance of a Bastille

flank itself with fresh-hewn mullions, spread out tyrannous wings; menacing Patriotism? New space for prisoners: and what prisoners? A d'Orleans, with the chief Patriots on the tip of the Left? It is said, there runs "a subterranean passage" all the way from the Tuileries hither. Who knows? Paris, mined with quarries and catacombs, does hang wondrous over the abyss; Paris was once to be blown up,— though the powder, when *we* went to look, had got withdrawn. A Tuileries, sold to Austria and Coblentz, should have no subterranean passage. Out of which might not Coblentz or Austria issue, some morning; and, with cannon of long range, *"foudroyer,"* bethunder a patriotic Saint-Antoine into smoulder and ruin! (*FR*, 2:128–29; first instance of emphasis added)

In Berlin, from Tuesday 31st May 1740, day of the late King's [Frederick Wilhelm's] death, till the Thursday following, the post was stopped and the gates closed. . . .

   Vaguely everywhere there has a notion gone abroad that this young King will prove considerable. Here at last has a Lover of Philosophy got upon the throne, and great philanthropies and magnanimities are to be expected, think rash editors and idle mankind. Rash editors in England and elsewhere, we observe, are ready to believe that Friedrich has not only disbanded the Potsdam Giants; but means to "reduce the Prussian Army one half" or so, for ease, (temporary ease, which we hope will be lasting) of parties concerned; and to go much upon emancipation, political rose-water, and friendship to humanity, as we now call it. (*FG*, 3:278–79)

Because epic represents what people believe, *The French Revolution* merges past and present, reader and history. Already in *Oliver Cromwell's Letters and Speeches*, past and present diverge into the past of Cromwell's large-type letters and speeches and the present of Carlyle's small-type narrative. In *Frederick the Great*, the reader and narrator are radically separated from the narrated past. Both of the passages above employ the present tense, but the passage from *The French Revolution* begins immediately in the present—narrator, readers, and historical actors are contemporaneous—whereas the passage from *Frederick* (typical of the latter work) begins in the past tense, a practice that contextualizes the event as a portion of the past that has no contact with the present.

   Frederick the Great also follows *Oliver Cromwell's Letters and Speeches* in abandoning the use of dramatized speech that unites the narrator and the historical actors in the first-person plural "we." The passage from

The French Revolution, like those discussed in chapter 3, represents polyphonic speech, capturing the paranoia, hyperbole, and fantasy of rumor in St. Antoine. The passage from *Frederick the Great*, by contrast, does not dramatize conflicting opinions and it keeps the narrator and historical audience distinct; there are two "we's," "we" who spread rumors in the past and "we" who "now call" ideas by different names. The latter groups the narrator and reader in an era separate from that of Frederick and his contemporaries, and the narrator further distances himself through irony by designating the speakers' ideas as "rash" and "idle" "political rose-water."

Finally, *Frederick the Great* fails to be epic because, like *Oliver Cromwell's Letters and Speeches*, it does not yield symbolic meaning. Although the thematic conflict between father and son, art and war, provides a symbolic structure for the history, this structure remains in the background, obscured by a forest of detail. As in *Cromwell*, the structure of the history is reduced to mere chronology, and the chapter titles— "Phenomena of the Accession," "At Reinsberg, 1736–1740," "Crown Prince Goes to the Rhine Campaign," "Battle of Kunersdorf"—refer to dates and events rather than symbolic actions. The kind of mythic episode and anecdote that revealed the meaning of the French Revolution most often turns out in *Frederick the Great* to be without meaning or, as in the case of the Jenny Geddes story in *Cromwell's Letters and Speeches*, without historical foundation. Whereas an anecdote like the story of "Margaret with the Pouch-mouth" might in *The French Revolution* have yielded some insight into events, Carlyle here relates it merely "for sake of the Bride's name," and while the folk myths that have arisen around the figure of Frederick might be "the Epic *they* could not write of him," more often than not Carlyle debunks these anecdotes rather than discovering their epic potential (1:135, 6:305). The pattern may be found most clearly in his two narratives of the "world-famous *'Moriamur pro Rege nostro Mariâ Theresiâ.'* " He first narrates the "poetic," and partly "mythical," version, a "very beautiful heroic scene" in which the Hungarian nobility answer Maria Theresa's pleas for aid with a chivalric oath to die for the queen. He then debunks the first version with a "prose" version in which the barons haggle for confirmation of their constitutional rights before they will swear fealty to the queen (4:259–62). By including both versions, Carlyle tries to have it both ways, but he clearly privileges the final debunking version, prose fact displacing poetic myth and symbol. Whereas he had once used the word "mythus" synonymously with "epic" to signify a culture's genuine beliefs, "mythic" now comes to mean simply a story that is untrue (e.g., 4:261, 7:324, 373, 8:7).[22]

Because Carlyle conceives epic as a closed and totalizing myth, especially at this point in his career, the impossibility of achieving authentic closure also means the impossibility of epic. *Frederick the Great* seeks totalizing closure by replacing the multiple voices of history—a plurality of dissenting factions that make closure impossible—with a multiplicity of narrators and narratives. Carlyle splinters himself into personae that represent different aspects of the historian—Scott's Dryasdust, Smollett's Smelfungus, Mr. Rigmarole, the aesthetician Sauerteig (and his aesthetic manifesto, the *Springwurzeln*), and Diogenes Teufelsdröckh—as well as the different stages of historical composition—a "predecessor" of the principal narrator, a "tourist" who has seen the sites of Frederick's battles, a satirical friend of the narrator, a writer whose notebooks the narrator has received, the narrator of an excerpt from an imbroglio of manuscripts, and the editor of the history. By including a representative of each stage of historical interpretation and composition Carlyle would seem to be creating a totality, a history that comprehends every aspect of the past. Yet the different stages of the process of writing history, especially the different historical perspectives, do not seem to add up to a whole so much as they produce a sense of fragmentation.

Carlyle's desire to achieve totality makes it almost impossible for him to decide how to use his historical sources, what to include or exclude. In *The French Revolution*, he revealed the meaning latent in historical documents by transforming them into dialogues and debates. In *Frederick the Great*, he does not perform this kind of transformation of historical documents; instead he simply quotes them at length as if he is unable to discover their latent meaning. Moreover, because he cannot decide which episodes are meaningful and which are not, he seems to feel compelled to include them all. The latter tendency is especially apparent in the practice of setting long passages in small type and the use of multiple parallel narratives that represent simultaneous historical actions. Passages in small type, which include direct quotations of documents like those just discussed, as well as narratives tangential to the main narrative and renarrations in greater detail of material already narrated, account for about one-fifth of the text (Peckham, 205–6). Tangential narratives, like the stories of Margaret with the Pouch-mouth or Laurence Sterne's father at the siege of Gibraltar, do not tell us much about Frederick or his era, but Carlyle includes them because he has no way of deciding what is relevant and what is merely interesting. Particularly indicative of Carlyle's uncertainty about whether he has successfully transformed his material into meaningful history are those passages that simply repeat and amplify the preceding narrative, as if he were trying to discover the second time around what he has missed the first. Instead of reassuring the reader that the narrative is now complete, such amplifications, by demonstrating the inadequacy of the preceding narrative, suggest the possibility of a still more complete narrative that would in turn displace the latter one, the whole process becoming an infinite regress in which one narrative displaces another in a necessarily failed attempt to achieve totality.

Carlyle's desire for totalizing closure was at odds with his desire for closure as the achievement of rest. The latter led him to predict almost as soon as he began writing that he would complete the work quickly, while the former led him to expand the book to twice the length he originally intended—over four thousand pages in six volumes—and to miss deadline after self-imposed deadline from 1856, just a year after he began writing, to 1864, when he was still a year away from finishing.[23] As if desperately trying to control the impulse to digress and repeat, he repeatedly asserts that he is omitting and abridging material, giving the reader the impression that the book might be much longer than it already is (e.g., 1:112, 132, 395, 2:223, 4:27, 28, 38, 50, 55, 103, 7:279, 8:181). Yet all of this work was not enough to "keep [his] heart at *rest*"; still restless after a long day's writing, he felt the need to take relief in horseback riding (*LL*, 1:182). The four-thousand-odd pages of *Frederick the Great* are the correlative of the thirty thousand miles he rode while writing it (*Rem.*, 133).

Carlyle's desire to finish writing *Frederick* and the impulse toward expansion that kept him from succeeding raised his anxieties to such a pitch that he "began to have an apprehension that [he] should never get [his] sad book on Friedrich finished, that it would finish [him] instead" (*LM*, 2:159).[24] If writing *Frederick the Great* was killing him, the impulse that extended the process to such a great length has to be regarded as suicidal. When Frederick, surrounded by a "world of enemies," suicidally throws himself into battle, Carlyle argues that it is not a matter of "puking up one's existence, in the weak sick way of *felo de se;* but, far different, that of dying, if he needs must, as seems too likely, in uttermost spasm of battle" (6:223, 253; see 249, 7:298). In writing *Frederick the Great*, Carlyle, who sometimes spoke approvingly of suicide, similarly threw himself into a labor that would allow him to lose consciousness of himself in the course of performing something like a public duty (Kaplan, 505).

Yet for all the effort he put into it, he was never even certain that Frederick was worth writing about (*NL*, 2:142, 149; *LL*, 2:139–40; *RWE*, 501, 505–6). Was Frederick a reincarnation of Friedrich Wilhelm or the incarnation of an era that "has nothing grand in it, except that grand universal Suicide, named French Revolution?"; was he, like Odin, a great originator, the "Creator of the Prussian Monarchy," or, like the man of letters, a belated hero, the "Last of the Kings?" (1:8, 3, 6). Because Friedrich Wilhelm is always prepared for war and never doubts the value of his martial ethos, he only needs to go to war once in his lifetime. Precisely because Frederick never fully embraces his father's values, he cannot complete the battle of life and must struggle incessantly against his anarchic enemies. Even in the long era of peace following the Seven Years' War, he cannot rest contentedly at Sans Souci, but drives his industrial regiments to death working on land reclamation projects:

> 'When, in the Marshland of the Netze, he counted more the strokes of the 10,000 spades, than the sufferings of the workers, sick with the marsh-fever in the hospitals which he had built for them; when, restless, his demands outran the quickest performance,—there united itself to the deepest reverence and devotedness, in his People, a feeling of awe, as for one whose limbs are not moved by earthly life. . . . And when Goethe, himself become an old man, finished his last Drama' (Second Part of *Faust*), 'the figure of the old King again rose on him, and stept into his Poem; and his Faust got transformed into an unresting, creating, pitilessly exacting Master, forcing-on his salutiferous drains and fruitful canals through the morasses of the Weichsel.' (8:126–27)[25]

Like Faust, Frederick wants to reclaim land so that he can found an ideal society on it, but the process of reclaiming the land destroys the very people who would inhabit his utopia.

Carlyle proclaims from the start of *Frederick the Great* that he has "renounce[d] ideals" and will "take-up with the mournfullest barren realities," that he has not produced a "Fabulous Epic" in which Frederick is invulnerable, but an "Epic of Reality" (1:17, 7:234–35). When he wrote *The French Revolution*, he had been interested in "what *has realized* itself," in "*How* Ideals do and *ought to* adjust themselves with the Actual" (*CL*, 7:24). Now the movement is in the opposite direction, the ideal emerging from the real, poetic myths displaced by prosaic facts. Carlyle wants to argue that art must proceed, not from the ideal, but from the real, the battle of existence. Instead of visionary art quelling the anarchy of war, military drill, he would argue in "Shooting Niagara," can become an art, progressing from "correct marching in line, to rhythmic dancing in cotillon or minuet" (*CME*, 5:42).[26] Appropriately, the only work of all Frederick's writings that Carlyle regards as having any merit is his *Art of War* (*FG*, 5:241).

The process of creating the Prussian state does not involve the attempt to realize an ideal as Samson had done in his monastery or Cromwell in the commonwealth. "Vater Fritz" is an impotent creator who has no children of his own; he has the power to create an orderly state, but his writings are incapable of creating cultural belief. Whereas Carlyle's belief in art, or the ideal, had once led him to imagine it as a force that could enable a society to rise above the battle of existence, art had now become for him merely the refinement of war.

SIX

The End of Writing

I N 1866, the year after Carlyle completed *Frederick the Great*, he trium-
phantly assumed the office of rector of the University of Edinburgh.
But three weeks later, when Jane Carlyle died, he plunged into de-
pression. In the following months, he divided his activities between
the private project of endeavoring to recover the domestic idyll, in
The Reminiscences, and the public attempt to restore the theocratic idyll
through his defense of Governor Eyre and his opposition to the Second Reform Bill, in "Shooting Niagara." During the last decade of
Carlyle's life, the debilities of old age, especially the palsy in his right
hand, made writing more and more difficult, and his literary output
slowed to a trickle.[1] But the silence of his last years was not the repose
he had always sought, the safe enclosure in the domestic idyll of tran-
quillity; it brought him no nearer the end of writing. On the contrary,
his continued yearning for the transcendental idyll left intact, even
made possible, the public world of economy he sought to escape.

Closing Failures in *The Reminiscences* and "Shooting Niagara"

Just a month after Jane Carlyle's death, Thomas began to write a series
of reminiscences, first of Jane herself; then of men they both knew
well, Edward Irving and Francis Jeffrey; and finally of two poets Carlyle had known only slightly, William Wordsworth and Robert Southey.
Written privately—whether or not he intended them to remain private was a point of controversy after his death—they sought, more
directly than any of his writings since the reminiscence of James Carlyle, to recapture the domestic idyll. They contrast a pastoral vision of
Scotland with the metropolis of London, and they make the process
of narrating a means of escape from present pain—his wife's death,
the chaos of contemporary society—into the past of memory.

163

Carlyle dwells insistently on the Scottish scenes in *The Reminis-cences*, clearly preferring them to the "London bits of *memorabilia*," which do "not disengage themselves from the general mass, as the earlier Craigenputtock ones" do (114). Using the contrast with Lon-don throughout *The Reminiscences*, always to the advantage of Scotland and Craigenputtoch, he revives the dream that the latter had been more congenial to literary production, that he could "do fully *twice* as much work in a given time there" (58). The Irving and Jeffrey of *The Reminiscences* both achieve their greatest successes in their native land and are ruined by London. Irving is "genially happy" in the "sunny islets" of Annandale, and Jeffrey achieves acclaim as the editor of the *Edinburgh Review* (229, 244). Each goes to London in search of greater success but only finds failure. Irving falls into heresy, loses his congregation, and dies; Jeffrey, forced to spend many "unwhole-some hours" in the "noisy hubbub of St. Stephen's," fails in Parliament, becomes "completely miserable," and is forced to return to Scotland to recover his health (331). By contrast, Carlyle, recognizing, during his 1824 sojourn, that London is "worse than Tartarus, with all its Phlegethons and Stygian quagmires," rejects the city in favor of the "russet-coated Idyll" at Hoddam Hill (281–82). Yet, by implying that in spirit he had never really left Scotland, that by remaining within the idyll of literature he had sustained the idyll even in London, he sup-presses the reverse possibility: that he can never escape the alienation of urban economy. In fact, although Carlyle frequently visited Scot-land, he never found permanent rest there, and he lived out the last years of his life in London. Like the heroes he had so often described, he could only achieve rest in death, and it was only in death that, ac-cording to his wishes, he returned permanently to Scotland and joined his parents in the Ecclefechan churchyard (Froude, *My Relations with Carlyle*, 71).

Carlyle's contradictory desires and aims in writing *The Reminiscences* are manifest in the contrast between his representation of Jane Carlyle as the center of the Scottish idyll and the pain he knew she suffered there. She is both the idyll itself—an "Eldorado" that "screen[s] [him] from pain"—and its creator—transforming darkness into light and creating "a little Eden round her" (163, 125, 70; see 305).[2] Carlyle had looked forward to Craigenputtoch in 1828 as a "green oasis," but had left it when the oasis withered and became a "Dunscore Desert"

(*CL*, 4:407, 7:280). In the reminiscence of Jane Carlyle, it takes Jane to make "the Desert blossom," to transform their "wild moorland home" into a "fairy palace" where they spent their "happiest days" (57). Through Jane, he suggests, the Scottish idyll could be made to bloom even in the deserts of London.

In writing *The Reminiscences*, Carlyle was not simply struggling to escape the alienations of literary commerce, however; he also sought, through the process of writing, relief from the guilt and remorse that followed Jane Carlyle's death. Although *The Reminiscences* are putatively about her and those who knew her, they frequently stray from her in order to dwell on genealogies, anecdotes, and chronologies related to her only tangentially, if at all. But he finds so much "solace" in the "refuge" of writing them that he cannot persuade himself to stop, even though he frequently chides himself for "defrauding" Jane (114; see 49, 55, 79, 167–69). Reluctant to reach the end of the narrative, he is driven to write the subsequent reminiscences, especially "Wordsworth" and "Southey," for which he had little enthusiasm—as much by the desire to sustain the solacing process of writing as to commemorate the lives of his mere acquaintances (307, 343).[3] Yet this desire to expand the narrative is at odds with the desire for closure represented by the Scottish idyll. Indeed, Carlyle expands the idyllic narrative, in which he represents Jane Carlyle as fundamentally happy, as a way of suppressing his guilty knowledge of the pain and sorrow he had in fact caused her (e.g., 125, 156).[4]

But if Carlyle narrated in order to forget the misery he had caused, he also wrote the reminiscence as a "religious course of worship" and a "little 'Shrine of pious Memory,'" in order to "expiate" it (89, 139; see 111, 155, 159, 275). Transferring his guilt about the pain he had caused Jane into guilt at indulging in "idle work" that has no public purpose, he makes his need to expiate a motive for more writing and for public action (79; see 90). The idealized image of Jane Carlyle he has created will inspire him to take part once again in public affairs. "I am gone, loved one," he imagines her saying to him, "work a little longer, if thou still canst; if not, follow!" (128; see 89, 157, 167). To imagine that Jane would command him to work—work that would inevitably take the form of writing, since "writing is [the] one thing [he] can do"—was to imagine that she forgave him for having been so obsessed with his own problems that he did not recognize her suffering

(*LL*, 2:369).[5] It was as much for himself as in obedience to her that he became advisor to the Eyre Defense Committee and wrote "Shooting Niagara."

The Eyre controversy and the question of reform were closely related in the public mind, and both were major topics of parliamentary debate in the spring of 1866, when England was disturbed by social unrest of a kind not seen since 1848. The Jamaica rebellion, brutally suppressed by Eyre, had taken place in the autumn of 1865; throughout 1866 there were Fenian disturbances both in Ireland and in England; and in July a riot broke out when public officials tried to prevent a public meeting in Hyde Park. In these circumstances, Disraeli, perceiving that reform was inevitable, introduced the bill that, after considerable modification, became law in August 1867.

"Shooting Niagara" responds directly to the Second Reform Bill— it was published in August 1867, the month in which it received its third and final reading—but also deals with the social unrest represented by the Hyde Park riots and the Jamaica rebellion. Like *Latter-Day Pamphlets*, "Shooting Niagara" is a bitter and despairing polemic in reaction to events both personal and public; its tone is altogether different from the mood of the inaugural address, delivered just two years earlier, that had concluded, like *Past and Present*, with the optimistic words from Goethe's "Symbolum": "We bid you be of hope!" (*CME*, 4:482). Although the criticisms in "Shooting Niagara" are directed against the reform bill, which it regards as symptomatic of England's social problems, it did not seek to reverse the bill (it appeared too late to affect the outcome of the parliamentary debate) but to urge a yet more radical reform that would bypass Parliament altogether. Even this was not entirely new, and Carlyle's analysis of England's social problems here remains fundamentally what it had been in *Chartism*, *Past and Present*, and *Latter-Day Pamphlets*. But he significantly altered his proposals by recasting them in terms of the shift from ideal to real he had made in *Frederick the Great* and in response to the Eyre controversy.[6]

In the first part of the essay, Carlyle appears to return to an earlier phase of his social criticism when he calls on a speculative (i.e., literary-religious) aristocracy to "restor[e] God and whatever was Godlike in the traditions and recorded doings of Mankind" (*CME*, 5:30);[7] an industrial aristocracy to restore justice and honesty by "build[ing]" an economy based, not on temporary contracts, but on relationships that will "stand till the Day of Judgment" (*CME*, 5:34); and a titled aristocracy to restore hierarchy and reign as kings on their estates. He imagines these religious, economic, and political aristocracies working quietly together, outside of the formal institutions of government, until they rise in the public esteem and their authority is acknowledged. The aim would be to change social institutions by changing the beliefs of the people; the public would obey these aristocracies, not because it was coerced, but because it had come to believe in them. But, as the essay proceeds, it becomes clear that the Carlyle of *Latter-Day Pamphlets* and *Frederick the Great*, who believes that no "argument of human intellect" can change his contemporaries, has not disappeared (*CME*, 5:4). Speculative aristocrats, he concludes, will continue to "waste themselves" in "Literature" (which in fifty years will sink "to the rank of street-fiddling"); the industrial aristocracy will continue producing "cheap and nasty" goods, despoiling the cities, and exploiting labor; and the political aristocracy, even the conservatives (he is thinking of the followers of Disraeli who supported the reform bill), will continue to confine themselves to self-serving parliamentary politics (*CME*, 5:24, 26).[8]

As in *Frederick the Great*, the ideal gives way to the real, and Carlyle turns to war, rather than art, as the means to transform the nation, imagining a scenario in which social disturbances like the Jamaican rebellion and the Hyde Park riots will multiply until England plunges into open civil war. In these circumstances, the literary aristocracy, which has no power, and the economic aristocracy, which has no ethos, will both be powerless, so it will be left to the political aristocracy to restore social order through military force. In contrast to the peaceful aristocrat, whom he initially depicts as "mould[ing] and manag[ing] everything, till both his people and his dominion correspond gradually to the *ideal* he has formed. . . . Till the whole surroundings of a nobleman [are] made noble like himself," he envisions a saving remnant of titled warriors turning their estates into training grounds where they establish order through military discipline (*CME*, 5:37; emphasis added).

Drawing on his portrait of Frederick and his defense of Governor Eyre, Carlyle thus envisions a radical transformation of society. When he argues that England cannot survive under common law, that it must embrace martial law, which, he claims, is "anterior to all written laws" and "coeval with Human Society," he is referring directly to the Eyre case and responding to Chief Justice Alexander Cockburn's six-hour peroration arguing that "the law of England knew no such thing as 'Martial law'" (*CME*, 5:12; Semmel, 153).[9] Several hundred people had been executed and many more flogged when Edward Eyre, the governor of Jamaica, declared martial law in response to a local uprising. Among those executed was George Gordon, an outspoken critic of the colonial government, who was illegally transported into the area where martial law was in effect and executed with Eyre's approval.

The issue that concerned many was that if Eyre could use martial law to punish Gordon, then martial law could also be declared in England to deprive citizens of their legitimate rights. Carlyle, too, considered the case relevant to England—the reference to the Eyre case is preceded by a discussion of the Hyde Park riots—but he reverses the terms; whereas others argued that, since what Eyre did would have been intolerable and illegal in England it was wrong to do it in Jamaica, Carlyle argues that the English aristocracy will need to act as Eyre had in Jamaica, that only military discipline can produce social order. As in *Frederick the Great*, he no longer imagines that the poetic hero can create a belief that will produce a social order, but insists that social order must be produced by coercive political power. Indeed, interweaving the various strands of his argument, he imagines Frederick the Great and Friedrich Wilhelm turning the Caribbean island of Dominica—a stand-in for Jamaica or even the British Isles—into a fertile kingdom that would embody his ideal of a martial and hierarchical society, the lower ground worked by a million black slaves and the upper portion of the island—"salubrious and delightful for the European"—occupied by a hundred thousand white slave masters (*CME*, 5:17). There was nothing in the politics of the day to drive Carlyle to this abhorrent vision; it was simply his inability to imagine any alternative—in particular, his inability to find a source of authority in literature and the processes of cultural formation.

The Eyre Controversy and the Dilemma of Literature

Like the Huxley-Wilberforce debate that signaled the victory of science over traditional religion despite much popular sentiment to the contrary, the Eyre controversy played out a conflict between literature and economy in which the men of letters won only a Pyrrhic victory over the advocates of classical liberalism. Even though Carlyle had turned to the institution of monarchy, rather than literature, as the means to oppose political economy and produce a social ethos with transcendental authority, he continued to write as a man of letters. In spite of the fact that he always considered it incapable of producing belief, it was increasingly the discourse of political economy, rather than literary discourse, that compelled belief. Because literature had withdrawn from the realm of political action into the transcendental idyll, it had not only failed as a worthy opponent to political economy, it had left political economy in possession of the realm of politics, thus helping to establish its authority.

In June of 1866, after a government commission removed Governor Eyre from office though arguing that his actions had been justified, John S. Mill and the Jamaica Committee decided to prosecute him for murder. When, in response, the Eyre Defense Committee was formed, Carlyle was the first prominent individual to join it. Since Mill was accompanied by a formidable group of public figures—Thomas Huxley, Frederic Harrison, Thomas Hughes, Herbert Spencer, John Bright, Charles Darwin, and Leslie Stephen—Carlyle felt it necessary to enlist an equally prominent group on the other side—John Ruskin, John Tyndall, Charles Dickens, Alfred Tennyson, and Henry Kingsley (see Ford; Workman; August, xxvii–xxxi; and Hall). The men on Mill's Jamaica Committee wrote in the scientific mode of economic discourse, the discourse of rationalized efficiency, while the authors on the Eyre Defense Committee employed the religiously inflected discourse of literature. Chief Justice Cockburn wrote his directions to the jury in the former mode, leaving little doubt that he thought Eyre should stand trial; but the grand jury, apparently more persuaded by the latter mode of discourse and reflecting widespread public sentiment, dismissed the case. The public could afford to follow the men of letters for, even setting aside other issues such as racial prejudice, they had no immediate interest in the case—which, however, did not stop them from embracing the fundamental principles espoused by Mill and taking the primacy of their own individual rights for granted. The same public that would allow the rights of a mulatto to be ignored already accepted many of the principles Mill put forward in respect of them.

Rather than regarding the discourses of literature and economy as diametrically opposed, it would be more accurate to see them as complementary, Mill's discourse providing the ideological ground for the dominant mode of conflictual social relations, and Carlyle's providing the middle classes with a compensatory vision of a secure social order. The discourse of economy claims to describe things as they are, while that of literature claims to describe things as they ought to be. Literature concedes that economy correctly analyzes and describes the world in history but insists that the world need not *be* in history, that if we were to return to the transcendental idyll, literature, not economy, would provide the "right" representation of reality. By confining its ability to define ethos to the transcendental or even to the private domestic sphere, literature legitimates economy, for the time being, in the public sphere. Carlyle could imagine ethos as a function of the social ideal, but he could not imagine it as part of a historical process; Mill could conceive of ethos as a social process, but could only see it in terms of the limits of the individual, not as the function of a social ideal.

The summer before the Jamaica rebellion, Mill had been elected to Parliament and sentiment in favor of a new reform bill was on the increase, but the prospects for passage remained slight because Palmerston resolutely opposed it. On the day Palmerston died (October 18, 1865), Carlyle, recognizing like his contemporaries that reform was now inevitable, sat down to draft a reply to Mill's *On Liberty*, the text that codified the classic principles of liberal individualism that would be embodied in the bill. Although Carlyle had been disturbed by the book when he first read it upon its appearance in 1859, it was only when Mill appeared to be on the verge of turning his principles into law that he felt compelled to respond.[10] The central issue that Carlyle's fragmentary response to *On Liberty* sought to address was the problem of ethos, how one controls the behavior of the self-interested individual. Defining justice in terms of the rights of individuals, Mill had insisted that individuals can be suppressed only when their actions infringe on the rights of others: "Advice, instruction, persuasion, and avoidance by other people if thought necessary for their own good, are the only measures by which society can justifiably express its dislike or disapprobation" (87). Carlyle attempted to refute Mill by arguing that this limitation of individual action does not provide a true ethos, that Mill's principle allows an individual to act wrongly so long as that wrong action does not affect anyone else. He concludes, as one might expect, that the solution is to discover a transcendental standard: "All turns on his course *being* verily Hellward, and of your persuasions, if they articulated themselves in the form of regulation, observable by human care & prudence and coercions and compulsions, being verily Heavenward" (Trela, "Review of Mill's *Liberty*," 25).

The Eyre case provided a symbolic arena for debating this conflict between the need for social and individual justice. Mill argued that it was a case of Gordon's individual rights under English law, and that English law did not allow martial law to displace common law. Carlyle argued that it was a matter of the social order as a whole: that it was "as if a ship had been on fire; the captain [i.e., Eyre] by immediate and bold exertion, had put the fire out, and had been called to account for having flung a bucket or two of water in the hold beyond what was necessary. He had damaged some of the cargo, perhaps, but he had saved the ship" (*LL*, 2:351–52). In the more positive form of his argument, Mill would make the forming of social consensus the historical process of defining social justice. But by taking the individual as the basis of his description of ethos, he provides a picture of society in perpetual conflict, individuals walled off from one another in self-defense. Carlyle attempts to provide a corrective by making society as a whole the basis of his analysis, but when, instead of seeking consensus as a historical and social process, he insists that governors and ruling classes have transcendental authority, he merely justifies authoritarian coercion.[11]

In his reminiscences of Edward Irving and Francis Jeffrey, written while he was working on the Eyre case, Carlyle represents the dilemma of literature situated midway between Irving's religious domain, in which he no longer believes, and Jeffrey's economic domain, in which he cannot bear to reside. In "Edward Irving," he assumes the position of the Voltairean skeptic in order to reject speaking in tongues and transcendental religion; in "Francis Jeffrey," he assumes the position of "mystic" in order to reject "dead Edinburgh Whiggism, Scepticism, and Materialism" (*Rem.*, 320; see 344). When Irving opposes the Reform Bill of 1832 as a "thing forbidden," Carlyle supports it (293); when Jeffrey assumes that Whig reform will truly transform society, Carlyle claims to become skeptical and to harbor a secret sympathy for John Croker Wilson and the Tory *Blackwood's Magazine* (328, 330). Because the law, consistent with the discourse of economy, is a self-referential system that ignores the question of real guilt or innocence in favor of its own processes, Jeffrey's "advocate morality" permits him to obtain acquittal for a murderer whose guilt seems certain. Carlyle concludes that the law is no longer concerned with justice, but has become enfolded in the economic system, the lawyer allowing his "intellect, [his] highest heavenly gift, [to be] hung up in the shop-window . . . for sale" (313). But Irving offers no alternative, his transcendental authority collapsing when he becomes isolated in a private world of Coleridgean moonshine. Both, for Carlyle, become self-enclosed, unable to author a social ethos.[12]

When in 1832 Carlyle discovered that he was becoming isolated in the private world of art at Craigenputtoch, he might have concluded that literature should engage in the public construction of values; but instead he decided to subordinate literature to the transcendental hero, who would discover, and compel society to accept, transcendental values. Carlyle's authoritarianism derived from the same division between private and public, transcendence and history, that underlay his early belief in literature. Because he continued to assume that the public domain consists of self-interested individuals, he always regarded the social process as fundamentally anarchic and therefore could never acknowledge that a just social order might be based on anything other than an apprehension of absolute and transcendental values. If the man of letters could not transmit those values peaceably through visionary insight, then the political dictator as divinely authorized hero would do it by force.

The alliance of literary culture and political authority against the depredations of political economy inevitably made its way into the works of Carlyle's contemporaries and successors even though they, more often than not, rejected his authoritarianism as well as his later anti-aestheticism. This alliance manifests itself directly in Matthew Arnold's *Culture and Anarchy*, which, like "Shooting Niagara," was written in response to the Hyde Park riots and the Reform Bill of 1867. Although Arnold seems to have preferred the first alternative offered by Carlyle in "Shooting Niagara"—using the authority of culture (i.e., literature) to create social order—he went even further, suggesting that culture can confer on the state the authority to coerce obedience from the masses (*Culture and Anarchy*, 96; see Wolf; Lloyd; Arac, *Critical Genealogies*, 135–36). Arnold means to say that culture will provide the state with the transcendental authority which will ensure that its laws are just—that, as Carlyle puts it, its course is "Heavenward."

But if culture does not truly possess transcendental authority—and it has been the thrust of this study to show that Carlyle and the Victorians were never able to establish how to verify such authority—then it merely serves to encourage the people to accept state coercion. Indeed, the Arnoldian principle of "disinterestedness"—his insistence that culture separate itself from the public domain and the political process—does not so much lend authority to the state as make the ethical imperatives of culture appear irrelevant to it. Like Carlyle's, Arnold's implicitly pastoral and idyllic notion of culture fails to become part of the process of creating social values, because it denies human history. It is of a piece with many other nineteenth-century visions of an idyll in which all human relationships are just and a haven from which the public domain can be disinterestedly criticized—for example, Dickens's "Christmas," Ruskin's "Gothic Eden," Tennyson's Round Table, Newman's primitive church, and the many versions of the preindustrial countryside, from Cobbett and Coleridge to Dickens and Eliot. But these idyllic communities finally fail as models for human society precisely because, as private transcendental spaces, they deny the historical process through which social consensus is continuously shaped and reshaped. With the possible exception of the later George Eliot, none of these writers—it is no coincidence that several joined Carlyle in the defense of Edward Eyre—was able to imagine that a community could create its own standards.

Literary culture, claiming that it can enable one to escape the alienations created by economy, still remains a retreat from the public sphere. If literature is to have public meaning, however, it must neither adopt the value-free discourse of economic efficiency nor continue to mimic the transcendental discourse of religious mysticism. Rather, it must enter the public domain of social dialogue and become genuinely critical. The idyllic vision of the nineteenth century did have a critical purpose; although its idylls were often retreats from society, they were also vantage points from which to criticize existing social structures (see Williams, *Culture and Society*, 43). Unfortunately, this critical method tended to reinforce the existing structures by setting up absolute polarities—implicit in the oppositions of transcendence and history, public and private—rather than dialectical contraries. Victorian social critics often portrayed the very voices of criticism as the source or sign of social fragmentation, the "dissidence of dissent" as the din of Babel. These critics, paradoxically, disliked criticism because they sought, like Carlyle, to achieve silence by silencing the opposition rather than by seeking ways to mediate among dissenting voices. Because its object was to make culture static, literature's participation in the process of cultural formation tended to be negative and limited. Only if literature can relinquish its claims to transcendental authority and enter into the collective historical process through which beliefs and laws are shaped can it eventually fulfill the mission that Carlyle and his contemporaries envisioned for it.

Abbreviations

The following abbreviations are used for Carlyle's collected and uncollected writings and selected frequently cited texts. Full bibliographical information may be found in Works Cited.

CL	*Collected Letters of Thomas and Jane Welsh Carlyle.* Ed. C. R. Sanders et al.
CME	*Critical and Miscellaneous Essays* (five volumes).
EL	James A. Froude. *Thomas Carlyle: A History of the First Forty Years of His Life.*
FG	*The History of Frederick the Great.* 8 vols.
FR	*The French Revolution.* 3 vols.
HGL	*Carlyle's Unfinished History of German Literature.* Ed. Hill Shine.
HHW	*On Heroes and Hero-Worship, and the Heroic in History.*
HL	*Lectures on the History of Literature.* Ed. J. Reay Greene.
HS	*Historical Sketches.* Ed. Alexander Carlyle.
Kaplan	Fred Kaplan. *Thomas Carlyle: A Biography.*
LDP	*Latter-Day Pamphlets.*
LJS	*The Life of John Sterling.*
LL	James A. Froude. *Thomas Carlyle: A History of His Life in London.*
LM	*Letters and Memorials of Jane Welsh Carlyle.* Ed. James Anthony Froude.
LMSB	*Letters of Thomas Carlyle to John Stuart Mill, John Sterling and Robert Browning.* Ed. Alexander Carlyle.
LS	*The Life of Schiller.*
NL	*New Letters of Thomas Carlyle.* Ed. Alexander Carlyle.
NLM	*New Letters and Memorials of Jane Welsh Carlyle.* Ed. Alexander Carlyle.
OCLS	*Oliver Cromwell's Letters and Speeches.* 5 vols.
PP	*Past and Present.*
Rem.	*Reminiscences.* Ed. Charles Eliot Norton.

RIJ   *Reminiscences of My Irish Journey in 1849.*
RWE   *The Correspondence of Emerson and Carlyle.* Ed. Joseph Slater.
Spedding   "Thomas Carlyle and Thomas Spedding: Their Friendship
           and Correspondence." Ed. Alexander Carlyle.
SR   *Sartor Resartus.*
TNB   *Two Note Books of Thomas Carlyle.* Ed. Charles Eliot Norton.
TR   *Two Reminiscences of Thomas Carlyle.* Ed. John Clubbe.
WM   *Wilhelm Meister's Apprenticeship and Travels.* 2 vols.
WR   *Wotton Reinfred.*

Notes

Preface

1. The importance of the work done on the early writings of Carlyle in the past thirty years should not be underestimated, and this study would not have been possible without it, yet it is nonetheless the case that the number of studies focused on *Sartor Resartus* continues to equal, or nearly equal, studies of all the other works combined. As G. B. Tennyson has written in his bibliographical essay on Carlyle, "What is now needed is for some of the serious and capable critical attention directed to *Sartor* and some of the techniques developed in modern *Sartor* and general Carlyle criticism—as in the works of Holloway, Tennyson, Levine, LaValley, and others—to be directed to other Carlyle works" ("Thomas Carlyle," 99–100). The tendency to focus on Carlyle's development up to the time of writing his masterwork, *Sartor Resartus*, has been present from the beginnings of modern Carlyle studies and has continued in recent years. Studies in this category include much of the best criticism of Carlyle, for example, C. F. Harrold's *Carlyle and German Thought*, Hill Shine's *Carlyle's Fusion of Poetry, History, and Religion by 1834*, G. B. Tennyson's *Sartor Called Resartus*, and Jacques Cabau's *Le Prométhée Enchaîné*. This tendency is most marked in otherwise sound and important studies that focus on the development of Carlyle's thought on particular issues rather than on particular works, but which nonetheless do not pursue the development of these ideas beyond the midpoint of his career, studies like Philip Rosenberg's *The Seventh Hero* and Ruth apRoberts's *Ancient Dialect*. Rosenberg stops his discussion with *Past and Present* (1843) because, he argues, Carlyle did not develop any "new insight, even a deplorable one" after that date. Rosenberg concludes that "these writings seem . . . scarcely worth reading and even less worth writing about" (p. x). One cannot help but notice that the later Carlyle does not accord very well with the very attractive Carlyle whom Rosenberg portrays in his book. It is only fair to add that there have been some excellent studies that do examine Carlyle's entire career, most notably George Levine's *The Boundaries of Fiction* as well as his "Use and Abuse of Carlylese," and Albert J. LaValley's *Carlyle and the Idea of the Modern*.

Chapter 1

1. Concommitant with these shifts in the authority of religious discourse were attacks on the hierarchical principle through which the institution of the

church was governed, the Reformation substituting less hierarchical or anti-hierarchical schemes like episcopacy, presbyterianism, and congregationalism for the Roman hierarchy (see Bendix, 293). In the nineteenth century, dissenters and utilitarians alike successfully challenged the union of church and state and the privileged position of the Anglican hierarchy.

2. I distinguish the rise of an explicit, written doctrine of patriarchy from the origins of patriarchy in Western culture. On the former, see Schochet, who argues that it does not become a full-fledged doctrine of political obligation until 1603 (16, 98); on the latter, see Lerner.

3. In addition, contemporary historians could point to changes in the English constitution—the former existence of feudalism, for example—as proof that government changes and that, therefore, it is not passed along genetically in unchanging form (see Pocock).

4. The word *literature* itself only came to designate artistic texts in the course of the nineteenth century (see Todorov; Williams, *Keywords*, 183–88; Kernan, 7, 259–64; and Parrinder, 20–21). René Wellek adds a corrective by insisting that there are important precedents for the modern usage, but his argument ultimately demonstrates that the word *literature* did not come to designate a body of imaginative texts until the late eighteenth century ("What Is Literature?" 16–23). In Gissing's *New Grub Street* (1891), Alfred Yule notes the evolution of the term: "And apropos of that, when was the word 'literature' first used in our modern sense to signify a body of writing? In Johnson's day it was pretty much the equivalent of our 'culture.'. . . His dictionary, I believe, defines the word as 'learning, skill in letters'—nothing else" (434).

5. Although Coleridge's *Constitution of Church and State* did not appear until after Carlyle's ideas were fairly well formed, it had been in progress for a long time and many of its ideas had appeared in Coleridge's earlier works.

6. Carlyle's knowledge of economic theory should not be underestimated. In the early 1820s, he translated the article on "Political Economy" by Simonde de Sismondi—one of the earliest critics of industrial capitalism—for Brewster's *Edinburgh Encyclopedia*. Carlyle's critique of laissez-faire appeared as early as 1831 when he wrote: "the principle of *Laissez-faire* is fast verging . . . to a consummation. *Let people go on,* each without guidance, each striving only to gain advantage for himself, the result will be this: Each, endeavouring by 'competition' to outstrip the others, will endeavour by all arts to manufacture an article (not better) only *cheaper* and *showier* than his neighbour" (*TNB*, 206; see also *WR*, 24; *SR*, 159; *HGL*, 5; *CL*, 5:183–84).

7. In so characterizing Carlyle, I am looking forward to his renewed interest in the civil wars in the late 1830s; but his sympathy with the Puritans and the Scottish rebels, whom he considered his own ancestors, was lifelong (see *CME*, 4:178).

8. Jacques Lacan's imaginary and symbolic realms have contributed to my

understanding of the dialectic described in this paragraph; it will be further explored in chapter 2.

Chapter 2

1. On the literary career in the nineteenth century, see Said, 236–75; Arac, *Commissioned Spirits*, 23.

2. The edition cited is a revision of an edition published in 1833. For a discussion of the representation of the family as a preindustrial idyll, see Davidoff et al. There is a similar relationship between family and pastoral in Dickens (see Marcus, chaps. 4 and 5; Welsh, chap. 9).

3. Carlyle represents the long course of ill health that began in 1790 and continued until his early death (at age forty-five) in 1805 as a correlative of Schiller's endless wanderings. Just as Schiller wandered in search of rest from wandering, so his "unceasing toil" in quest of emotional health produced illness (105). The relationship between Carlyle's own dyspepsia and his quest for psychic health will be discussed in chapter 3.

4. Tennyson dates the poem before 1825, and David Masson dates it before 1821 (Tennyson, 62, n. 45). Tarr and McClelland agree that, although the poem could have been composed as late as 1830, the early 1820s seems the most likely date (135–36).

5. He had finished translating the second part of *Wilhelm Meister* just before beginning these attempts at fiction, and its influence is clear. Apart from its opening, *Wotton Reinfred* has much more in common with *Meister* than with *Werter*. Like Meister, Reinfred sets out on a journey after losing his beloved to another man. The House in the Wold, where freethinkers engage in highly philosophical conversations, resembles Lothario's castle, where Wilhelm discovers a secret society of men dedicated to higher knowledge. Wotton discovers his rival in the House in the Wold, just as Meister encounters the husband of the countess he had nearly fallen in love with in Lothario's castle. Finally, *Wotton Reinfred* owes a great deal to the style and narrative methods of *Wilhelm Meister*.

6. "Illudo Chartis" also records the father's death, which apparently occurs sometime after he sends Stephen to the university. No mention is made of the death of the mother in either narrative. The stern father motif also occurs in other narratives, especially the lives of Burns and Goethe (*CME*, 1:293; *WM*, 1:13).

7. That it is truly an ideal society and an Elysium is also questionable. Although the inhabitants discuss transcendentalism, it is not certain that they live transcendentally. Carlyle's semiparodic representation of the Coleridgean figure Dalbrook will be discussed below in chapter 3.

8. In addition to Schiller and Goethe, Carlyle most frequently draws on

his depiction of Richter in producing his representation of Teufelsdröckh. The title of the chapter under discussion echoes his description of Richter's childhood as "idyllic" (*CME*, 2:109–10).

9. In addition to the biographical and fictional narratives Carlyle used as resources for his construction of Teufelsdröckh's career, he undoubtedly drew on *Wilhelm Meister*, in which the father/son relationship anticipates *Sartor Resartus* in a number of ways. Wilhelm comes into conflict with his father over his career, Wilhelm wishing to study art instead of going into commerce like his father. Wilhelm's father had sold off his own father's collection of art, including a painting of a king's son dying of love for the father's bride. (Similarly, Schiller's *Don Carlos*—a play concerned with monarchical authority—involves a father who condemns his son to death and marries his son's beloved, turning his Garden of Eden into a desert of despair [*LS*, 64]). While on his journey, Wilhelm is introduced to the works of Shakespeare, who becomes his substitute father, and inevitably becomes obsessed with the play that revolves around the relationship of father and son, *Hamlet* (1:244). Finally, the death of Wilhelm's father frees him to commit himself to art and the search for knowledge, and Wilhelm reaches an important stage when he recognizes in himself the father of Felix and adopts Mignon as his daughter.

10. The early death of the father may also be found in the biographies of Richter and Werner. Werner, like Teufelsdröckh, subsequently becomes a "Wandering Jew" (*CME*, 1:131).

11. Carlyle was also drawing on *Wilhelm Meister's Travels*, subtitled *The Renunciants* (*CME*, 2:15; *SR*, 191; see also 186, n. 4).

12. Not long thereafter, according to another late report, Carlyle admitted to his friend Irving that he had lost his faith in Christianity (*Rem.*, 225). Note, however, that David Masson reports the episode as the end of a process rather than a critical event in itself, claiming that it was "from that first well-remembered reading of Gibbon in twelve days, at the rate of a volume a day, that he dated the extirpation from his mind of the last remnant that had been left in it of the orthodox belief in miracles" (263–64). What counts here is the imaginative reconstitution of events, not their "reality." There is no precise date at which one can fix Carlyle's loss of faith; we know only from the letters that the sufferings of disbelief intensified around 1819 (see *EL*, 1:64–68; Kaplan, 48–59; Allingham, *Diary*, 232, 253, 268; Wilson, 1:78, 132–33, 145–47).

13. He seems to have begun learning German both to study mineralogy and to read the authors he had learned of through Mme. de Staël (*CL*, 5:136; see Campbell and Tarr). While Carlyle might have found the idea of literature as replacement for religion in Coleridge, he always attributed it to the Germans. Although it seems likely that he had read Coleridge's criticism, I can find no references to it in Carlyle's writings before 1823 (*TNB*, 46–47; Shine, *Carlyle's Early Reading*, 69, no. 455).

14. See *CME*, 3:16, 58, 119; *LS*, 46; *WM*, 1:113. His second major review article, "The State of German Literature" (1827), summed up his view of German literature as a new religious creed, the article's conclusion equating religion and literature (*CME*, 3:85). Correlatively, writers, like Jeffrey, about whom Carlyle had reservations were excluded from the priesthood of literature (*TNB*, 175).

15. The linkage between poetry and revelation, prophecy, and inspiration appears frequently in Carlyle's early writings (see *TNB*, 211; *LS*, 201; *CME*, 2:94–95; *HGL*, 5; *SR*, 224).

16. The comparison of poet and king, ruler, lawmaker appears repeatedly in his writings. He claimed that the "writer of the first Book in a language . . . must be ranked by the nation he writes for, infinitely higher than any conqueror or lawgiver" (*HGL*, 28). In comparing the institution of literature to the church, he had also called it "our Senate, our whole Social Constitution" (*CME*, 2:369). He compared Burns to a legislator and argued that Johnson's true calling was not for literature but for the more active political arena, "as Statesman (in the higher, now obsolete sense), Lawgiver, Ruler" (*CME*, 1:287, 3:92; see also *SR*, 45; *TNB*, 139; *HGL*, 28; *CME*, 1:287, 2:369, 3:92).

17. See also *CME*, 2:372, 398. Shakespeare is also implicitly a king, since he "knew (*kenned*, which in those days still partially meant *can-ned*) innumerable things" (*CME*, 3:142–43).

18. This description appeared in a letter to Goethe describing his projected (and never completed) history of German literature. In this letter, Goethe's era explicitly succeeds an era of skepticism. A similar pattern and attitude may be seen as late as 1832 (*CL*, 6:123; see *CME*, 3:178).

19. One must take into account the circumstance that Carlyle was a young author seeking to ingratiate himself with the master. He certainly had reservations about Goethe, but in a letter to a friend he did claim, in spite of these reservations, that he "could sometimes fall down and worship" this adopted father (*CL*, 2:437; see Ikeler, 27–29, 73–77).

20. The novels were "Illudo Chartis," *Wotton Reinfred*, and an epistolary novel he proposed to coauthor with Jane Welsh (*CL*, 2:229–31). He did manage to complete a short story, "Cruthers and Jonson," in 1822 (published 1830).

21. Carlyle also implicitly compares his father's building to texts in two later statements in the reminiscence discussed below (7, 33). Linda Peterson's reading of *Sartor Resartus* as a text that employs the hermeneutic technique of biblical interpretation is equally appropriate to the "Reminiscence of James Carlyle," which could be regarded as an interpretation of the meaning of his father's life for him (chap. 2).

22. As C. F. Harrold notes, Carlyle alludes to the etymological derivation of pontiff from the Latin "*pons + facere,* bridge builder, originally applied to Roman Magistrates whose sacred function it was to superintend the building

and demolition of bridges." The word was later "applied to priests at Rome, then to the Pope" (*SR*, 79, n. 5). The theme of the bridge as medium connecting the natural and supernatural worlds also occurs in Tieck's "The Elves," a work Carlyle translated for *German Romance* (see Cabau, 120–21, 168–73).

23. Kaplan notes, significantly, that Margaret Carlyle actively opposed the separation decided upon by James (24). Carlyle does attempt to argue that his education did not separate him from his father and family. His father, he says, had disregarded the warning that if he educated his son, he would "grow up to despise his ignorant parents" and had later assured him that the prophecy had not been fulfilled (*Rem.*, 12). But the fact that Carlyle needs assurance in itself betrays his anxiety that education has separated them, and the metaphorical resonances are clear when he writes that, after going to school at age ten, he "was never *habitually* beside" his father again (28).

24. Froude describes Carlyle's "real passion" for his mother, their mutual "passionate attachment of a quite peculiar kind," and asserts that the "strongest personal passion" that Carlyle "experienced through all his life was his affection for his mother" (*EL*, 1:35, 47, 239). He also argues that the attachment persisted even after Carlyle's marriage, depicting Carlyle and his mother driving about in a gig, "smoking their pipes together, like a pair of lovers—as indeed they were" (*LL*, 1:178). Kaplan concurs and expands Froude's reading (e.g., 24; see also Cabau, 193–235).

25. In formulating this discussion, I have in mind Lacan's discussions of the imaginary and symbolic realms, his associated oedipal theory of the *nom du père*, and his critique of ego psychology. Of course, Lacan's critique of ego psychology means that a writer's works cannot be traced to any origin in the individual; the notion that the self is constituted socially suggests, rather, a dialectic that undermines the opposition of self and society (see also Jameson, Lemaire, and Ragland-Sullivan).

Chapter 3

1. Although Carlyle was living in relative isolation in southwestern Scotland, he followed these events closely in the newspapers (see *CL*, 5:130, 161, 216). In late August, he would have seen Mill's letters on the revolution, which appeared anonymously in the *Examiner* (Mill, *Earlier Letters*, 12:59–67).

2. See *TNB*, 160, 163, on the relationship between judge and criminal (*SR*, 60) and the vision of the clothes flying off the court (*SR*, 61). See also *TNB*, 164–66, and *CL*, 5:153; in the latter, a letter of August 30, Carlyle makes reference to "natural Supernaturalism." The first notebook passage occurs just after Carlyle notes that he had received writings from the St. Simonian Gustave d'Eichthal four weeks earlier. Since he received the packet around July 23 (see *CL*, 5:133), this would date the entry as about August 20. Both this letter

(which mentions the July revolution) and the notebooks juxtapose mention of the St. Simonians and the use of the clothing metaphor. In his response to the St. Simonians, Carlyle employed, perhaps for the first time, the "tone and Phraseology of Teufelsdröckh" (*CL*, 5:136, n. 3). Although much of the material that Carlyle would include in *Sartor Resartus* had been gathering for nearly a decade (for example, in *Wotton Reinfred*), passages written before this date do not employ the clothing metaphor. In *Sartor Resartus*, for example, the passage on the figurativeness of language is expressed in terms of the clothing metaphor; but the earlier version of the passage, written in the latter half of 1829, does not use it (*SR*, 73; *TNB*, 141–42).

3. Carlyle informed his brother on September 18 that he was planning to *"write something of* [his] *own,"* and, on October 10, he spoke of actually being at work on it (*CL*, 5:164, 171).

4. Other details indicate Teufelsdröckh's sympathy with the revolution. The Editor suggests he may be headed for London, where the reform agitation was under way; Teufelsdröckh responds to news of the July revolution with a German version of the revolutionary song, *Ça ira*; and we are also told that he has been communicating with the revolutionary St. Simonians. On the relationship between what Carlyle himself said of the St. Simonians and this passage, see *CL*, 5:136, and *TNB*, 158–59.

5. Carlyle sympathized with the "poor wretches" who threatened to strike and riot in Glasgow in late 1819 and early 1820 (*CL*, 1:242; see also 212, 218, 224–25, 252–53, 254; *Rem.*, 212–13, 222). He may even have had firsthand experience of these riots, since one occurred in Edinburgh in August 1812, a summer that he spent mostly there (Logue, 33, 41; Kaplan, 32).

6. It also elaborates the familiar notion of the "fabric" of society (see *SR*, 62). On the general notion of the tissue of society and social interconnectedness, see the chapter "Organic Filaments" and 52, 53, 60, 70, 71, 89, 95, 132, 245.

7. "Custom," Teufelsdröckh writes, persuades us that "the Miraculous, by simple repetition, ceases to be Miraculous . . . thus let but a Rising of the Sun, let but a Creation of the World happen twice, and it ceases to be marvellous, to be noteworthy, or noticeable" (259, 57). Puns on habit and costume appear throughout *Sartor* (35, 59, 72–73, 171, 223, 260–61, 266; see also the chapter on symbols, esp. 218).

8. In *The French Revolution*, Carlyle will represent this as the sansculottic tendency toward cannibalism, and already in *Sartor Resartus* he is concerned with the Malthusian anxiety that we will end up "universally eating one another" (*SR*, 227). He also frequently complains that the utilitarian "Profit-and-Loss Philosophy" replaces the soul with the stomach (e.g., 232).

9. From "The State of German Literature" (1827) forward, Carlyle depicts as mere hodmen authors who do not treat literature as religion (*CME*, 1:59;

see *CL*, 4:271, 5:152–53, 6:329; *TNB*, 144). He also contrasts those who build (e.g., Goethe) with those who burn or destroy (e.g., Voltaire; see *WM*, 1:28). The masonry metaphor can be found throughout *Sartor Resartus* (see esp. 54, 250, 263).

10. About 1830, his insistence that literature will be the new liturgy receives an ironic twist when he begins saying that "journalism," which he always despised, rather than "literature," is the new religion. Teufelsdröckh writes, for example, that "Journalists are now the true Kings and Clergy," for the liturgy of journalism is an ironic one that destroys "ancient idols" rather than producing a new belief (*SR*, 45, 252; see *CME*, 2:77; *TNB*, 263; *HGL*, 5).

11. Since the hero's authority derives from God, not the people, Teufelsdröckh rejects representational government that assumes popular authority. "Not that we want *no* Aristocracy," Carlyle wrote in his notebook at this time, "but that we want a *true* one" (*TNB*, 179). Here Carlyle departs from Mill in "Spirit of the Age," who argues that authority has shifted from governors, who had been the only ones with sufficient knowledge to govern, to representatives of the people now sufficiently knowledgeable to choose their own governors (*Newspaper Writings*, 253–58).

12. Whether or not he might have found a publisher under other circumstances, Carlyle became convinced that nothing could be done while the English had their minds on the reform bill (*CL*, 5:376, 436, 6:14, 16, 24, 64).

13. Several years earlier, DeQuincey had made almost identical objections to Carlyle's translation of *Wilhelm Meister*, complaining of its "lawless innovation," "licentious coinages," and "neoteric slang" (192–97). Anticipating the defense of *Sartor*'s style discussed below, Carlyle inscribed this episode in *Sartor Resartus* (Vanden Bossche, "Polite Conversation"). It is an index of Carlyle's own accommodation to English culture that he later conceded that DeQuincey had been right to admonish him (Shepherd, 2:276).

14. For example, Teufelsdröckh's wanderings enact the Editor's statement that his birth is an exodus; his "watch-tower" home becomes the "watch-tower" of German philosophy (20, 6); he sees a clock and jail on his way to his first school and then becomes a prisoner of time (127); as a child, he "sew[s]" books into a "volume" and as an adult writes a "Clothes-Volume" (102, 79).

15. These techniques are described in Cabau, 140; Caserio, 31–32; Edwards, 99; Gilbert, 433–36; Leicester, 11, 15; M. Roberts, 404; and Haney, 319ff. This is not to deny that *Sartor Resartus* draws on a long tradition of religious and literary symbolism and figuration, but it can be argued that even the extravagance of *Sartor*'s allusions to biblical, classical, and German texts, as well as contemporary thought and events, does not provide any real external reference (i.e., to a tradition that precedes and grounds the text), since it makes use of them apart from the system of meanings to which they were formerly attached. Along these lines, Linda Peterson has recently argued that

Carlyle employs a Straussian hermeneutics of intertextuality that finds meaning through the relation between texts rather than, as in traditional theories of revelation, through appeal to the single divine author (54–57).

16. When *Sartor* finally appeared in Fraser's, the reactions were almost entirely unfavorable (*EL*, 2:461). It should be noted that all of the responses to *Sartor Resartus* discussed here came after the 1834 publication, but they indicate attitudes that were surely apparent earlier, as Carlyle's statements about his feeling of isolation, discussed below, indicate. I am concerned with how his contemporaries responded to the rhetoric of *Sartor Resartus*; for detailed analyses of this rhetoric, see Holloway, chap. 2; Tennyson, *Sartor*; Levine, *Boundaries of Fiction* and "The Use and Abuse of Carlylese"; Brookes; and Landow, *Elegant Jeremiahs*.

17. Mill complained, among other things, that Carlyle's phraseology "fails to bring home [his] meaning to the comprehension of most readers" (*Earlier Letters*, 12:176). When he later published Carlyle's "Mirabeau," Mill first attempted to smooth out some of its "quaint" usages and then defended its style to his friends (see 202, 307, 334).

18. In another letter, he described a visit during which Irving gave him an article by one Thomas Carlyle (!) that he claimed was "'given him' by the spirit!" Carlyle found it "to be simply the insanest Babble, without top bottom or centre, that ever was emitted even from Bedlam itself" (*CL*, 6:132; see also *Rem.*, 298ff.; Skabarnicki, "Annandale Evangelist").

19. Carlyle's phrasing—"At some Hotel of the Sun, Hotel of the Angel, Gold Lion, or Green Goose, or whatever hotel it is, in whatever world-famous capital City, his chariot-wheels have rested"—makes it clear that Green Goose is meant to be a typical name for the kind of inn Cagliostro stopped at, not an actual place (*CME*, 3:279).

20. It is worth emphasizing in the context of the preceding discussion that, while Carlyle employs something like Romantic irony in *Sartor Resartus*, he does not intend to destablize meaning completely. In this respect, I concur with those critics who insist that Carlyle intends his irony to be limited by his insistence on an ultimate ground of meaning (e.g., Fleishman 128; McGowan, 60–69). A number of recent studies have treated Carlyle as a Romantic ironist (see Dale, "*Sartor Resartus*," 293–312; Haney, 307–33; Jay, 92–108; Mellor, chap. 4; and Morris, 201–12).

21. Later, Carlyle associated contemporary English literature with industrial mechanization as well as urban capitalism. "Literature, too," he wrote in "Signs of the Times," "has its Paternoster-row mechanism, its Trade dinners, its Editorial conclaves, and huge subterranean, puffing bellows; so that books are not only printed, but, in a great measure, written and sold, by machinery" (*CME*, 2:62). Mechanization, he claimed elsewhere, was helping to make literature a commodity, just another "species of Brewing or Cookery"

(*CL*, 5:149). Through such comments, Carlyle attempts to sustain a distinction between literature and the mere products of print (see *TNB*, 170).

22. He never tired of repeating the story of society's neglect of Burns as proof that, when judged by the laws of supply and demand, poets will never be considered valuable (*CME*, 1:258; see also 42–43).

23. The metaphor of hunger in this sentence connects novel writing both with the Cagliostric quackery that eats and destroys rather than creates, and with the important theme of cannibalism in *The French Revolution*, which will be discussed below (see also *CL*, 6:396). Carlyle frequently complained in his letters of the 1830s that hunger might drive him from the profession of literature. One could argue, of course, that hunger forced him to stay with it.

24. There have been a number of discussions of Carlyle's use of epic devices and the influence of Homer on his writings, but little on his conception of epic until Mark Cumming's *A Disimprisoned Epic*. I would suggest that Carlyle did not so much attempt to make the *The French Revolution* epic because he read Homer, but read Homer because he wanted to make his next work epic (see LaValley, 139–52; Farrell, 215–31; Clubbe, "Carlyle as Epic Historian" and "Epic Heroes"; J. Rosenberg, 39–48; Cumming, "Disimprisonment of Epic").

25. In the early nineteenth century, there were nearly as many definitions of epic as there were critics and no consensus on what constituted the epic canon. Thus, while Carlyle drew on recent scholarship, he had considerable freedom in how to define epic (Foerster, 31–34; see also Jenkyns, chap. 9; Turner, chap. 4). Mark Cumming's study confirms and provides considerable evidence beyond that presented here that Carlyle was reshaping epic to suit his own literary ends. Cumming demonstrates how Carlyle combines romance, satire, elegy, farce, tragedy, emblem, fragment, allegory, phantasmagory, and so on to create a heterogeneous form. However, I would note that Cumming tends to discuss these genres as opposed pairs, pitting a univocal against a multivocal, or closed versus open, form (emblem versus fragment, for example, or allegory versus phantasmagory). Cumming suggests that multivocality undermines univocality, whereas I find that the desire for univocality and closure persists in tension with multivocality.

26. The shift in Homeric criticism paralleled the shift from Percy's minstrel theory to Ritson's "productions of obscure or anonymous authors" (Hustvedt, 265). These two areas of study come together with biblical criticism in Herder's comparison of Homer, early Hebrew poets, and German folk songs (Myres, 75, 81).

27. The phrase "songs and rhapsodies" was used to describe the *Iliad* by Richard Bentley in 1713 and became a commonplace in later Homeric studies (cited in Myres, 49; see also Dale, *Victorian Critic*, 81–82, esp. n. 36). Henry Hart Milman, citing Henry Nelson Coleridge's comparison between the Robin

Hood legends and the Homeric poems, complained that Homer's epics were being turned into a "minstrelsy of the Grecian border" (124–25). Carlyle read Ritson's *Fairy Tales* and *Ancient Songs and Ballads* in 1831 (*TNB*, 213).

28. As Turner notes, Carlyle was an exception among early Victorians in his acceptance of Wolf's hypothesis. Carlyle may have accepted it in part because Goethe had hailed it (see Myres, 86; Grafton et al., 27).

29. Wolf's *Prolegomena to Homer* (1795) accordingly was largely modeled on Eichhorn's analysis of the Bible (Grafton et al., 18–26). Carlyle himself frequently compared Homer to the Bible (e.g., *TNB*, 188; *CME*, 3:176; *CL*, 7:135, 138).

30. This conception of epic as a totalizing worldview—"how the World and Nature painted themselves to the mind in those old ages"—appears early in Carlyle's writings (*CME*, 1:351; see 3:161; *TNB*, 187). It also was something of a commonplace (Turner, 136; Myres, 63).

31. We see here the term "epic" taking over the role played by "myth" in Carlyle's earlier writings. In 1828, he had written that the Faust legend was a "Christian mythus," an "embodiment of a highly remarkable belief," which in this sense "may still be considered true," and, of course, he had used the term "Mythus" in *Sartor Resartus* to denote a cultural belief (*CME*, 1:154–55). Epic takes the place of myth, enabling Carlyle to emphasize a text's factual and historical basis rather than its transcendental and imaginative qualities.

32. A letter to his brother, for example, distinguishes Gibbon's *Decline and Fall* from "general literature" (*CL*, 2:467–68).

33. Carlyle accepted Wolf's hypothesis that Homer could not write (see *HL*, 17). He also associated the invention of writing, especially of printing, with the onset of the modern era (see *SR*, 40, 246; *HGL*, 5).

34. Still one of the best discussions of Carlyle's use of history, especially its antihistorical strain, is René Wellek's "Carlyle and the Philosophy of History." On Carlyle as historian and historical writer, see J. Rosenberg; Dale, *Victorian Critic*; Jann, chap. 2; and Culler, chap. 3. Dale's discussion, like Wellek's, emphasizes the caution with which one must discuss Carlyle's historicism (7–8, 55–58).

35. While, as Carlyle quickly saw, Mill had been influenced by the St. Simonians, Carlyle traced this cyclical model of history to the Germans. Indeed, he wrote to the St. Simonian Gustave d'Eichthal that the idea that revelation may be found in the "acted *History of Man*" is the "Religion of all Thinkers . . . for the last half century: of Goethe . . . Schiller, of Lessing, Jacobi, Herder" (*CL*, 5:278–79). On the origins of this concept in Carlyle's writings, see Wellek, "Carlyle and the Philosophy of History," and Shine, *Carlyle and the Saint-Simonians*.

36. On the pervasive desire to escape history in Victorian culture, see Welsh, chap. 13. Carlyle's use of tripartite structures in *Sartor Resartus, The*

French Revolution, Past and Present, and elsewhere is also related to this tripartite historical model. The cyclical pattern of creation and destruction is most fully elaborated in the (organic) image of the phoenix that is reborn from its own ashes and in the organic cycle of growth and decay (*SR*, 244; see 40, 47, 56, 122, 177, 200, 216, 244).

37. He began it by February 16, 1832, a month after his father's death (*CL*, 6:124). In the reminiscence, he had compared his father to Samuel Johnson, and later in life he noted that his feelings about his father were "traceable" in the essay on Johnson (*Rem.*, 7; *CL*, 6:105).

38. The letters mention only the first four books, but Clubbe reasonably suggests that Carlyle read as far as book 6 ("Carlyle as Epic Historian," 126). The commentaries mentioned here are the ones he requested in a letter to Henry Inglis (*CL*, 7:92, 137–38; see 132). He may have read others from his own library or from other sources. It is certain, for example, that he had read Wolf by the time he lectured on the history of literature in 1838, for he refers to him there, and it seems most likely that he read him in 1834 during his period of concentrated Homer study (*HL*, 16–19).

39. It is worth recalling that in "Illudo Chartis" Stephen Corry's father decides to send him to the University of Edinburgh "in the ever memorable year of 1795," an event that the narrator compares to "a second birth" (King, 167).

40. Holloway briefly discusses Carlyle's "dramatization of discussion" through the use of fictional personae in *Sartor Resartus, Past and Present,* the introduction to *Oliver Cromwell's Letters and Speeches,* and *Latter-Day Pamphlets,* but he does not connect it to the dramatization of discussions by historical personae in *The French Revolution* (27).

41. This mode of historical narrative is so prevalent that Emile Benveniste designates it simply *histoire* (208–9; see White, intro.). Conventional historians have long objected to Carlyle's historical style. Recently, for example, Hugh Trevor-Roper complained of the "over-dramatization . . . highly personal judgments . . . rhetorical interruptions . . . [and] grotesque egotism" of Carlyle's histories (732).

42. I cite the edition of 1839, but this volume appeared in 1833. I choose Alison because his history represents contemporary practice and Carlyle had some acquaintance with it (see *CL*, 6:373).

43. C. F. Harrold has estimated that such commentaries constitute nearly a third of *The French Revolution* ("Carlyle's General Method," 1150).

44. One effect of this practice is Carlyle's even-handed sympathy for virtually every historical figure in spite of his personal judgments of them. Although he admires Mirabeau and Danton more than Robespierre and Louis XVI, he endeavors to see why they acted in the way they did and how historical circumstances shaped them (e.g., 3:106–7, 285–86). See especially the deaths of Mirabeau, Marat, Marie Antoinette, Philippe d'Orléans, and Mme. Roland (2:146, 3:169–70, 194–95, 207–11).

45. For further discussion of the antinarrative quality of *The French Revolution*, see Caserio, 30–43; Leicester, 8; J. Rosenberg, 58ff.; Vanden Bossche, "Prophetic Closure," 212.

46. Carlyle's error about the distance to Varennes, the topic of much controversy among historians, is discussed in Ben-Israel, 142–43 (see also J. Rosenberg, 71). The point here is that Carlyle's error reveals only that he was more concerned with the symbolic import of the event—that the inability of the monarchy to move swiftly in flight indicated its inability to govern—rather than literal facts.

47. Carlyle's use of mock epic has been previously noted by LaValley (139–52, 146, 159) and J. Rosenberg (64–66). Both Rosenberg and LaValley provide an important corrective to those who do not take the mock-epic element into account in their discussions of Carlyle's use of epic form, but I think Rosenberg is mistaken when he argues that Carlyle is "boast[ing]" that "speech is more useful than song" (52–53). As the theme of speech in *The French Revolution* makes clear, Carlyle "speaks" only because singing has become impossible (see also LaValley, 147). Cumming, in turn, by deemphasizing epic devices and concentrating on Carlyle's reshaping of epic, provides a corrective to Rosenberg and LaValley.

48. Once again, Carlyle echoes Burke, who had written "let them not break prison to burst like a *Levanter*, to sweep the earth with their hurricane and to break up the fountains of the great deep to overwhelm us" (*Reflections*, 66–67). Unlike Carlyle, however, Burke does not equate the building of the state with the Bastille, nor does he regard it as having become a prison.

49. On the importance of the metaphor of fire in the works preceding *The French Revolution*, see Cabau, 12ff., and passim.

50. Note that the earliest meaning of the word *fabric* is an edifice or building, yet *fabric* also evokes Carlyle's clothing metaphor and its connotations of an organic network of human relations (see also *Reflections*, 24).

51. Carlyle's analysis deviates from Burke's, however. Burke refers repeatedly to the *assignat*, the paper money issued by the revolutionary government, as a sign of its moral bankruptcy (*Reflections*, 44, 60, 62, 273–75). Carlyle also treats the *assignat* as an example of the insubstantiality of the acts of the revolutionary government, but he regards the problem of producing worthless banknotes as the product of the old regime that bankrupted the government and was the first to substitute paper for gold, a point that Burke glosses over in his analysis (*FR*, 2:8).

52. Allusions to Babel appear throughout the history: e.g., a "confusion of tongues" (1:41); a "jargon as of Babel" (1:100); "as many dialects as when the *first* great Babel was to be built" (2:27).

53. Carlyle here follows Burke (and Coleridge, who states the case more obliquely) in arguing that it is virtually impossible to base a constitution on abstract political principles (*Reflections*, 35–38 et al.).

54. The difference between Carlyle and Goethe can be discerned in Carlyle's essay on "Goethe's Works" (1832), written about a year after he completed *Sartor Resartus*. In this essay, Carlyle adapts the three phases of religion of *Wilhelm Meister* and the three stages in Teufelsdröckh's conversion to describe Goethe's own career. The three phases in *Wilhelm Meister* are the Ethnic, the Philosophical, and the Christian (*WM*, 2:267). In Carlyle's narrative of Goethe's life, the first phase, the period dominated by the "pestilential fever of Scepticism" manifested in *Werter*, precedes the three phases of religion and corresponds to Teufelsdröckh's Everlasting No. The third phase, in which Goethe rises from the "ashes" of "Denial" into "Reverence" and the "deep all-pervading Faith" of *Wilhelm Meister's Travels*, corresponds to the Christian phase of religion and Teufelsdröckh's Everlasting Yea (*CME*, 2:431–32). To describe the intervening period, which clearly corresponds to the Centre of Indifference, Carlyle combines the first two phases of religion, the Pagan and Ethnic. Whereas the phases described in *Wilhelm Meister* are progressive stages of religious development, Carlyle disregards this when he combines the first two, presumably as erroneous delusions, in favor of the last. Similarly, his Teufelsdröckh does not really progress from No to Centre to Yea, but suddenly discovers the Everlasting Yea. This is how Carlyle dealt with the problem of closure raised by *Wotton Reinfred*. There, closure was premature, Wotton almost immediately discovering the House in the Wold, the Eden of German transcendentalism, rather than reaching it through progressive self-understanding. In *Sartor Resartus*, all apparent moments of closure prior to the Everlasting Yea turn out to be illusions. The House in the Wold of *Wotton Reinfred* becomes the Waldschloss (castle in the wood) where Teufelsdröckh falls in love with Blumine and believes he has discovered, or returned to, Eden. Teufelsdröckh himself undermines this moment of closure, by describing his vision of paradise ironically as a mere "Calenture . . . whereby the Youth saw green Paradise-groves in the waste Ocean-waters" (147–48).

55. Teufelsdröckh concludes with the maxim often repeated in *Sartor Resartus*: "Doubt of any sort cannot be removed except by Action" (196). Closely related is his transformation of "Know thyself" into "Know what thou canst work at" (163). In "Characteristics," Carlyle laments that "Opinion and Action" have been "disunited," and longs for the time when the "former could still produce the latter" (*CME*, 3:15).

56. Closely related is the association between speculation, wandering, and illness that Carlyle had already established in *The Life of Schiller* (see 105). In "Characteristics," Carlyle's dyspepsia becomes the "dyspepsia of Society," and he seeks to recover the period of life before pain makes us aware of our bodies, the idyllic childhood when "the body had not yet become the prison-house of the soul" (*CME*, 3:20, 2). On Carlyle's dyspepsia, see Kaplan, 59, 63–64, 87, 120.

57. This last passage draws almost word for word on one of Carlyle's descriptions of Coleridge (*CL*, 3:90–91; see 6:233, 261). Before he had met him, Carlyle had already put him down as "mystical," placing him in the same category as Fox and Böhme (*CL*, 2:468). His famous description of Coleridge in *The Life of John Sterling* draws heavily on the reports in these letters (*LJS*, 52–62).

58. The aristocracy, Carlyle writes, has "nearly ceased either to guide or misguide" (1:12). On Louis's incapacity for action and decision, see 2:137, 180, 223–24, 264, 286.

59. For a cogent summary of these problems, see Brantlinger, 67, 76–77. Brantlinger also argues, as I do below, that the revolution is endless, because the political process provides no solutions to the social problems that produced it (chap. 3, passim).

60. Carlyle borrowed the speech from his essay "The Diamond Necklace" (see Leicester, 15–17).

Chapter 4

1. The first in English, that is; I except the German translation of *The Life of Schiller* that appeared with Carlyle's name in 1830.

2. My argument finds support in Patrick Brantlinger's assertion that Carlyle dispassionately criticizes all parties in *The French Revolution* and that he identifies the French aristocracy, Girondins, and Jacobins with the English Tories, Whigs, and Radicals (chap. 3 passim). My argument is that, in spite of his distrust of partisan politics, Carlyle at this point hoped to intervene in them to forward his own proposals for reform.

3. The tensions between Carlyle and the radicals are evident in Mill's maneuvers after he received Carlyle's first contribution, "Mirabeau," in which Carlyle had sought controversy by criticizing Etienne Dumont, a French follower of Bentham. Mill made deletions and added a note advising readers that the author's opinion did not reflect that of the editors. Carlyle objected to the deletions and restored the passages when the essay was published in his collected essays. Carlyle contributed to the *London and Westminster* for only a short period, in 1837–38, when he was still in need of the income that review articles brought. By the time he became serious about the Chartism project in 1839, it appeared that the *London and Westminster* was about to fold. When Mill offered to publish "Chartism" there as a "final shout," he decided that "the thing [was] too good for that purpose" and turned down the offer (*CL*, 11:221; see 19, 45, 206).

4. Carlyle wrote to Lockhart on May 20, when the bed chamber crisis of May 7–13, 1839, seemed certain to bring in a Tory ministry, but the crisis was resolved and the Whigs stayed in power until 1841. In discussing Carlyle's

relationship to the political parties and their literary vehicles I do not intend to exclude *Fraser's Magazine*, a Tory journal in which Carlyle published more frequently than anywhere else. But Carlyle never considered it a vehicle for his social criticism because, unlike the major reviews which examined books from the perspective of party ideology, *Fraser's* was a literary magazine, more committed to jeux d'esprit than party politics (see D. Roberts, 79; Houghton, *Wellesley Index*, 2:303ff.).

5. See also Morgan (Seigel, 28) and the review "*Chartism*" in the *Monthly Chronicle* (101–2). Carlyle's desire to be accounted a Tory may have shaped his reading of the *Morning Chronicle* (December 31, 1839) review which asserts, more equivocally than Carlyle's letter implies, that he is "no friend to the present Ministry, or to either the Whig or the Radical section of the Liberal party" but also insists that his views are opposed to the Tory line of the *Quarterly Review*. The *Spectator* lavished praise on *Chartism* and quoted several passages from it ("Topics of the Day," 9–11).

6. This is an inference from Carlyle's reply; Mill's letter is lost. Carlyle's critique dates from the passage of the New Poor Law in 1834, when he complained that the law assumed "that the condition of the Poor people is— improving! . . . 'Well gentlemen,' I answered once, 'the Poor I think will get up some day, and *tell* you how improved their condition is'" (*CL*, 8:117).

7. See *Tait's Edinburgh Review* in Seigel, *Critical Heritage*, 166–67; Lady Sydney Morgan, 27; "*Chartism*," *Monthly Chronicle*, 98, 104; and Herman Merivale in Seigel, *Critical Heritage*, 280. Several reviewers were quick to point out that the emigration proposal was not new. Both proposals were part of his program to radicalize the Tory party, since one faction of the radical party did support emigration and it was the Tory party, as he argued in *Chartism*, that was holding up the establishing of a national system of education.

8. The first two lecture series, on the histories of German literature and European literature, looked to his past as a literary critic, which by this time was nearly over (the essays on Walter Scott and Varnhargen von Ense published in 1838 were to be his last written on literary figures). The third series, on modern revolutions, also drew heavily on his previous writings and researches. As the *Times* reported, "the reader of Mr. Carlyle's works will have seen these sentiments many times before" ("Mr. Carlyle's Lectures," 5). To a certain extent, of course, *On Heroes and Hero-Worship* also drew upon previous work. When he finished the third lecture, he wrote that the lectures were not "a new story" to him, but that the "world seemed greatly astonished at it" (*CL*, 12:192).

9. Carlyle had decided on the topic of heroes by February (*CL*, 12:58, 64). Since his plan to give six lectures remained consistent throughout, it would seem to indicate that the alteration of his plan did not mean adding a lecture but simply reversing the order of the last two. This may explain the chrono-

logical anomaly of his returning to Cromwell and the seventeenth century in the final lecture, following the lecture on eighteenth- and nineteenth-century men of letters.

10. On the general notion of the Carlylean hero, see Lehman; Grierson; DeLaura; P. Rosenberg, 188–203; and LaValley, 236–52.

11. Martin Bidney has demonstrated that the successive heroes are "diminishing" reincarnations of the first hero, Odin. LaValley rightly argues that the man of letters is the weakest of the heroes, but mistakenly assumes that the form of *On Heroes* was meant to be linear and progressive (250–51; see also Donovan).

12. If Lehman is correct that Fichte's man of letters—as a man who manifests the divine in history—underlies Carlyle's conception of the hero (75 et al.), then there is a special irony in this lecture, for in it Carlyle transfers the authority originally conceived as the privileged realm of the poet to the divinity / king and portrays the man of letters as incapable of achieving it. In this sense, Lehman's argument that the hero theory was complete by 1832 must be modified (88).

13. Not only had Carlyle published several essays on Goethe, but he had also concluded his first two series of lectures with Goethe. Since it is safe to assume that many members of his audience had attended the earlier lectures, it seems all the more surprising that he would imply that they knew Rousseau, Odin, or Mahomet better than Goethe.

14. Donovan notes that DeLaura inconsistently makes "Hero as Man of Letters" rather than "Hero as King" the climax of *On Heroes and Hero-Worship* (Donovan, n. 18; DeLaura, 719; see also Bidney, 60).

15. In 1833, when Carlyle was still deciding whether or not to write on the French Revolution, he regarded Knox rather than Cromwell as the kind of reformer that England needed (*CL*, 6:303; see 260–61). But by 1840, when he lectured on heroes, Knox had been replaced by Cromwell, and Knox was treated only briefly in the "Hero as Priest."

16. We know the earlier lectures only from newspaper reports, but these reports make clear that Carlyle was already attempting to rebut the prevailing view of Cromwell. Although it approved of most of the lectures, the *Examiner* censured the discussion of Cromwell in terms that suggest Carlyle was trying to rehabilitate his reputation ("The Lectures of Mr. Carlyle," 294).

17. Forster, 48.E.36, Victoria and Albert Library, London, fol. 96. Some portions of this manuscript have been published in "A Preface by Carlyle" in Fielding and Tarr, which I will cite when appropriate.

18. Similar statements may be found throughout his manuscripts and letters. One is a "conservative," he wrote, "who brings back the Past vitally visible into the Present living Time" (Fielding and Tarr, 18). His struggles to find a proper form for his history persistently emphasize that he is striving to write

more than history, that "the epic of the Present is the thing always to write; the epic of the Present not of the past and dead" (Fielding and Tarr, 16). He frequently portrays his inability to make progress on Cromwell as a failure to make the past live: "By Heaven's blessing, we belong not to the 17 centy; we are alive here, and have the honour of belonging to the nineteenth!" (Forster, fol. 52; see also fol. 54). He also wrote in January 1840 that he had been reading about Cromwell, but he did "not see how the subject can be presented *still alive*. A subject dead is not worth presenting" (*CL*, 12:16).

19. His complaints that a book on Cromwell was "impossible," which began in mid-1842, have an especially despairing resonance, since in *Chartism* he had derided the utilitarians for deeming social reform "impossible" (an admonition he would repeat in *Past and Present*). Carlyle always complained about the difficulty of writing, but his complaints about Cromwell in his letters and journals were unusually frequent (e.g., *LL*, 1:215, 238–39, 300, 339; *CL*, 13:129, 263, 14:199, 204, 210–11, 214, 239; *NL*, 1:302, 304). The Forster manuscripts are also sprinkled with expressions of frustration about his inability to "get begun" (see fols. 23, 52, 53 v., 60 v., 61, 65, 66 v., 69, 87, 92 v., 93, 94, 97, 98, 98 v., 99, 102, 104, 111 v., 112 v., 170 v.).

20. At one point in the Forster manuscripts following a passage that he apparently felt failed to revive the past, he admonishes himself: "But in fact thou shalt know what is dead and not seek to revive it, but leave the dead to bury their dead" (fol. 65).

21. D. J. Trela has argued, against Kaplan, J. Rosenberg, and LaValley, that *Oliver Cromwell's Letters and Speeches* was not a "failure" (Cromwell *in Context*, 5 et al.). But, as Kaplan demonstrates, Carlyle himself regarded the project as a failure, at the very least because he had originally intended to write a history or biography but had to settle for an edition of historical papers (310).

22. Forster, fol. 93, begins: "Gazing with inexpressible trembling curiosity into those old magic tombs of our Fathers [. . .] I can see a city in considerable emotion." The verses, written in Scots dialect, are transcribed in Tarr and McClelland (63–64; see also 65). The dramatic scenario is discussed below. In addition to the list of "Moments" in the Forster manuscript, the *Historical Sketches* contains a page labeled "*Moments, again*" that outlines the book as a series of "scenes" (fol. 206).

23. The manuscript is published in Fielding, "Unpublished Manuscripts—II." I will cite page numbers from this text. Although the scenario is dramatic, Carlyle does not abandon his epic intention. In the introductory notes, he discusses biography as "epic," and the twelve acts suggest the model of classical epic in twelve books. In another passage in the manuscripts, Carlyle tries to create some drama by imagining a dialogue between Cromwell and his doctor (Forster, fol. 101).

24. Although he considered it only a short-term measure, he had become

a firm supporter of repeal (see *CL*, 13:143, 216, 14:225). At this point, he was torn between hoping for a Whig majority sufficient to repeal the Corn Laws and a Tory leader willing to do so. His faith in the Tories was slight enough that he could still hope for the election of his Whig friend Edward John Stanley in the 1842 elections (*CL*, 13:181–82, 186). In letters to his Tory friend Richard Monckton Milnes, he chastised the Tories for supporting the Corn Laws and predicted that Peel would surprise everyone by supporting repeal (*CL*, 13:152, 194, 311).

25. The circumstantial evidence seems conclusive. The Manchester Insurrection was a seminal topic of *Past and Present*, the subject of the opening chapters and the title of book 1, chapter 3. The letters to Jane Carlyle link his new writing with the Manchester Insurrection, and at this time he was having difficulty writing on Cromwell. Nine days after writing to Jane, he hinted to Emerson that he was working on a book other than the one on Cromwell (*RWE*, 328). Carlyle's comment, in the letter to Jane, that he does not know what he is working at, is to the point; he knew he was not working on Cromwell, and only later would this new writing take shape as *Past and Present*. See Kaplan, 293, 579, n. 62.

26. The details of this episode have been discussed elsewhere. See Richard Altick's introduction to *Past and Present*, xii–xiii et al.; Kaplan, 294–95; *LL*, 1:296–308.

27. Carlyle was attacking the Whigs, much to Sewell's satisfaction, but his views were hardly orthodox enough to satisfy the Anglican divine, who began his review by asserting that Carlyle's works "contain many grave errors: they exhibit vagueness, and misconception, and apparently total ignorance in points of the utmost importance." Although Sewell found Carlyle's criticism of society "forcible, acute, true, and in many respects wise," he complained that Carlyle wanted to discard old institutions instead of revitalizing them (446, 461).

28. For the passage Carlyle refers to, see Seigel, *Critical Heritage*, 81–82. Although Merivale was explicitly reviewing *The French Revolution*, his review may well have been prompted by *Chartism* and the political infighting among the parties it prompted. After Sewell's review appeared in September, for example, several newspapers commented on it, each taking up the cry of one or the other party (see *CL*, 12:284, n. 3). The evidence for the influence of *Chartism* is that Merivale reviewed the second edition of *The French Revolution* that appeared some three years after the history was first published yet just some six months after *Chartism* had attacked the Whig government. Although the review does not explicitly mention *Chartism*, it specifically alludes to Carlyle's proposals for emigration and education (Seigel, *Critical Heritage*, 82). Carlyle saw it as a Whig response, readily believing early reports that its author was Macaulay (then a member of the Whig cabinet).

29. The Quaker appears in *Past and Present* as "Friend Prudence" (276). Carlyle's letter of February 1, 1843, to Marshall, written as he was completing *Past and Present* and advising Marshall to "*be* a real king, and guide, and just *Law-ward* (antique for 'Lord') or Preserver of God's Law among your people," continues to focus on the need for a "*real* Aristocracy, in place of a false imaginary Aristocracy" (Hilles Box 25, Beinecke Library, New Haven, 2–3).

30. Later that year he read a history of the Carlyle family and bemusedly suggested that he might have been a duke (*CL*, 14:174).

31. These are joined by an astonishing number of speakers represented as more generalized figures: personifications—working Mammonism, Unworking Dilettantism, Enlightened Philosophies, Captains of Industry, Humanity of England, Millocracy; typical individuals—the idle reader of newspapers, the parents who killed their child in the Stockport cellar, the pope, the king, a royal subject, a man in a horsehair wig, he of the shovel-hat, a drill sergeant, a Hapless Fraction, an Industrial *Law-ward,* and the Irish widow; typical groups—the poor at St. Ives, millions of workers, interrogative philosophers, the moneyed class, the English, the Community, aristocrats, "vested interests," Spinners, future men, Lancashire Weavers, Upholsterers and French Cooks, Transcendental friends, Socinian Preachers; historical groups and individuals—the workers massacred at Peterloo, the French at the Bar of the Convention, William the Norman bastard, Howel Davies the bucanier, King Redbeard; and institutions—Parliament, the Legislature, and the Anti-Slavery Convention.

32. Landow discusses the prophetic aspects of the two introductory paragraphs but does not note the differences discussed here (*Elegant Jeremiahs,* 41–43).

33. As in his representation of the French nation in *The French Revolution,* he portrays the working class as inarticulate, requiring a leader to voice their needs; he thus subsumes these voices to his own in the debate with his nonworking-class audience. Unable to imagine anything but a hierarchical social order, Carlyle dismisses all thought of the working class fending for itself. Although the title of *Chartism* seems to indicate that it is about the working-class social movement, Carlyle sees Chartism only as a sign of the times—a symptom, not a solution. Because workers are isolated from one another by laissez-faire economy—"each [is] unknown to his neighbour," he had argued in *Chartism*—they are not able to "take a resolution, and act on it, very readily" (*CME,* 4:201).

34. Although the "past" of *Past and Present* refers to the twelfth century, the title of one chapter, "Two Centuries," refers us to the seventeenth, and the present is measured as often against Cromwell's era as against Samson's (see 24–25, 221–23, 251–52, 257, 265). Furthermore, it is the settlement of 1660,

rather than the Reformation, that opens up the gulf between the lost paradise of the past and present-day chaos (167).

35. Although Philip Rosenberg provides one of the most cogent analyses of the limitations of Carlyle's social critiques, I think he is mistaken to suggest that Carlyle might somehow have produced a critique like Marx's (e.g., 166–67). The alternative that Rosenberg wishes Carlyle had discovered was precluded by Carlyle's refusal of a rigorous historicism and his insistence on the necessity for transcendental authority.

36. Carlyle's interest in land reclamation preceded his interest in emigration. In 1829, he had written in his notebook that the political economists had erred in their comparison of manufacture to improving wastelands: "the improved land remains an *addition* to the Earth *forever*" (*TNB*, 143). In the 1830s, his concerns for the laboring population led him to favor emigration as a solution, and it may, in fact, have been his effort to describe the situation of Scottish peasants driven to emigration by hardhearted landlords that led him to write *Chartism* (*CL*, 11:203–4). Although he had counseled against emigration in the 1820s, by the early 1830s he was talking about emigrating himself and eventually did help his brother Alexander emigrate to Canada (*CL*, 1:156, 2:30, 54, 84, 6:355–56, 353, 360, 386, 8:146, 9:162–64). Carlyle preferred government-supported to individual emigration, because the schemes for the former offered the opportunity for a heroic leader to create a new society. In 1835, he grew so enthusiastic about the man he thought was to lead a colony in South Australia that he said he wanted to go himself when he had finished writing *The French Revolution* (*CL*, 8:10–11). Emigration was also one area where Carlyle still agreed with his friends among the philosophic radicals. Both the Mills and Charles Buller were among a faction of the radicals that supported Edward Gibbon Wakefield's plan for government-sponsored emigration and colonization, although they supported it on the principle that it would produce ordered colonies rather than that it would reduce the supply of labor in England (Shepperson, 15–19; see Carrothers, 91–93). On Carlyle's personal interest in emigrating, see *CL*, 12:202, and Fielding, "Carlyle Considers New Zealand."

37. One problem that arises in *Latter-Day Pamphlets* is that Carlyle's reliance on the commercially minded middle class ends up justifying the very commercial spirit he had condemned in *Past and Present*, but this contradiction emerges already in the earlier text when he praises the colonizers for turning the "desert-shrubs of the Tropical swamps" into "Cotton-trees" (*PP*, 170).

38. Jeremiah, 6:14, 8:11. It is cited in the context of criticism of political economy by Coleridge (*Lay Sermons*, 141) and Carlyle (*PP*, 245; see also *SR*, 232). It is also echoed by the narrator of Tennyson's *Maud* (part 1, ll. 21–28).

39. Indeed, Carlyle's opinion of literature continued to decline in these years. He persisted in advising against the profession of literature (*CL*, 14:26)

and in advising poets to write prose (*CL*, 13:155, 14:22; *NL*, 1:283; *RWE*, 353). He even came to feel that German literature, since the death of Goethe, was worthless (*CL*, 14:3).

40. In the lectures on modern revolutions, Carlyle had depicted the Puritan revolution as the beginning of the era of modern revolutions, although he had also attempted to differentiate it from later revolutions. The dramatic scenario for Cromwell depicts the end of Cromwell's era as holding "France and Revol*n* in germ," an idea suggested on the last page of the *Letters and Speeches* as well (Fielding, "Unpublished Manuscripts—II," 10; *OCLS*, 4:207–8).

41. The dramatic scenario mentions the "various speech" of a group of Scots gathered around Jenny Geddes; groups discussing what the people and nobility think of the trial of Strafford; "troopers' dialogues" about Oliver; and an interchange involving "an astrologer, hunger, steeple, women in the trenches" (Fielding, "Unpublished Manuscripts—II," 8–10).

42. For example, 1:165, 178, 305, 394, 2:148, 179, 243, 260, 3:196, 4:77. On occasion, he also uses the first-person technique to represent Parliament, the political instrument of the Puritans (e.g., 1:256, 4:17). There are, of course, a very few exceptions (e.g., 1:120–22, 2:208, 246). In the latter half of the text, where the speeches dominate, the technique is hardly used at all.

43. The typographical conventions discussed here are those of the first, and as far as I can determine, all subsequent editions until the Centenary Edition, which breaks with the previous practice. The Centenary prints the narrative in the same size type as the letters and puts the letters in italics. The conventions for printing the speeches are unchanged.

44. Conventional modern historians, of course, consider these interpolations "Carlyle's greatest fault as an editor" rather than a means of enlivening historical documents (Frith, I:xxxviii).

45. The major manuscript versions of the episode are the passage in the *Historical Sketches* manuscript (*HS*, 299–310), the Forster manuscript (fol. 105), and the dramatic scenario (in which the Geddes anecdote is the most detailed episode). The latter concludes with the remark, "Could *nothing be made* of this?" (Fielding, "Unpublished Manuscripts—II," 9).

46. Carlyle's care in establishing the date manifests how seriously he pursued the subject. His letter of 1839 is already seeking information about the historical basis of the anecdote. He again sought information in 1840 and 1841, at which time David Laing informed him that Jenny Geddes was probably not historical (*CL*, 12:300, 13:74–78; see esp. 75–76, n. 7). Carlyle traced the appearance of the Geddes myth to the successive editions of Richard Baker's *Chronicle of the Kings of England*. In his copy of the *Chronicle*, now at the Carlyle House, Chelsea, he has noted in the margin alongside the passage on Gaddis: "This is not in the Edit[n] of 1665 (the 4th), and it is as here in the 6th of 1674: the 5th I have not seen, nor yet ascertained the year of" (458). In the *Letters*

and Speeches, he remarks that the passage makes its first appearance in the fifth edition of 1670 and that it had been anticipated by a pamphlet of 1661 (1:96–97, n. 3).

47. "The Nigger Question" is the title of the 1853 and all subsequent versions of Carlyle's essay, originally published in 1849 as "The Negro Question." Whenever possible, I will specify the version to which I am referring by the appropriate title. "Negro/Nigger Question" will refer nonspecifically to both editions.

48. Carlyle complained on several occasions about the slowness with which Parliament acted once it finally committed itself to repeal (Marrs, 629, 631, 634–35). Furthermore, he regarded repeal of the Corn Laws—which he thought more likely to benefit the middle class than the poor—only the first act toward major reform (*RWE*, 391).

49. Carlyle was at first inclined to treat the Irish Question, like the English one, as a problem of an irresponsible aristocracy, and, as late as 1848, he was satirizing the "Rakes of Mallow" (i.e., the Irish aristocracy) for presuming that ownership of a piece of "sheepskin" gave them a right to turn "the hard-won potato they [i.e., Irish peasants] have earned in hard travail from the bosom of their mother Earth" into "claret and champagne, into horse-furniture, house furniture, incidental expenses and the delicacies of the season" for their own pleasure ("Rakes of Mallow," MS 1213, Beinecke Library, New Haven, fol. 1 v.; see 2 v.). Dating of the manuscript is difficult, since it is a transcription of various notes prepared by his secretary, Joseph Neuberg, when he began writing *Latter-Day Pamphlets*. Although internal evidence dates parts of the manuscript to 1848, other portions could have been written as early as 1846.

50. Letter to John Grey, April 17, 1847, Hilles box 24, Beinecke Library, New Haven f. 2 v.

51. The following discussion seeks to add further evidence to the persuasive case made by Kaplan that Carlyle began by intending to write about Ireland (341). In addition to the argument put forward here, there is further evidence of Carlyle's preparation to write such a book in the reading he did in anticipation of the 1849 journey to Ireland. This reading included Jocelyn's and the Bollandists' lives of Saint Patrick as well as the saint's own *Confessio* (Duffy, 136–39; Allingham, *Diary*, 129–30, 137). Carlyle's brief manuscript on the Bollandists' *Acta Sanctorum*, however, does not deal with Saint Patrick or Ireland (Bowdoin, 1878, Brunswick, Me.). His further reading is indicated by material in his library at the Carlyle House, Chelsea, which includes James Fraser's *Hand Book for Travellers in Ireland* and a collection of tracts by Jasper W. Rogers, including *Facts for the Kind-Hearted of England! as to the Wretchedness of the Irish Peasantry, and the Means for Their Regeneration*. The "Rakes of Mallow" manuscript, which focuses on the vicissitudes of laissez-faire (see above, n. 49), provides the only other indication of where his writings on Ireland were tend-

ing. A related manuscript is "Leave It Alone; Time Will Mend It," which uses the same language concerning laissez-faire as the "Rakes" manuscript (see Kaplan, 352; "Rakes," fols. 12–14).

52. "Louis-Philippe," *The Examiner*, March 4, 1848; reprinted in Shepherd, 2:365–69 (see also *RWE*, 439; *LL*, 1:461, 462–63). In another article, published later that spring, Carlyle suggested that Russell would follow Louis Philippe into exile if he did not take charge of the Irish problem. "Ireland and the British Chief Governor," *The Spectator*, May 13, 1848; reprinted in Shepherd, 2:391–98.

53. In addition to the two articles mentioned above, Carlyle published "Legislation for Ireland" and "Irish Regiments of the New Era" in the *Examiner* and *Spectator*, respectively, on May 13, 1848; both are reprinted in Shepherd.

54. In an unpublished manuscript, Carlyle defended the argument that it was the "destiny" of England to rule Ireland while insisting that he did not mean to say that England was superior to Ireland (Harnick, 31). In a passage not published by Harnick (it is written on a small sheet that accompanies the manuscript), his metaphor of the body politic, suggesting that England as the head must not cut off its legs simply because it cannot clothe them properly, implies a natural subordination of Ireland to England ("The English Talent for Governing," Beinecke Library, New Haven).

55. By this time, he felt that religion had been degraded into sentimentalism (*LL*, 2:20, and "Model Prisons") and literature had become "Phallus-Worship" (Kaplan, 332–33, and "Phallus-Worship," 22).

56. On May 11—he was at work on the sixth pamphlet in late April and finished the seventh by the end of May—he wrote to his mother that he might stop at eight or ten pamphlets, and he did not make the decision to stop at eight until June 27 (Kaplan, 354). Carlyle always seems to have the epic model before him and, as Seigel points out, the *Aeneid* and *Paradise Lost* have twelve books ("*Latter-Day Pamphlets*," 159, 162–63).

57. Elsewhere he wrote that he did not have "the slightest thought of quitting" until he had "fired twelve cannon-salvoes (red-hot balls occasionally) thro' the infinite Dung heap which the English Universe seem[ed] to [him] to consist of at present" (Gray, 285).

58. All the elements of the framing device were added in 1853 except for Carlyle's introduction describing the setting and one description of indignant auditors leaving the room (*CME*, 4:354). The seven additions of 1853 dramatize the progressive audience reaction. At first there are mere shows of emotion (351, 354), then the first departures (354, 357). After this point, those still present become increasingly enthusiastic, "increase" their attention (357), laugh at the speaker's humor (359, 383), become silent (367), and, finally, "assent" (379). Both August and Levine comment on the artistry of the frame and how it invites the reader to identify with the represented audience. What

I would stress is that the strategy is intended to test the audience, to drive away nonbelievers rather than make us into believers. Note that, apart from August's introduction and notes, I do not cite his edition (see note on texts).

59. Michael Goldberg notes that this seems hyperbolic in light of the fact that Carlyle was published, as he admits in the same letter, that year in the *Spectator* and the *Examiner*. However, Carlyle is probably making reference to the fact that the article was cut by Forster, and he was forced to divide it between newspapers because of editorial objections to length and content ("Prospects of the French Republic," 22).

60. Carlyle blamed Russell for failing to deal with the principal problem facing England, the Irish Question (see Spedding, 755). During his journey to Ireland in 1849, he kept his distance from Russell's government by traveling in the company of the nationalist Gavan Duffy and turning down an invitation from Lord Clarendon, the chief British administrator in Ireland (see Kaplan, 342; *RIJ*, 49).

61. Carlyle's attacks on sentimental opposition to capital punishment in the *Pamphlets* may also be traced to this discussion of the massacres (see *OCLS*, 2:51–52; *LDP*, 73–79). Elsewhere he suggests that the good governor will lay on the "whip" (*RIJ*, 74; *CME*, 4:376).

62. The evolution of Carlyle's conception of the industrial regiments stretches back to the discussion of work in *Past and Present*. In 1844, he compared his labor in writing *Oliver Cromwell's Letters and Speeches* to the labor of the "170,000 men [who] had to die . . . draining the Neva Bog" in order to build St. Petersburg (Faulkner, 158). He first proposed that unemployed Irish be organized in regiments to drain the Bog of Allen and perform other public works projects that would make the land fertile in his 1848 article, "Irish Regiments of the New Era." Later that year, he read and inquired about a report in the *Times* of just such a project in France (*NL*, 2:61; Spedding, 750–51). During his tour of Ireland, he found most hope in projects that involved draining bogs and improving farming techniques; at one stop, he asked the proprietor of a model farm if he would like to have "2000 labourers already fed and clothed to your hand (such as sit in the Killarney workhouse idle at this moment)?" (*RIJ*, 133; see 53–54, 129–31, 203ff.; Duffy, 431). All of this suggests that Wilson is in error to argue that the idea came from Andrew Fletcher, a seventeenth-century political writer that Carlyle was reading about 1850; if anything, Carlyle was seeking further support for his ideas in Fletcher (Wilson, 4:252–53; see Goldberg and Seigel, *Latter-Day Pamphlets*, 531, n. 63).

63. Although Gallagher does not discuss "The Negro Question," this and the following paragraph are much indebted to her *Industrial Reformation of English Fiction* (chap. 1, esp. 6–21). On Carlyle's specific knowledge of this debate, see Campbell, "Carlyle and the Negro Question Again," and Christianson, "Writing of the 'Occasional Discourse.'"

64. Carlyle continued to use the horse metaphor in the later pamphlets

(see 96–97, 101–2, 152, 237–38, 244). These passages allude directly to the issues of "The Negro Question" by making reference throughout to the colonies and the freed slaves; at one point, for example, Hodge's horse is referred to as "Black Dobbin." In the 1853 "Nigger Question," Carlyle attempted to soften the effect of the analogy by arguing that Farmer Hodge should be compelled by law to "treat his horses justly" (*CME*, 4:370).

65. Mill anticipates many of the questions discussed here, including the point that slaveowners were motivated by "love of gold" rather than high ideals, and that Carlyle equates the noble task called for by the gods with the production of spices. Mill responds by asking whether the gods judge that "pepper is noble, freedom . . . contemptible" (*Essays on Equality*, 88, 91).

66. Carlyle was again running counter to a tide of popular sentiment. He must have had in mind the exposés of the sweated garment trade that had recently appeared in the *Morning Chronicle*, and the plight of seamstresses had been a cause célèbre since Mary Furley, a homeless and desperate seamstress, attempted suicide and inspired Thomas Hood's "Bridge of Sighs" earlier in the decade. Hood's poem had, in turn, inspired numerous popular paintings and prints. The dilemma of the seamstress was the subject of other contemporary social commentary, including Hood's "Song of the Shirt" (1843), Elizabeth Gaskell's *Mary Barton* (1848), and Richard Redgrave's painting "The Seamstress" (1844, 1846).

67. "The Nigger Question" is, if anything, more racist than "The Negro Question." Not only did Carlyle alter the title from "Negro" to the more offensive "Nigger," but he repeated the idea that "the Black gentleman is born to be a servant," as well as the assertion that blacks and whites were created differently by God and blacks belong at the bottom of the social hierarchy (*CME*, 4:368, 371, 361). The 1853 version also provided further support for anti-abolitionists by suggesting that slavery could be made just (*CME*, 4:368–72). For a different point of view, see Tarr, "Emendation as Challenge." Although the Governor Eyre controversy will be discussed below, it is relevant here for the light it sheds on this debate. Gillian Workman has recently argued that Carlyle's "involvement in the Eyre controversy" was not a result of "racist views" and that "Carlyle's language in describing the Negro . . . was surely more a rhetorical device than an expression of racial disgust" (85). In light of Carlyle's overtly racist comments, it is hard to make sense of this distinction. Even if rhetoric can be separated from meaning, which is doubtful, Carlyle's belief in racial inequality is difficult to square with the idea that his writings are merely some kind of Swiftian satire. If he had not harbored racial prejudices, how else could he have responded to the Eyre furor in these words: "Nay (*privately very!*) if Eyre had shot the whole Nigger population, and flung them into the sea, would it probably have been much harm even to *them*, not to speak of *us*?" (Bliss, 388; see also Hall, esp. 177–82).

68. Carlyle's racial prejudices were not limited to these groups. Already in *Past and Present*, he had portrayed medieval Jewish moneylenders as "insatiable . . . horseleech[es]" and approved of the use of torture to force them to abandon claims for payment of debt (64, 65, 182; see 96). Nor were his prejudices confined to medieval moneylenders. After Disraeli opposed Peel on Corn Law repeal, Carlyle rarely mentioned his name without adding an anti-Semitic slur, depicting him as Judas, the merchant of Venice, and a descendent of the impenitent thief; this may have led him, in 1848, to oppose a bill that would allow Jews to sit in Parliament (*LDP*, 171; *NL*, 2:124, 125, 141, 143, 148; *LL*, 1:450–52; see also Gross, 30–31). Carlyle did, of course, befriend educated members of the Irish middle class and denied that he had any anti-Celtic prejudice in *Oliver Cromwell's Letters and Speeches* (1:407). Yet other evidence suggests a strong prejudice, as does, for example, his tendency to classify the Irish by "types" (*RIJ*, 12, 19).

69. Hepworth Dixon, who may, of course, have read this reply to "The Negro Question" in *Fraser's*, also noted, in the *Athenæum*, how often Carlyle invoked "'the Immortal Gods,' 'the Immensities,' 'the Eternities,' and such like personages" (126).

70. Asked by a young man from Manchester for advice on pursuing a career in literature, Carlyle replied that if he really intended to do "*a man's work* in literature" and not merely entertain, he could not expect to make a living from the career (*LL*, 1:440). In his journal, Carlyle had recently written that he no longer believed in "Art" and now considered it "one of the deadliest *cants*" (*LL*, 1:453; see also *RWE*, 395).

Chapter 5

1. Although the quotation appears in a passage in which Wilson cites a letter of 1847, the reference to *Pamphlets* suggests a later date, probably 1850. Wilson's documentation is scanty, and it seems likely that he has run together quotations from two different letters here.

2. See also Wilson, 5:85; Reid, 1:494–95; Shepherd, 2:152; Kaplan, 397; and Fielding, "Carlyle's Unpublished Comments on the Northcote-Trevelyan Report."

3. See LaValley, 304, 308. Robert Keith Miller is misled by Carlyle's preference for prose over poetry into concluding that Carlyle was opposed to Sterling's choice of literature for a career, but the narrative represents Carlyle, notwithstanding his ambivalence toward literature, pushing Sterling toward that career in preference to the religious vocation (41).

4. Sterling had been attacked in 1848 by the high church *English Review* in an article entitled "On Tendencies towards the Subversion of Faith." The cause was then taken up by the even more fervent Evangelical paper, *The*

Record, which attacked him repeatedly in the spring of 1849. One of his worst offenses was that he "did not scruple to avow that he regard[ed] Carlyle as being a truly inspired Isaiah!" (Tuell, 364).

5. Tuell, 272–80, 292–300, 337–50; Harding, passim. Harding argues that, while Sterling differed with the church on certain questions, he was fundamentally orthodox. Tuell and Harding were not the first to note that Carlyle distorted Sterling's religious career; it was already recognized by some of his contemporaries. See, for example, the review "Carlyle's Life of Sterling," in the *Christian Observer*.

6. Another instance of Carlyle's shaping of Sterling's biography is discussed by Anne Skabarnicki in "Too Hasty Souls."

7. See the discussion of Coleridge above, chap. 3. Gerald Mulderig demonstrates how Carlyle set Sterling against Coleridge but does not note the similarities between them. My argument is that Carlyle's literature did not turn out to be any more satisfactory than Coleridge's religion. Although Sterling was active while Coleridge was inactive, Sterling's activities had no more practical issue than did Coleridge's endless talk.

8. Carlyle gave Sterling this advice repeatedly between 1837 and 1842, and he may well have given it both before and after those dates (*CL*, 10:128–29, 234–35, 12:187, 263, 321, 348, 13:132, 14:22, 23). A good example of his advice to aspiring poets may be found in his exchange of letters with W. C. Bennett. In 1847, Bennett sent Carlyle a sonnet, and Carlyle replied with his customary advice on seeking a better career than literature. When, in 1853, Bennett sent a pamphlet on educational reform, Carlyle replied enthusiastically that it was "much more melodiously 'poetical' . . . than the best written verses are" (Shepherd, 2:9, 135).

9. His acquiescence to Browning, after reading *Men and Women* (1855), is phrased in almost the same way: "I do not at this point any longer forbid you *verse*, as probably I once did. I perceive it has grown to be your dialect, it comes more naturally than prose. . . . Continue to write in verse, if you find it handier" (*LMSB*, 299–300).

10. Other reviews noting the change in tone include Gilfillan, esp. 717; "*The Life of John Sterling*," *Examiner*, esp. 659; "John Sterling and His Biographers," *Dublin University Magazine*, esp. 185–86; George Eliot (in Seigel, *Critical Heritage*, 377); Francis Newman (in Seigel, *Critical Heritage*, 380); John Tulloch (in Seigel, *Critical Heritage*, 393). Of course, Carlyle was only half pleased that a book he considered "light" and unimportant received a better reception than his other recent works (Marrs, 685).

11. The *North British Quarterly* and George Gilfillan in the *Eclectic Review* charged him with "Nihilism" and "despair" (*North British*, 245; Gilfillan, 721, 720). Even the *Spectator*, which had published Carlyle's articles on Ireland in 1848 and attributed "an attractive charm" to the new book, complained that

he "has no right . . . to weaken or destroy a faith which he cannot or will not replace with a loftier" (Brimley, 1024).

12. Prince Albert had proposed the pension, but Lord Aberdeen turned it down on the grounds of Carlyle's "Heterodoxy" (*NL*, 2:157). When Carlyle was nominated for the office of rector of the University of Glasgow, the Scottish papers attacked him for denying "that the revealed Word of God is 'the way, the truth, the life'" (Wilson, 5:131; see *NL*, 2:170–71).

13. This manuscript, written in November 1852, was printed by Froude in *EL*, 2:8–15. I cite the more accurate transcription of Murray Baumgarten in "Carlyle and 'Spiritual Optics.'" Other manuscripts produced during this period include "On the project of appointing to the civil service by merit alone" (Beinecke Library, New Haven), a manuscript on constitutional government (National Library of Scotland), and another arguing that the aristocracy only survived historically because they "were the beautifullest" (National Library of Scotland; reprinted in Trela, "Carlyle and the Beautiful People"). The letters of the early 1850s also abound with opinions on recent political and cultural events: Irish land reform (Duffy, 450, 454; *NL*, 2:121–22); education reform (Wilson, 5:19, 24; Shepherd, 2:135); the Great Exhibition of "Wind-ustry" (*LMSB*, 287; *RWE*, 468; *NL*, 1:106; *LL*, 2:84; Sadler, 286); Napoleon III's coup (Wilson, 5:25; *NL*, 2:119); changes in the English cabinet (Wilson, 5:25–26; *NL*, 1:124–25, 141; Sadler, 289); and the Crimean War (*RWE*, 506; *LL*, 2:163–64).

14. Concerned, like *The Life of John Sterling*, with the problem of Jesuitism, this manuscript records the attempt of the Catholic Guise family to repress the truth of the Reformation, a process that only brings back the repressed truth with greater violence in the French Revolution (27, 61; the same point is made in *FG*, 1:223). Comparisons with the French Revolution of 1789 appear throughout (e.g., 39, 45, 46).

15. Carlyle published a few very minor writings between the time he completed *The Life of John Sterling* and 1855, when he became immersed in *Frederick the Great*, and after 1855 there is little in the way even of manuscripts addressing current issues. Only "Ilias (Americana) in Nuce" (1863), which was only half a page long and was aimed primarily at America, not England, sought controversy.

16. In addition to the implicit comparison in *Frederick the Great*, Carlyle explicitly compared James Carlyle and Friedrich Wilhelm in the 1866 *Reminiscences* (333). The fact that he conceived the figure of Friedrich Wilhelm in terms of the figure of his own father explains how he could write so approvingly of a figure whom others find barbarous.

17. In referring to the first half of the history, I mean to indicate the structural rather than literal division of the work. Carlyle had planned four volumes, two covering the period up to the death of Friedrich Wilhelm and

two on the reign of Frederick the Great, but the second half grew on him as he wrote and became, in the first edition, four volumes in itself. Thus the completed edition totaled six volumes. Carlyle's original intention can still be discerned in the division of the work into books. The first two volumes have ten books and the last four have eleven (originally intended to be ten). To indicate this division of the work into two parts, I will refer to the first two volumes as the first half and the last four volumes as the second half of the history. Note, however, that citations are from the Centenary Edition, which has eight volumes, the "second half" beginning at 3:278.

18. Previous commentary has noted the oedipal conflict in the first two volumes but assumed that it is resolved when Frederick submits to Friedrich Wilhelm. J. Rosenberg, for example, argues that the last four volumes lack the coherence that this theme gives to the first two (163–65). My argument is that the father/son conflict persists in the last four volumes, which fail for formal rather than thematic reasons.

19. Carlyle is very insistent on this point, repeating it several times: "Not the Peaceable magnanimities, but the Warlike, are the thing appointed Friedrich . . . henceforth"; war is his "inexorable element," while "Peace and the Muses" are "denied him" (3:395, 4:363, 5:196). Carlyle shaped his representation of Frederick's life to emphasize the victory of Bellona over the Muses. While 70 percent of the final four volumes (eight of the eleven books) represent Frederick's wars, the period of the wars only occupied 27 percent of the historical time covered. Carlyle condenses the ten years' peace between the Silesian wars and the Seven Years' War, as well as the final twenty-three years of Frederick's life, each into one book.

20. Carlyle again shapes his narrative to deemphasize Frederick's interest in the arts. While he represents Voltaire as seeking trouble in the controversy, Nancy Mitford suggests that Frederick actually set Maupertius and Voltaire against one another (11–12). Mitford also points out that Carlyle never mentions Frederick's interest in the rococo art of Watteau (3; see 12).

21. In another passage, Carlyle's phrasing similarly suggests that Voltaire is an inverted Dante. Just as *The Divine Comedy* "belongs to ten Christian centuries, only the finishing of it is Dante's," the "Theory of the Universe" of the eighteenth century is "not properly of Voltaire's creating, but only of his uttering and publishing" (*HHW*, 98; *FG*, 3:193).

22. Another example is an anecdotal "bit of modern chivalry" performed at the Battle of Fontenoy that has been "circulating round the world . . . for a century." Carlyle discovers a "small irrefragable Document" demonstrating that the truth is "quite the reverse" and concludes that the story, which does not belong to the folk but to the literary French, is a product of "French Mess-rooms" (5:98–100).

23. Carlyle began the actual writing of *Frederick the Great* in the spring of

1855, and already in the spring of 1856, and again that summer, he was writing that he hoped to send the "First half of [his] wretched Book" to press in the autumn (*NL*, 2:178; *RWE*, 511). Yet it was two years later, in June 1858, before he could report that he had only a sheet and a half of the first two volumes to write, and even so there were further delays (*NL*, 2:192). At work on what he initially thought of as the second pair of volumes, he again optimistically reported early in 1859 that he planned to finish in a year (Duffy, 583). Yet, in late 1860, he admitted that his work went "very slow[ly]" and he was still not "yet *quite* done" with the second of the planned ten—it turned out to be eleven—books (*NL*, 2:209). The process of delay continued until the autumn of 1864, when he could finally say with confidence that the history would soon be finished; even then he was still some six months away from finishing it (*NL*, 2:225, 226; see also 225; *RWE*, 534; Duffy, 588; Allingham, *Letters*, 135).

24. Phrases like "If I live to get out of this last Prussian Scrape" and "if I live to finish" occur frequently in his letters (Spedding, 759; *RWE*, 496; Marrs, 719). He also compared writing *Frederick the Great* to being "choked," "nearly ended," and "nearly killed" (*RWE*, 526; Marrs, 740–41; *RWE*, 551; see *LL*, 2:188, 247–48; Duffy, 578; Spedding, 760).

25. Carlyle quotes his, or possibly Neuberg's, faithful translation of Gustav Freytag's *Neue Bilder aus dem Leben des deutschen Volkes* (397–408).

26. A letter of 1856, in which Carlyle is concerned to argue that Frederick's tactics had still not been improved upon and that Napoleon had not introduced any genuine innovations, suggests that Carlyle's detailed accounts of Frederick's intricate military maneuvers and tactics may partially be accounted for by his desire to see in them Frederick's true artistic genius (Wilson, 5:208–9).

Chapter 6

1. Even in the early 1870s, Carlyle continued to produce occasional public pronouncements. Nonetheless, for the last five years of his life, he was nearly silent, and from 1879 to his death in early 1881, there is almost no recorded writing. Since Froude is selective in his quotations, it is difficult to tell when the journal ends, but there seem to be no entries after 1878, the year of his last published piece of writing. The last letter of those published is a letter of February 8, 1879, to his brother John, who died in September of that year (*NL*, 2:341). Letters to most other correspondents stopped earlier, about 1875–76 (see *RWE*, 587; Cate, 208; Copeland, 248; Marrs, 788; Duffy, 606).

2. LaValley appropriately describes the Jane Carlyle of *The Reminiscences* as a sun goddess (330). Carlyle describes her as sunny (51, 58), bright (155, 317), shining (69, 128), and luminous (128); he also praises her lambency (99), brilliancy (99), and irradiation (123; see also 126, 133–34, 302). The epitaph

he wrote for her refers to her "bright existence" and "clearness of discernment" and describes her as "the light of his life" (*LM*, 2:392; see also *LL*, 2:369).

3. Examples abound. About midway through "Edward Irving," he writes that although the manuscript should probably be "*burnt* when done," he will continue with it because it calms and soothes him (307). After finishing "Lord Jeffrey," he writes "I must carefully endeavour to find out some new work for myself" (341). But the compulsion to narrate was so strong that after writing that he has "no wish or need to record" Jane Carlyle's death, he goes on to do so (164).

4. This perhaps needs to be qualified by the fact that the reminiscence has never been published in the form that Carlyle apparently envisioned, namely, alongside Jane Carlyle's diary of April 15–July 5, 1856, in which he discovered just how great her pain had been, that she had even feared she was dying (see *NLM*, 87–109). Nonetheless, Carlyle does insist that she was happy in spite of this and other evidence of her unhappiness. LaValley argues that he may have been prompted by "guilt" and a "need to delude himself about the central meaning of his life" to create a "loving and overpoweringly important Jane" (329).

5. He learned from her diary at this time that while he was boring her with his struggles to write the account of the battle of Mollwitz she "felt convinced she was dying" (134). His schedule while writing *Frederick the Great* allowed her only one half-hour a day of his time. He also realized that he was so obsessed with working that he refused to take the time to buy a carriage for her, a purchase that might have prevented the accident that he clearly felt hastened her death (145).

6. Some of the rhetoric is new, but Carlyle's most incisive criticisms owe more to his friend Ruskin than to his own insights. While the early Ruskin had been profoundly influenced by Carlyle, the influence was by this time running in the other direction. For example, he had not for a long while, if ever, been concerned, as he is in "Shooting Niagara," with the soot and squalor of industry and the pollution of streams, but these were major themes of Ruskin's criticism of industry (see *CME*, 5:31, 47). By this date, Carlyle had read the first volume of *Stones of Venice* (Cate, 61), the third and part of the fourth volumes of *Modern Painters* (Cate, 72–73, 75), *Unto This Last* (Cate, 89), the "Essays in Political Economy" (Cate, 100, 103–4), and *Ethics of the Dust* (Cate, 113).

7. The section in which this passage appears was not included in *Macmillan's Magazine* where the essay first appeared, but it did appear when the essay was reprinted as a pamphlet later that year.

8. This appeared in the passage that was not included in *Macmillan's*. See previous note.

9. Semmel explains that "Martial law could only be legally employed when

used to suppress a revolt; when used to punish a crime, it was illegal" (146; see 128ff.).

10. Mill had sent a copy to Carlyle when the book was published (Wilson, 5:340). At the time, Carlyle found the reasoning powerful and praised it as "serious, ingenious, clear," but he could not accept its fundamental argument and went on to register his "perfect and profound dissent for the basis it rests upon" (*NL*, 2:196; see Larkin, 74). The manuscript of the response Carlyle wrote in 1865 is transcribed in Trela, "A New (Old) Review." Carlyle worked only two days, October 18–19, 1865, before abandoning the critique. Trela, who remarks that it is "surprising" Carlyle would return to *On Liberty* six years after reading it, seems not to have noticed that Mill had recently been elected to Parliament or that Carlyle began writing on the day of Palmerston's death.

11. Carlyle's defense of Eyre has sometimes been confused with his implicit proslavery arguments in "The Negro Question" and "Ilias in Nuce." Those writings had used the argument that slavery constitutes a potentially superior form of relationship between employers and workers to industrial capitalism. But the Eyre controversy had to do with the relationship between governors and governed, not employers and employed. The merits of his earlier argument aside, Carlyle's argument in this case has to do with sustaining social order—saving the ship—rather than creating just social relationships, and the charge against Eyre was not that he intervened paternalistically to make the Jamaicans work—the action Carlyle advocated in "The Negro Question"—but that he had treated them ruthlessly and unjustly.

12. Carlyle strongly identifies with, yet vehemently rejects, both positions. His narrative of Irving—the "uncommon man" who arrives in London to great acclaim, holds audiences captive with "Rhadmanthine expositions of duty and ideal," but then has his "Prophecy" rejected as heresy—closely parallels his own career (232, 283, 278; see 254, 288ff.). Although he does not identify as closely with Jeffrey, he cannot help discovering affinities with the man he classes as the greatest literary critic of his time and a "Scotch Voltaire" (340, 341; see Skabarnicki, "Annandale Evangelist," 27–28). The latter suggests an indirect link as well, since there are numerous affinities between Carlyle and the Voltaire of *Frederick the Great* who, like Carlyle, is a solitary Ishmael (3:187, 4:409, 5:237 et al.), considers giving up literature when condemned for his heterodoxy (4:453), writes on Mohammed, and becomes dyspeptic (5:333).

Works Cited

Carlyle's Published Works

With the exception of *Past and Present* and *Sartor Resartus*, all citations of Carlyle's works are to the Centenary edition edited by H. D. Traill. I have cited Richard D. Altick's edition of *Past and Present* and C. F. Harrold's edition of *Sartor Resartus*. I cite the Centenary edition (and Harrold's, which is based on it) because of its general availability. However, recent scholarship has discovered severe corruption of the text in the Centenary, especially regarding accidentals like capitalization and hyphenation peculiar to Carlyle's style. I have therefore checked all citations (with the exception of Altick's *Past and Present*, which was based on the first edition) against first editions and silently emended all accidentals to conform to the first edition. Emendations of substantives, of which there are only a handful, are indicated in the notes. The following list of editions of works published in Carlyle's lifetime includes the editions collated as well as the editions cited in this study.

Thomas Carlyle. *The Collected Poems of Thomas and Jane Welsh Carlyle*. Ed. Rodger L. Tarr and Fleming McClelland. Greenwood, Fla.: Penkevill, 1986.

——. *Critical and Miscellaneous Essays*. 4 vols. Boston: James Monroe, 1838.

——. *The French Revolution*. 3 vols. London: James Fraser, 1837.

——. *German Romance*. 2 vols. Edinburgh: William Tait, 1827.

——. *The History of Friedrich II of Prussia*. 6 vols. London: Chapman and Hall, 1858–65.

——. *Latter-Day Pamphlets*. Ed. Michael K. Goldberg and Jules P. Seigel. Canada: Canadian Federation for the Humanities, 1983.

——. *The Life of Friedrich Schiller*. London: Taylor and Hessey, 1825.

——. *The Life of John Sterling*. London: Chapman and Hall, 1851.

——. *Oliver Cromwell's Letters and Speeches*. 2 vols. London: Chapman and Hall, 1845.

——. *On Heroes and Hero-Worship, and the Heroic in History*. London: James Fraser, 1841.

——. *Past and Present*. Ed. Richard Altick. Boston: Houghton Mifflin, 1965.

211

————. *Sartor Resartus*. Ed. C. F. Harrold. Indianapolis: Odyssey, 1937.

————. *Sartor Resartus. Fraser's Magazine* 8 (1833): 581–92, 669–84; 9 (1834): 177–95, 301–13, 443–55, 664–74; 10 (1834): 77–87, 182–93.

————. "Shooting Niagara: And After?" *Macmillan's Magazine* 16 (1867): 319–36.

————. *Shooting Niagara: And After?* London: Macmillan, 1867.

————. *Wilhelm Meister's Apprenticeship*. Edinburgh: Oliver and Boyd, 1824.

————. *Works of Thomas Carlyle*. Ed. H. D. Traill. 30 vols. London: Chapman and Hall, 1896–99.

Sources of Carlyle's Uncollected Writings, Letters, and Journals

Allingham, E. A. H., and E. Baumer Williams, eds. *Letters to William Allingham*. 1911. London: Longmans, 1971.

Allingham, William. *Diary*. 1907. Fontwell, Sussex: Centaur, 1967.

Baumgarten, Murray. "Carlyle and 'Spiritual Optics,'" *Victorian Studies* 11 (1968): 503–22.

Bliss, Trudy, ed. *Thomas Carlyle: Letters to His Wife*. London: Gollancz, 1953.

Brooks, Richard A. E. *Journey to Germany, Autumn 1858*. New Haven: Yale University Press, 1940.

Carlyle, Alexander, ed. *Historical Sketches*. London: Chapman and Hall, n.d.

————. *Letters of Thomas Carlyle to John Stuart Mill, John Sterling and Robert Browning*. New York: Stokes, 1923.

————. *New Letters and Memorials of Jane Welsh Carlyle*. London: Lane, 1903.

————. *New Letters of Thomas Carlyle*. 2 vols. London: Lane, 1904.

————. "Thomas Carlyle and Thomas Spedding: Their Friendship and Correspondence." *Cornhill Magazine* 123 (1921): 516–37, 742–68.

Carlyle, Thomas. "Peter Nimmo," *Fraser's Magazine* 3 (1831): 12–16.

————. *Reminiscences of My Irish Journey in 1849*. New York: Harper, 1882.

————. *Wotton Reinfred*. In *Last Words of Thomas Carlyle*. London: Longmans, Green, 1892.

Cate, George Allan, ed. *The Correspondence of Thomas Carlyle and John Ruskin*. Stanford: Stanford University Press, 1982.

Clubbe, John, ed. *Two Reminiscences of Thomas Carlyle*. Durham: Duke University Press, 1974.

Copeland, Charles Townsend, ed. *Letters of Thomas Carlyle to His Youngest Sister*. Boston: Houghton, 1899.

Duffy, Gavan. "Conversations and Correspondence with Thomas Carlyle." *The Contemporary Review* 61 (1892): 120–52, 279–304, 430–56, 577–608.

Faulkner, Peter. "Carlyle's Letters to Charles Redwood." *Yearbook of English Studies* 2 (1972): 139–80.

Fielding, K. J. "Unpublished Manuscripts—II: Carlyle's Scenario for *Cromwell*." *Carlyle Newsletter* 2 (1980): 6–13.

———. "Carlyle's Unpublished Comments on the Northcote-Trevelyan Report. *Carlyle Annual* 10 (1989): 5–13.

Fielding, K. J., and Rodger Tarr, eds. "A Preface by Carlyle." *Carlyle Past and Present*. London: Vision, 1976.

Froude, James Anthony, ed. *Letters and Memorials of Jane Welsh Carlyle*. 2 vols. in 1. New York: Scribners, 1883.

———. *My Relations with Carlyle*. London: Longmans, Green, 1903.

———. *Thomas Carlyle: A History of the First Forty Years of His Life, 1795–1835*. 2 vols. London: Longmans, 1890.

———. *Thomas Carlyle: A History of His Life in London, 1834–1881*. 2 vols. London: Longmans, 1919.

Gray, W. Forbes. "Carlyle and John Forster: An Unpublished Correspondence." *Quarterly Review* 268 (1937): 271–87.

Greene, J. Reay, ed. *Lectures on the History of Literature Delivered by Thomas Carlyle April to July 1838*. New York: Scribners, 1892.

Harnick, Phyllis. "Point and Counterpoint: Carlyle and Mill on Ireland in 1848." *Carlyle Newsletter* 7 (1986): 26–33.

Kaplan, Fred. "'Phallus-Worship' (1848): Unpublished Manuscripts III—A Response to the Revolution of 1848." *Carlyle Newsletter* 2 (1980): 19–23.

———. *Thomas Carlyle: A Biography*. Ithaca, N.Y.: Cornell University Press, 1983.

King, Margaret P. "'Illudo Chartis': An Initial Study in Carlyle's Mode of Composition." *Modern Language Review* 49 (1954): 164–75.

Larkin, Henry. "Carlyle and Mrs. Carlyle: A Ten-Years' Reminiscence." *British Quarterly Review* 74 (1881): 28–85.

Marrs, Edwin W., Jr., ed. *The Letters of Thomas Carlyle to His Brother Alexander Carlyle*. Cambridge: Harvard University Press, 1968.

Norton, Charles Eliot, ed. *Reminiscences*. 1887. London: Dent, 1972.

———. *Two Note Books of Thomas Carlyle*. 1898. Mamaroneck, N.Y.: Appel, 1972.

Reid, T. Wemyss. *The Life, Letters, and Friendships of Richard Monckton Milnes, First Lord Houghton*. 2 vols. London: Cassell, 1890.

[Sadler, Thomas]. "Carlyle and Neuberg." *Macmillan's Magazine* 50 (1884): 280–97.

Sanders, Charles Richard, Kenneth J. Fielding, Clyde de L. Ryals, Ian Campbell, et al., eds. *Collected Letters of Thomas and Jane Welsh Carlyle*. Durham: Duke University Press, 1970–.

Shepherd, Richard Herne. *Memoirs of the Life and Writings of Thomas Carlyle*. 2 vols. London: Allen, 1881.

Shine, Hill, ed. *Carlyle's Unfinished History of German Literature*. Lexington: University of Kentucky Press, 1951.

Slater, Joseph, ed. *The Correspondence of Emerson and Carlyle*. New York: Columbia University Press, 1964.

Tarr, Rodger L., ed. "The Guises." *Victorian Studies* 25 (1981): 7–80.

Trela, D. J. "Carlyle and the Beautiful People: An Unpublished Manuscript." *Carlyle Newsletter* 5 (1984): 36–41.

———. "A New (Old) Review of Mill's *Liberty*: A Note on Carlyle's and Mill's Friendship." *Carlyle Newsletter* 6 (1985): 23–27.

Tuell, Anne Kimball. *John Sterling: A Representative Victorian*. New York: Macmillan, 1941.

Wilson, David Alec. *Carlyle*. 6 vols. London: Kegan, Paul, 1923.

Other Works Cited

Abbott, Wilbur Cortez. *Conflicts with Oblivion*. Cambridge: Harvard University Press, 1935.

Adrian, Arthur A., and Vonna H. Adrian. "Frederick the Great: 'That Unutterable Horror of a Prussian Book.'" In Fielding and Tarr, 177–97.

Alison, Archibald. *History of Europe from the Commencement of the French Revolution in 1789 to the Restoration of the Bourbons in 1815*. Edinburgh: Blackwood, 1839.

apRoberts, Ruth. *The Ancient Dialect: Carlyle and Comparative Religion*. Berkeley: University of California Press, 1988.

Arac, Jonathan. *Commissioned Spirits: The Shaping of Social Motion in Dickens, Carlyle, Melville and Hawthorne*. New Brunswick, N.J.: Rutgers University Press, 1979.

———. *Critical Genealogies: Historical Situations for Postmodern Literary Studies*. New York: Columbia University Press, 1987.

Arnold, Matthew. *Culture and Anarchy*. Ed. J. Dover Wilson. 1932. Cambridge: Cambridge University Press, 1969.

Ashton, T. S. *The Industrial Revolution: 1769–1830*. 1948. London: Oxford University Press, 1968.

August, Eugene R., ed. Introduction. *Thomas Carlyle: The Nigger Question, John Stuart Mill: The Negro Question*. New York: Appleton, 1971.

Baker, Lee C. R. "The Diamond Necklace and the Golden Ring: Historical Imagination in Carlyle and Browning." *Victorian Poetry* 24 (1986): 31–46.

Baker, Richard. *Chronicle of the Kings of England*. London: Tooke and Sawbridge, 1684.

Bakhtin, Mikhail. *The Dialogic Imagination*. Trans. Caryl Emerson and Michael Holquist. Ed. Michael Holquist. Austin: University of Texas Press, 1981.

Barthes, Roland. "From Work to Text." In *Image-Music-Text*, trans. Stephen Heath, 155–64. New York: Hill and Wang, 1977.

———. "Le Discours de l'histoire." *Informations sur les sciences sociales* 6.4 (1967): 65–75.

Bendix, Reinhard. *Kings or People: Power and the Mandate to Rule.* Berkeley: University of California Press, 1978.

Ben-Israel, Hedva. *English Historians on the French Revolution.* Cambridge: Cambridge University Press, 1968.

Benveniste, Emile. *Problems in General Linguistics.* Trans. Mary E. Meek. Coral Gables, Fla.: University of Miami Press, 1971.

Bidney, Martin. "Diminishing Epiphanies of Odin: Carlyle's Reveries of Primal Fire." *Modern Language Quarterly* 44 (1983): 51–64.

Brantlinger, Patrick. *The Spirit of Reform: British Literature and Politics, 1832–1867.* Cambridge, Mass.: Harvard University Press, 1977.

Briggs, Asa. *The Age of Improvement: 1783–1867.* New York: McKay, 1959.

[Brimley, George]. "Carlyle's *Life of John Sterling.*" *Spectator* 24 (1851): 1023–24.

Brookes, Gerry H. *The Rhetorical Form of Carlyle's* Sartor Resartus. Berkeley: University of California Press, 1972.

Brown, Richard Harvey. *Society as Text: Essays on Rhetoric, Reason, and Reality.* Chicago: University of Chicago Press, 1987.

Burke, Edmund. *Reflections on the Revolution in France.* Ed. Thomas H. D. Mahoney. Indianapolis: Bobbs, 1955.

Cabau, Jacques. *Le Prométhée Enchaîné: Essai sur la genèse de l'œuvre de 1795 à 1834.* Paris: Presses Universitaires de France, 1968.

Campbell, Ian. "Carlyle and the Negro Question Again." *Criticism* 13 (1971): 279–90.

———. "Edward Irving, Carlyle and the Stage." *Studies in Scottish Literature* 8 (1971): 166–73.

Campbell, Ian, and Rodger Tarr. "Carlyle's Early Study of German: 1819–21." *Illinois Quarterly* 34 (December 1971): 19–27.

"Carlyle's Life of Sterling." *Christian Observer* 52 (April 1852): 262–76; rpt. *Littell's Living Age* 33 (1852): 470–76.

Carrothers, W. A. *Emigration from the British Isles with Special Reference to the Development of the Overseas Dominions.* London: King, 1929.

Carter, April. *Authority and Democracy.* London: Routledge, 1979.

Caserio, Robert L. *Plot, Story, and the Novel: From Dickens and Poe to the Modern Period.* Princeton: Princeton University Press, 1979.

"Chartism." *Monthly Chronicle* 5 (1840): 97–107.

Christianson, Aileen. "Carlyle and Universal Penny Postage." *Carlyle Newsletter* 4 (1983): 16–19.

———. "On the Writing of the 'Occasional Discourse on the Negro Question,'" *Carlyle Newsletter* 2 (1980): 13–19.

Clubbe, John, ed. *Carlyle and His Contemporaries.* Durham: Duke University Press, 1976.

———. "Carlyle as Epic Historian." In *Victorian Literature and Society: Essays*

Presented to Richard D. Altick, ed. James R. Kincaid and Albert J. Kuhn, 119–45. Columbus: Ohio State University Press, 1984.

———. "Epic Heroes in *The French Revolution*." In *Thomas Carlyle 1981: Papers Given at the International Thomas Carlyle Centenary Symposium*, ed. Horst W. Drescher, 165–85. Scottish Studies 1. Frankfurt: Lang, 1983.

Coleridge, Samuel T. *Lay Sermons*. Ed. R. J. White. Princeton: Princeton University Press, 1972.

———. *On the Constitution of the Church and State*. Ed. John Colmer. Princeton: Princeton University Press, 1976.

Collmer, Robert G. "Carlyle, Francia, and Their Critics." *Studies in Scottish Literature* 14 (1979): 112–22.

Culler, A. Dwight. *The Victorian Mirror of History*. New Haven: Yale University Press, 1985.

Cumming, Mark. "Carlyle, Whitman, and the Disimprisonment of Epic." *Victorian Studies* 29 (1986): 207–26.

———. *A Disimprisoned Epic: Form and Vision in Carlyle's* French Revolution. Philadelphia: University of Pennsylvania Press, 1988.

Dale, Peter Allan. "*Sartor Resartus* and the Inverse Sublime: The Art of Humorous Deconstruction." In *Allegory, Myth, and Symbol*, ed. Morton W. Bloomfield, 293–312. Cambridge: Harvard University Press, 1981.

———. *The Victorian Critic and the Idea of History*. Cambridge: Harvard University Press, 1977.

Davidoff, Leonore, Jean L'Esperance, and Howard Newby. "Landscape with Figures: Home and Community in English Society." In *The Rights and Wrongs of Women*, ed. Juliet Mitchell and Ann Oakley, 139–75. Harmondsworth: Penguin, 1976.

DeLaura, David J. "Ishmael as Prophet: *Heroes and Hero-Worship* and the Self-Expressive Basis of Carlyle's Art." *Texas Studies in English* 2 (1965): 705–32.

[DeQuincey, Thomas]. "Goethe's *Wilhelm Meister's Apprenticeship*." *London Magazine* 10 (1824): 189–97.

Derrida, Jacques. "The Law of Genre." In *On Narrative*, ed. W. J. T. Mitchell, 51–77. Chicago: University of Chicago Press, 1981.

[Dixon, Hepworth]. "*The Life of John Sterling*." *Athenæum* 1251 (1851): 1088–90.

Donovan, Robert A. "Carlyle and the Climate of Hero-Worship." *University of Toronto Quarterly* 42 (1973): 122–41.

Eagleton, Terry. *The Function of Criticism: From* The Spectator *to Post-Structuralism*. London: Verso, 1984.

Edwards, Janet Ray. "Carlyle and the Fictions of Belief: *Sartor Resartus* to *Past and Present*." In Clubbe, *Carlyle*, 91–111.

Farrell, John P. *Revolution as Tragedy: The Dilemma of the Moderate from Scott to Arnold*. Ithaca, N.Y.: Cornell University Press, 1980.

Fielding, K. J. "Carlyle Considers New Zealand." *Landfall* 129 (1979): 51–60.

Fielding, K. J., and Rodger L. Tarr, eds. *Carlyle Past and Present*. London: Vision, 1976.

Fleishman, Avrom. *Figures of Autobiography: The Language of Self-Writing in Victorian and Modern England*. Berkeley: University of California Press, 1983.

Foerster, Donald M. *The Fortunes of Epic Poetry: A Study in English and American Criticism, 1750–1950*. Washington, D.C.: Catholic University of America Press, 1962.

Ford, George H. "The Governor Eyre Case in England." *University of Toronto Quarterly* 17 (1948): 219–33.

Foucault, Michel. *The Order of Things*. New York: Vintage, 1970.

Fraser, James. *Hand Book for Travellers in Ireland*. London: Longmans, 1844.

Freytag, Gustav. *Neue Bilder aus dem Leben des deutschen Volkes*. Leipzig: Hirzel, 1862.

Frith, C. H. Introduction. *The Letters and Speeches of Oliver Cromwell with Elucidations by Thomas Carlyle*. Ed. S. C. Lomas. London: Methuen, 1904.

Galbraith, John Kenneth. *Economics in Perspective: A Critical History*. Boston: Houghton Mifflin, 1987.

Gallagher, Catherine. *The Industrial Reformation of English Fiction: Social Discourse and Narrative Form, 1832–1867*. Chicago: University of Chicago Press, 1985.

Gaskell, Peter. *Artisans and Machinery: The Moral and Physical Condition of the Manufacturing Population Considered with Reference to Mechanical Substitutes for Human Labour*. 1836. London: Cass, 1968.

Gilbert, Elliot. "'A Wondrous Contiguity': Anachronism in Carlyle's Prophecy and Art." *PMLA* 87 (1972): 432–42.

Gilfillan, George. "*The Life of John Sterling*." *Eclectic Review* 104 (1851): 717–29.

Gissing, George. *New Grub Street*. Ed. Bernard Bergonzi. Harmondsworth: Penguin, 1968.

Goldberg, Michael. "A Universal 'howl of execration': Carlyle's *Latter-Day Pamphlets* and Their Critical Reception." In Clubbe, *Carlyle*, 129–47.

———. "Prospects of the French Republic." *Carlyle Newsletter* 4 (1983): 19–23.

Graff, Gerald. *Literature Against Itself: Literary Ideas in Modern Society*. Chicago: University of Chicago Press, 1979.

Grafton, Anthony, Glenn W. Most, and James E. G. Zetzel. Introduction. *Prolegomena To Homer*. By F. A. Wolf. Princeton: Princeton University Press, 1985.

Grierson, Herbert. *Carlyle and Hitler*. Manchester, Eng.: University of Manchester Press, 1930.

Gross, John. *The Rise and Fall of the Man of Letters*. London: Weidenfeld and Nicolson, 1969.

Hale, Edward Everett. "James Russell Lowell and His Friends." *The Outlook* (1898): 46. Cited in Evelyn Barish Greenberger. *Arthur Hugh Clough: The Growth of a Poet's Mind.* Cambridge, Mass.: Harvard University Press, 1970.

Hall, Catherine. "The Economy of Intellectual Prestige: Thomas Carlyle, John Stuart Mill, and the Case of Governor Eyre." *Cultural Critique* 12 (1989): 167–96.

Haney, Janice. "'Shadow-Hunting,' Romantic Irony, *Sartor Resartus,* and Victorian Romanticism." *Studies in Romanticism* 17 (1978): 307–33.

Harding, Anthony. "Sterling, Carlyle, and German Higher Criticism: A Reassessment." *Victorian Studies* 26 (1983): 269–85.

Harrold, C. F. *Carlyle and German Thought, 1819–1834.* New Haven: Yale University Press, 1934.

——. "Carlyle's General Method in *The French Revolution.*" *PMLA* 43 (1928): 1150–69.

Hartman, Geoffrey. "Romanticism and Anti-Self-Consciousness." In *Beyond Formalism: Literary Essays, 1958–1970,* 298–310. New Haven: Yale University Press, 1970.

Holloway, John. *The Victorian Sage: Studies in Argument.* London: Macmillan, 1953.

Houghton, Walter E. *The Victorian Frame of Mind, 1830–1870.* New Haven: Yale University Press, 1957.

——, ed. *Wellesley Index to Victorian Periodicals: 1824–30.* Toronto: University of Toronto Press, 1972.

Hustvedt, Sigurd Bernhard. *Ballad Criticism in Scandanavia and Great Britain during the Eighteenth Century.* New York: American Scandanavian Foundation, 1916.

Ikeler, A. Abbott. *Puritan Temper and Transcendental Faith: Carlyle's Literary Vision.* Columbus: Ohio State University Press, 1972.

Jameson, Fredric. "Imaginary and Symbolic in Lacan: Marxism, Psychoanalytic Criticism, and the Problem of the Subject." *Yale French Studies* 55–56 (1977): 338–95.

Jann, Rosemary. *The Art and Science of Victorian History.* Columbus: Ohio State University Press, 1985.

Jay, Paul. *Being in the Text: Self-Representation from Wordsworth to Roland Barthes.* Ithaca, N.Y.: Cornell University Press, 1984.

Jenkyns, Richard. *The Victorians and Ancient Greece.* Cambridge: Harvard University Press, 1980.

"John Sterling and His Biographers." *Dublin University Magazine* 39 (1852): 185–99.

Kaplan, Fred. "'Phallus-Worship' (1848): Unpublished Manuscripts III—A Response to the Revolution of 1848." *Carlyle Newsletter* 2 (1980): 19–23.

Kern, Fritz. *Kingship and the Law in the Middle Ages.* Oxford: Blackwell, 1939.

Kernan, Alvin. *Printing Technology, Letters, and Samuel Johnson.* Princeton: Princeton University Press, 1987.

Lacan, Jacques. *Ecrits: A Selection.* Trans. Alan Sheridan. New York: Norton, 1977.

Landow, George P. *Elegant Jeremiahs: The Sage from Carlyle to Mailer.* Ithaca, N.Y.: Cornell University Press, 1986.

———. *Images of Crisis: Literary Iconology, 1750 to the Present.* Boston: Routledge, 1982.

———. " 'Swim or Drown': Carlyle's World of Shipwrecks, Castaways, and Stranded Voyagers." *Studies in English Literature* 15 (1976): 641–55.

LaValley, Albert J. *Carlyle and the Idea of the Modern.* New Haven: Yale University Press, 1968.

"The Lectures of Mr. Carlyle on the Revolutions of Modern Europe." *Examiner* 12 (May 1839): 293–94.

Lehman, B. H. *Carlyle's Theory of the Hero: Its Sources, Development, History and Influence on Carlyle's Work.* Durham: Duke University Press, 1928.

Leicester, H. M. "The Dialectic of Romantic Historiography: Prospect and Retrospect in *The French Revolution.*" *Victorian Studies* 15 (1971): 5–17.

Lemaire, Anika. *Jacques Lacan.* Trans. David Macey. Boston: Routledge, 1977.

Lentricchia, Frank. *After the New Criticism.* Chicago: University of Chicago Press, 1980.

Lerner, Gerda. *The Creation of Patriarchy.* Oxford: Oxford University Press, 1986.

Levine, George. *The Boundaries of Fiction.* Princeton: Princeton University Press, 1966.

———. "The Use and Abuse of Carlylese." In *The Art of Victorian Prose,* ed. George Levine and William Madden, 100–26. Oxford: Oxford University Press, 1966.

"The Life of John Sterling." *British Quarterly Review* 15 (1852): 240–53.

"The Life of John Sterling." *Examiner* 18 (October 1851): 659–61.

Lloyd, David. "Arnold, Ferguson, Schiller: Aesthetic Culture and the Politics of Aesthetics." *Cultural Critique* 2 (1985–86): 137–69.

Locke, John. *Two Treatises of Government.* Ed. Peter Laslett. Cambridge: Cambridge University Press, 1960.

Logue, Kenneth J. *Popular Disturbances in Scotland: 1780–1815.* Edinburgh: Donald, 1979.

Lotman, Jurij. *The Structure of the Artistic Text.* Trans. Ronald Vroon. Ann Arbor: Michigan Slavic Contributions, 1977.

McGowan, John P. *Representation and Revelation: Victorian Realism from Carlyle to Yeats.* Columbia: University of Missouri Press, 1986.

MacIntyre, Alasdair. *After Virtue.* 2d ed. Notre Dame: University of Notre Dame Press, 1984.

Marcus, Steven. *Dickens from Pickwick to Dombey.* New York: Simon, 1965.

Masson, David. *Edinburgh Sketches and Memories.* London and Edinburgh: Black, 1892.

Mellor, Anne. *English Romantic Irony.* Cambridge, Mass.: Harvard University Press, 1980.

[Merivale, Herman]. "Carlyle on the French Revolution." *Edinburgh Review* 71 (1840): 411–45.

Mill, John Stuart. *The Earlier Letters of John Stuart Mill: 1812–1848.* Ed. Francis E. Mineka. Toronto: University of Toronto Press, 1963.

———. *Essays on Equality, Law, and Education.* Ed. John M. Robson. Toronto: University of Toronto Press, 1984.

———. *Newspaper Writings.* Ed. Ann P. Robson and John M. Robson. Toronto: University of Toronto Press, 1986.

———. *On Liberty.* Ed. David Spitz. New York: Norton, 1975.

Miller, David A. *Narrative and Its Discontents: Problems of Closure in the Traditional Novel.* Princeton: Princeton University Press, 1981.

Miller, Robert Keith. *Carlyle's* Life of John Sterling: *A Study in Victorian Biography.* Ann Arbor: UMI, 1987.

[Milman, Henry Hart]. "Origins of the Homeric Poems." *Quarterly Review* 44 (1831): 121–68.

Mitford, Nancy. "Tam and Fritz: Carlyle and Frederick the Great." *History Today* 18 (1968): 3–13.

Moore, Carlisle. "*Sartor Resartus* and the Problem of Carlyle's Conversion." *PMLA* 70 (1955): 662–81.

———. "Thomas Carlyle and Fiction: 1822–1834." In *Nineteenth-Century Studies,* ed. Herbert Davis, et al., 131–77. 1940. New York: Greenwood, 1958.

Morgan, Edward Victor. *A History of Money.* Baltimore: Penguin, 1965.

Morgan, Lady Sydney. "Chartism." *The Athenæum* 637 (1840): 27–29.

Morris, Wesley. *Friday's Footprint: Structuralism and the Articulated Text.* Columbus: Ohio State University Press, 1979.

"Mr. Carlyle's Lectures on the Revolutions of Europe." *Times,* 10 May 1839, 5.

Mulderig, Gerald P. "The Rhetorical Design of Carlyle's *The Life of John Sterling.*" *Journal of Narrative Technique* 14 (1984): 142–50.

Myres, John L. *Homer and His Critics.* Ed. Dorothea Gray. London: Routledge, 1958.

Parrinder, Patrick. *Authors and Authority: A Study of English Literary Criticism and Its Relation to Culture, 1750–1900.* London: Routledge, 1977.

Peckham, Morse. "*Frederick the Great.*" In Fielding and Tarr, 198–215.

Peterson, Linda. *Victorian Autobiography: A Tradition of Self-Interpretation.* New Haven: Yale University Press, 1986.

Pitkin, Hanna Fenichel, ed. *Representation*. New York: Atherton, 1969.

Pocock, J. G. A. *The Ancient Constitution and the Feudal Law: A Study of English Historical Thought in the Seventeenth Century*. Cambridge: Cambridge University Press, 1957.

Popkin, Richard H. *The History of Scepticism from Erasmus to Spinoza*. Berkeley: University of California Press, 1979.

Ragland-Sullivan, Ellie. *Jacques Lacan and the Philosophy of Psychoanalysis*. Urbana: University of Illinois Press, 1986.

Richardson, Thomas C. "Carlyle's *Chartism* and the *Quarterly Review*." *Carlyle Annual* 10 (1989): 50–55.

Roberts, David. *Paternalism in Early Victorian England*. New Brunswick, N.J.: Rutgers University Press, 1979.

Roberts, Mark. "Carlyle and the Rhetoric of Unreason." *Essays in Criticism* 18 (1968): 397–419.

Rogers, Jasper W. *Facts for the Kind-Hearted of England! as to the Wretchedness of the Irish Peasantry, and the Means for Their Regeneration*. London: James Ridgway, 1847.

Rosenberg, John D. *Carlyle and the Burden of History*. Cambridge, Mass.: Harvard University Press, 1985.

Rosenberg, Philip. *The Seventh Hero: Thomas Carlyle and the Theory of Radical Activism*. Cambridge, Mass.: Harvard University Press, 1974.

Ryals, Clyde de L. "Thomas Carlyle and the Squire Forgeries." *Victorian Studies* 30 (1987): 495–518.

Said, Edward. *Beginnings: Intention and Method*. Baltimore: The John Hopkins University Press, 1975.

Schochet, Gordon J. *Patriarchalism in Political Thought: The Authoritarian Family and Political Speculation and Attitudes Especially in Seventeenth-Century England*. New York: Basic Books, 1975.

Seigel, Jules P. "Carlyle and Peel: The Prophet's Search for a Heroic Politician and an Unpublished Fragment." *Victorian Studies* 26 (1983): 181–95.

———. "*Latter-Day Pamphlets*: The Near Failure of Form and Vision." In Fielding and Tarr, 155–76.

———. *Thomas Carlyle: The Critical Heritage*. New York: Barnes, 1971.

Semmel, Bernard. *The Governor Eyre Controversy*. London: MacGibbon and Kee, 1962.

[Sewell, William]. "Carlyle's Works." *Quarterly Review* 66 (1840): 446–503.

Shell, Marc. *The Economy of Literature*. Baltimore: The John Hopkins University Press, 1978.

Shepperson, W. S. *British Emigration to North America: Projects and Opinions in the Early Victorian Period*. Minneapolis: University of Minnesota Press, 1957.

Shine, Hill. *Carlyle and the Saint-Simonians: The Concept of Historical Periodicity*. Baltimore: The Johns Hopkins University Press, 1941.

———. *Carlyle's Early Reading to 1834*, University of Kentucky Libraries Occasional Contribution 57. Lexington, Ky.: Margaret I. King Library, 1953.

———. *Carlyle's Fusion of Poetry, History, and Religion by 1834*. 1938. New York: Kennikat, 1967.

Sigman, Joseph. "Adam Kadmon, Nifl, Muspel and the Biblical Symbolism of *Sartor Resartus*." *English Literary History* 41 (1974): 233–56.

Skabarnicki, Anne. "Annandale Evangelist and Scotch Voltaire: Carlyle's *Reminiscences* of Edward Irving and Francis Jeffrey." *Scotia* 4 (1980): 16–24.

———. "Too Hasty Souls: Goethe's Eurphorion in Carlyle's *Life of John Sterling*." *Carlyle Newsletter* 6 (1985): 27–34.

Sterrenburg, Lee. "Psychoanalysis and the Iconography of Revolution." *Victorian Studies* 19 (1975): 241–64.

Tarr, Rodger L. "Emendation as Challenge: Carlyle's 'Negro Question' from Journal to Pamphlet." *Papers of the Bibliographical Society of America* 75 (1981): 341–45.

———. "Thomas Carlyle and Henry M'Cormac: Letters on the Condition of Ireland in 1848." *Studies in Scottish Literature* 5 (1968): 253–56.

Tennyson, G. B. *Sartor Called Resartus: The Genesis, Structure, and Style of Thomas Carlyle's First Major Work*. Princeton, N.J.: Princeton University Press, 1965.

———. "Thomas Carlyle." In *Victorian Prose: A Guide to Research*, ed. David J. De Laura, 33–104. New York: Modern Language Association, 1973.

Thackeray, William M. *The Letters and Private Papers of William Makepeace Thackeray*. Ed. Gordon N. Ray. Cambridge, Mass.: Harvard University Press, 1945.

Todorov, Tzvetan. "The Notion of Literature." *New Literary History* 5 (1973): 5–16.

"Topics of the Day." *Spectator* 4 (January 1840): 9–11.

Trela, D. J. *Cromwell in Context: The Conception, Writing and Reception of Carlyle's Second History*. Edinburgh: Carlyle Newsletter, 1986.

Trevor-Roper, Hugh. "Thomas Carlyle's Historical Philosophy." *TLS*, 26 June 1981, 731–34.

Turner, Frank M. *The Greek Heritage in Victorian Britain*. New Haven: Yale University Press, 1981.

Vanden Bossche, Chris R. "Fictive Text and Transcendental Self: Carlyle's Art of Biography." *Biography* 10 (1987): 116–28.

———. "Polite Conversation or Revolutionary Style: An Allusion to DeQuincey's Review of *Wilhelm Meister* in *Sartor Resartus*." *Carlyle Newsletter* 3 (1982): 44–47.

———. "Prophetic Closure and Disclosing Narrative: *The French Revolution* and *A Tale of Two Cities*." *Dickens Studies Annual* 12, ed. Michael Timko, Fred Kaplan, and Edward Guiliano, 209–21. New York: AMS, 1983.

———. "Revolution and Authority: The Metaphors of Language and Carlyle's Style." *Prose Studies* 6 (1983): 274–89.

Weaver, Frederick Stirton. "Thomas Carlyle on Dr. Francia: The Functional Role of the Carlylean Hero." *Ideologies and Literature* 3 (1980): 105–15.

Wellek, René. "Carlyle and the Philosophy of History." *Philological Quarterly* 23 (1944): 55–76. Rpt. in René Wellek, *Confrontations*, 82–113. Princeton: Princeton University Press, 1965.

———. "What Is Literature?" In *What Is Literature?* ed. Paul Hernadi, 16–23. Bloomington: Indiana University Press, 1978.

Welsh, Alexander. *The City of Dickens.* 1971. Cambridge, Mass.: Harvard University Press, 1986.

White, Hayden. *Metahistory: The Historical Imagination in Nineteenth-Century Europe.* Baltimore: The Johns Hopkins University Press, 1973.

Williams, Raymond. *Culture and Society: 1780–1950.* 1958. New York: Columbia University Press, 1983.

———. *Keywords.* New York: Oxford University Press, 1985.

Wolf, Michael. "The Uses of Context: Aspects of the 1860s." *Victorian Studies* 9, Supplement (1964): 47–63.

Workman, Gillian. "Thomas Carlyle and the Governor Eyre Controversy: An Account with Some New Material." *Victorian Studies* 18 (1974): 77–102.

Index

Aberdeen, George Hamilton-Gordon, earl of, 205

Action, 37, 45, 51, 87–89, 97, 100–101, 103–4, 106, 114, 116, 118, 125–26, 139–40, 148–49, 152; deferred, 45, 51, 83–84, 86, 116, 125, 143; epic as, 103–4; political, 161, 165; versus writing, speech, speculation, 83–89, 100, 147, 190. *See also* Closure; Writing

Adrian, Arthur A., and Vonna H., 152

Aeneid, 58, 200

Albert (prince consort), 205

Alison, Archibald, 64–66, 68, 188

Altick, Richard, 195

Anarchy, viii, 59, 69, 70–71, 73, 76, 86–87, 110–13, 115, 117–20, 148, 155–56, 161, 162, 172

Anstey, Thomas, 90

ApRoberts, Ruth, 177

Arac, Jonathan, 72, 172, 179

Aristocracy, 94, 95–97, 105, 127, 128, 131, 166–68, 191, 205

Arnold, Matthew, 3, 12, 172–73; *Culture and Anarchy*, 3, 172

Athenaeum, 51–52, 203

Audience, 47–48, 62, 90–91, 93, 104–5, 106–7, 126, 131–32

August, Eugene R., 131, 200

Authority: Carlyle's, 1, 15, 30–33, 38–39, 48, 52, 54, 62, 90, 107, 139–40, 144, 147; coercive, viii, 107, 113, 119, 125–26, 131, 133, 135–36, 138, 156, 167–68, 171, 172–73; concept of, 13; destruction or absence of, ix, 1, 11, 20, 28, 70–71, 73–74, 84, 86, 99, 100, 101, 118, 142, 168, 172; of language, 6–7; literary, vii, 7–8, 14, 17, 24, 29–33, 45–48, 151, 168, 172; paternal, 16–18, 23, 26, 29, 33–39, 141, 142, 148–49, 152; political, 3–5, 9, 11, 30, 34–35, 45, 71, 92, 168, 172; politi-

cal supersedes literary, 92, 97, 101, 119, 149, 153, 155, 172, 193; political supersedes religious, 101, 115, 171–72; through rebellion, 13, 18–19, 27, 29, 39, 46, 70–71, 74, 86, 117–20, 138–39, 143, 149, 154; rebellion against, 17, 39, 134–35; recovery of, 11, 20, 27, 28, 33, 36, 39, 44, 70, 78, 89, 97, 99–101, 112, 117, 138; religious, 28–29, 34, 45; search for, viii–ix, 11, 13–14, 28, 40–41, 80, 88, 99, 101; shift of, ix, 1–8, 177, 184; transcendental, viii, 1, 2–4, 10, 12, 30, 33, 43–44, 49–50, 55, 58–59, 78, 87, 98, 107, 100, 112, 113, 171, 173–74, 181, 184, 197. *See also* Constitutions; Father

Authors: Editor of *Sartor* as, 78; the French as, 75–76, 78–83; of Prussia, 155–56; Teufelsdröckh as, 80–83. *See also* Legislative bodies; Literary career

Autophagy, or consumption, 51, 83–86, 137, 183, 186

Babel, 75, 77, 83, 118, 151, 174, 189

Baker, Richard, 198

Bakhtin, Mikhail, 68

Baring, Bingham, 143

Baring, Harriet, 143

Barthes, Roland, 64, 76

Bastille, 53, 72, 73, 189. *See also* Prison motif

Battle motif, 9, 16, 115, 122–23, 132, 147, 148–49, 154–56, 160–62, 167, 206. *See also* Industrial regiments; Law: martial

Belatedness, 116, 149, 161

Ben-Israel, Hedva, 189

Bendix, Reinhard, 4, 5

Bentham, Jeremy, 10, 94, 191

Bentley, Richard, 186